GMAT® 5-Hour Quick Prep

by Lisa Zimmer Hatch, MA, Scott A. Hatch, JD, and Sandra Luna McCune, PhD

A Wiley Brand

GMAT® 5-Hour Quick Prep For Dummies®

Published by: **John Wiley & Sons, Inc.,** 111 River Street, Hoboken, NJ 07030-5774, www.wiley.com

Copyright © 2024 by John Wiley & Sons, Inc., Hoboken, New Jersey

Published simultaneously in Canada

For general information on our other products and services, please contact our Customer Care Department within the U.S. at 877-762-2974, outside the U.S. at 317-572-3993, or fax 317-572-4002. For technical support, please visit https://hub.wiley.com/community/support/dummies.

Wiley publishes in a variety of print and electronic formats and by print-on-demand. Some material included with standard print versions of this book may not be included in e-books or in print-on-demand. If this book refers to media such as a CD or DVD that is not included in the version you purchased, you may download this material at http://booksupport.wiley.com. For more information about Wiley products, visit www.wiley.com.

Library of Congress Control Number: 2023950098

ISBN 978-1-394-23171-3 (pbk); ISBN 978-1-394-23173-7 (ebk); ISBN 978-1-394-23172-0 (ebk)

SKY10063502_122723

Table of Contents

Start Here

Y ou've decided to go back to school to earn your Master of Business Administration (MBA) degree. Good for you. There's only one catch, and it's a big one: The program you're applying to requires that you take the Graduate Management Admission Test (GMAT) to prove that you have the brain power to succeed. Now what? You have no idea what's on the test, and even if you did, years have passed since you studied that material or took a comprehensive standardized exam covering it. You need a primer on what the test covers, a brief refresher in those subject areas, and a little practice to get your rusty brain working like a well-oiled machine. Welcome to *GMAT 5-Hour Quick Prep For Dummies*.

About This Book

GMAT 5-Hour Quick Prep For Dummies distills everything you need to know to succeed on the GMAT into a six-block, five-hour mini-study guide. Here's a rundown of what you'll find in each block and about how much time each block is likely to take you to complete:

>> **Block 1 (20 minutes):** Find out what you need to know about registering for the GMAT, the topics covered, how to prepare, and how the test is scored.

>> **Block 2 (1 hour):** Get up to speed on verbal skills and knowledge, discover how to read faster with better comprehension, sharpen your critical-thinking skills, and practice answering GMAT's verbal questions.

>> **Block 3 (1 hour, 20 minutes):** Refresh your memory and build your math skills in topic areas including numbers, operations, algebra, statistics, and sets. Answer sample math questions and develop techniques for solving problems faster and improving your chances when you need to guess.

>> **Block 4 (40 minutes):** Wrap your brain around the four key question types in the Data Insights section of the test, improve your ability to extract insights from graphic data such as tables and charts, and tackle data sufficiency questions, which challenge your ability to analyze data.

>> **Block 5 (1 hour, 30 minutes):** Take an abridged sample GMAT test, check your answers, and identify subject areas where you may need to focus your remaining prep time.

>> **Block 6 (10 minutes):** Find quick tips on how to answer more questions correctly and improve your score.

Foolish Assumptions

To target the content of this book to your specific needs, we made a few foolish assumptions about you:

>> You're planning to apply to an MBA program, and at least one of the schools on your list requires that you take the GMAT as part of its admissions process.

>> You're highly motivated to score high on the GMAT, because you're applying for admission to a competitive program.

>> You're not quite sure what's covered on the GMAT.

>> Your knowledge and skills in at least one section of the GMAT are a little rusty — perhaps you've been out of school for some time but you have life and work experience that can boost your score despite your time outside of academia.

Icons Used in This Book

Icons appear throughout this book to highlight especially significant portions of the text. These little pictures in the margins alert you to content that demands your close and careful attention.

This icon highlights *really* important information to remember even after you close the book.

Throughout the book, we give you insights into how you can enhance your performance on the GMAT. The tips give you juicy guidance on how to answer questions faster and improve your odds of getting them right.

Your world won't fall apart if you ignore our warnings, but your score may suffer. Heed these cautionary pointers to avoid making careless mistakes that can cost you points.

Whenever you see this icon in the text, you know you're going to get to practice the particular area of instruction covered in that section with a question like one you may see on the test. Our examples include detailed explanations of how to answer GMAT questions most efficiently and accurately while avoiding common pitfalls.

Where to Go from Here

We know that everyone who uses this book has different strengths and weaknesses, so this book is designed for you to read in the way that best suits you:

>> To reap the full benefits of this book, start with Block 1 and familiarize yourself with the GMAT, proceed through Blocks 2–4 to review all subject areas you'll be tested on, take the abridged sample test in Block 5, and wrap up your test prep with the ten test-taking tips presented in Block 6.

>> If you're a math whiz and need to brush up only on your verbal skills, take the same approach, but skim through Block 3, focusing only on your weakest math skills.

>> If you've been writing proposals every day for the last ten years, you can probably skim through the verbal coverage in Block 2.

>> Whatever approach you take, we strongly recommend that you invest some time in Block 4 regardless of your math prowess or verbal genius, because the GMAT uses the Data Insights questions to separate the master from the novice. We also recommend that you take the abridged sample exam in Block 5 to identify any areas you may need to work on a little more.

Wherever you go from here and whatever you choose to do in addition to working through this book to prepare for the GMAT, we wish you all the best in your pursuit of your MBA.

Block **1**

GMAT Overview in 20 Minutes

The GMAT doesn't have to be a daunting ordeal. A little knowledge and preparation can help calm your nerves, and that's exactly what this block delivers. Here you discover your test-taking options and how to register for the GMAT, get a brief overview of what's on the test, obtain step-by-step guidance on how to prepare for it, and gain insight into how the test is scored and how your scores will be used.

Signing Up for the GMAT

Which MBA programs to apply to isn't the only decision you have to make. After you've figured out where you want to go, you have to make plans for the GMAT. You need to choose which format works best for you and determine the ideal time to take the test.

Deciding where to take the test

You can take the GMAT online at home or at a designated testing center, the choice is yours. Regardless of where you take it, the GMAT e-content and interface are the same. In this section, we present the key factors to consider when deciding whether to take the GMAT at home or at a designated testing center.

Taking the GMAT online at home

You may choose to take the GMAT online exam in the comfort of your home on your own computer. Before you take the exam, you download the special secure software and set up your test space. A human proctor virtually oversees the online exam throughout the testing experience, and you're responsible for meeting the stringent specifications for setting up the testing environment. Here are the advantages of taking the online exam:

>> **The online format is available even more often than the options provided at testing centers.** You can take the online GMAT 24 hours a day, 7 days a week, and you can register 24 hours before an open slot.

>> **The testing environment is familiar.** As long as you set up the testing environment following the required guidelines, you can test from any location.

>> **You don't have to worry about traffic or other commuting issues.** It's hard to get lost when you're commuting from your bedroom to your home office.

Taking the GMAT at a testing center

You can also opt to take the GMAT at a testing center. Although testing at home may seem more desirable, you may choose the testing center for the following reasons:

>> **The testing center provides all supplies.** You don't have to worry about a reliable Internet connection or purchasing your own whiteboard for notes.

>> **You aren't responsible for securing your environment.** To maintain the integrity of the home testing experience, you must follow stringent guidelines. Testing at a center guarantees that you won't be penalized for an interruption by a family member or fail to pass a room scan.

Registering for the GMAT

The first step in the GMAT registration process is scheduling an appointment, but don't leave it to the last minute. Depending on the time of year, appointment times can fill up quickly. You may have to wait at least a month for an open time. To determine what's available, you can go to the official GMAT website at www.mba.com. From there, you can choose an online test appointment or testing location and find out what dates and times are available. When you find a date and time you like, you can register online or over the phone.

TIP

When choosing a test date and time, consider your schedule and the time of day you generally feel most mentally alert. The GMAT is no longer just an 8 a.m. Saturday morning option. You can take the test any day of the week except Sunday, and, depending on the test center, you may be able to start at a variety of times. Many centers offer 8 a.m. testing times, but some have other options, even 6:30 at night.

Knowing What's on the Test

The GMAT is a standardized test, which means lots of questions to answer in a short period, no way to cram for them or memorize answers, and very little chance of scoring 100 percent. The skills tested on the GMAT are those that leading business schools have decided are important for MBA students: data insights, quantitative reasoning, and verbal reasoning.

Checking out how the GMAT is structured

The following table presents a summary of the structure of the GMAT by Sections:

Section	Data Insights	Quantitative	Verbal
Time	45 minutes	45 minutes	45 minutes
Number of questions	20	21	23
Question type(s)	Data sufficiency Table analysis Two-part analysis Graphics interpretation Multi-source reasoning	Basic arithmetic Algebra Statistics and probability Problem solving	Reading comprehension Critical reasoning
Avg. time/question	2 minutes, 15 seconds	2 minutes, 9 seconds	1 minute, 57 seconds

TIP

The GMAT Select Section Order option allows you to complete those three sections in any order you choose.

Knowing what you're being tested for

Standardized tests are supposed to test your academic potential, not your knowledge of specific subjects. The GMAT focuses on the areas that admissions committees have found to be relevant to MBA programs. The sections that follow are an introduction to the three GMAT sections. Most of this book explains exactly how to approach each one.

Leveraging your data literacy skills

The GMAT Data Insights section has 20 questions consisting of two question types:

>> **Data sufficiency questions** present you with two statements and ask you to decide whether the problem can be solved by using the information provided by the first statement only, the second statement only, both statements, or neither statement.

>> **Integrated reasoning (IR)** questions test your ability to read and evaluate charts, graphs, and other forms of presented data. You'll examine a variety of data representation and answer questions based on the information. IR questions come in the following three types:

- Table analysis and graphics interpretation questions require you to glean insights from data presented in a graphic format (table or chart).

- The two-part analysis questions present a problem and related data, provided in two columns, and instruct you to choose a piece of information from each column to solve the problem.

- Multi-source reasoning questions provide you with a bunch of information from which you have to decide what piece or pieces of data actually give you what you need to know to solve the problem.

Quizzing your quantitative skills

The GMAT Quantitative section consists of 21 questions to assess your proficiency in arithmetic, algebra, data interpretation, and probability and statistics. This section is comparable to other standardized math assessments in terms of its format and question types. To succeed on this section, you will need to employ your problem-solving skills to answer multiple-choice questions, choosing the best response from five possible options.

Validating your verbal skills

The GMAT Verbal section consists of 23 multiple-choice questions of two general types:

>> **Reading comprehension** requires you to answer questions about written passages on a number of different subjects.

>> **Critical reasoning questions** require you to analyze logical arguments and understand how to strengthen or weaken those arguments.

Navigating the computerized test

All three sections of the computerized GMAT are available only in *computer-adaptive test* (CAT) format. The first question of each section is of medium difficulty. If you consistently answer questions correctly, the computer will challenge you with more difficult questions. Conversely, if you choose enough wrong answers, the computer presents you with easier questions. Your score isn't based solely on how many questions you answer correctly or incorrectly, but also on the average difficulty level of the questions you answer correctly. Theoretically, you could miss several questions and still get a very high score, so long as the questions you missed were among the most challenging.

At the conclusion of each section, you are assigned a level of ability, which is used to score your performance. This method of evaluation is designed to ensure that test takers are assessed based on their individual capabilities.

Answering in an orderly fashion

Because each question is based on your answers to previous questions — you can't skip questions, nor can you return to a previous question to revise your answer, although you do have an opportunity to review and edit your responses after completing the section. You can edit only three answers, time permitting.

Observing time limits

The time limit for each section is 45 minutes, and this has two important implications for your test strategy: First, your score is based on the number of questions you answer correctly, so if you run out of time before answering all the questions, you miss those points. Second, you won't have a chance to go back to review any questions.

REMEMBER

Technically challenged, take heart! You need only minimal computer skills to take the computerized GMAT. All you need to know is how to select answers by using either the mouse or the keyboard.

Preparing for the GMAT

During the weeks or months leading up to your scheduled GMAT exam, you'd be wise to prepare for it so you're ready to answer even the trickiest questions. To use your remaining time most efficiently, take the following steps to prepare:

1. Set a target score.

Research the programs you're applying to and find out the average score of accepted students. Generally, a score between 650 and 690 is good and anything over 700 is great. 800 is perfect, not to mention rare.

2. Take a practice test to establish your baseline score and identify your weakest areas.

You can take the abridged practice GMAT in Block 5 of this book or another practice test. The GMAT Official Starter Kit + Practice Exams 1 & 2 software is available for free download at www.mba.com/exam-prep/gmat-official-starter-kit-practice-exams-1-and-2-free. This kit provides two-full-length official practice exams — a total of 90 IR, quantitative reasoning, and verbal practice questions that adapt in difficulty as you improve. Better yet, it provides a computer version of the test that simulates the real test-taking experience.

TIP

Use one of the tests in the GMAT Official Starter Kit as your diagnostic. Work through Blocks 2, 3, and 4 to review your weakest subjects. Then take the second official GMAT practice test to gauge your improvement.

3. Develop a detailed study plan and put it in writing.

Include dates and times of your study sessions and practice exams and how long you're willing to commit to each study session. The blocks in this book facilitate your ability to plan your study sessions. For example, if you have five weeks between now and your scheduled GMAT, you can plan to complete Blocks 2–5 over the course of the first three weeks, take a second practice exam the fourth week, and review during week 5.

4. Identify fundamentals in math and verbal subject areas that you struggle with.

Although the GMAT isn't like a typical math, reading, or English test, it requires foundational knowledge and skills in all those subject areas. To answer certain math questions, for example, you'll need to know how to solve for variables or calculate the area of basic shapes. To answer Verbal questions, you'll need to understand concepts such as thesis and tone and grammar rules such as subject-verb agreement and parallel structure.

5. Review math and verbal subject areas you struggle with.

Consult the relevant blocks in this book to review the areas you have the most trouble with on the test. If you feel that you need additional information and practice, consult books or websites for more guidance and sample questions/problems.

REMEMBER

Whether you're planning to take the GMAT online at home or at a testing center, a couple days before your scheduled test, confirm your appointment date, time, and time zone in your email confirmation.

If you're taking the exam at a testing center, take the following steps the day before your scheduled exam:

1. Review the Exam Policies.

GMAT policies are extensive and cover everything from eligibility and identification requirements to minimum system requirements for taking the online version at home. Visit www.mba.com/exams/gmat-exam/register/exam-policies.

2. **Plan your route to the test center location and account for travel time and potential delays.**

   Take a test run to the facility, so you're familiar with the route and the location of the specific building and test room. Know how you're getting to the test center (for example, driving your car, getting a ride, or using public transportation or a rideshare service).

3. **Plan to arrive 30 minutes early, so you have plenty of time to find the room and check in.**

4. **Bring a valid photo ID (with your photo and your name that exactly matches the name you used to register for the exam).**

5. **Get a good night's sleep before the exam, so you'll wake up feeling well rested.**

If you're planning to take the GMAT online at home, take the following steps a week before your scheduled exam time, so you have time to procure the hardware and whiteboard you'll need:

1. **Review the system requirements to ensure that your computer (desktop or laptop) meets the specifications of the GMAT software. (Tablets and other mobile devices are prohibited.)**

   Visit www.mba.com/exams/gmat-exam/plan-for-exam-day/taking-the-exam-delivered-online for details. This page includes a link for running a system check to ensure that your computer has a functioning webcam and microphone and that your operating system, browser, and Internet connection meet the minimum requirements.

2. **If you plan to use a whiteboard during the exam, obtain one that meets the GMAT requirements.**

   The board can be no larger than 12 x 20 inches (30 x 50 centimeters). You can have up to two dry-erase markers and one dry-erase eraser.

3. **Clear your desk and workspace of any prohibited items.**

   Basically, you can have your computer, whiteboard (with markers and eraser), water in a clear container, a box of tissues and any medical devices or supplies you need. Mobile phones, headphones, earbuds, watches, wallets, purses, bags, books, notepads, and just about anything else is prohibited, so the sparser your surroundings, the better. For additional details, visit www.mba.com/exams/gmat-exam/plan-for-exam-day/taking-the-exam-delivered-online.

   Prior to the exam, the person supervising your exam session will inspect your testing area via your webcam to identify and have you remove any prohibited items.

REMEMBER

4. **Get a good night's sleep before the exam, so you'll wake up feeling well rested.**

Getting Up to Speed on GMAT Scoring

Okay, you know the GMAT's format and how many questions it has and so on. But what about what's really important to you, the crucial final score?

Interpreting your score

Each section of the GMAT is scored on a scale from 60 to 90, in 1-point increments, and contributes equally to the GMAT total score. The GMAT total score is on a scale of 205 to 805, in 10-point increments. So, the maximum total score you can earn on the GMAT is 805. However, your section scores are determined by more than just the number of questions you get right. Scoring is based on three factors:

>> **The difficulty of the questions you answer:** The questions become more difficult as you continue to answer correctly, so getting tough questions means you're doing well on the test.

>> **The number of questions you answer:** If you don't get to all the questions in a section, your score is reduced by the proportion of questions you didn't answer. So, if you failed to answer 5 of the 21 Quantitative questions, for example, your raw score would be reduced by about 24 percent: After converting the raw score to the scaled measure, this loss could significantly decrease your percentile rank.

>> **The number of questions you answer correctly:** In addition to scoring based on how difficult the questions are, the GMAT score also reflects your ability to answer those questions correctly.

Deciding whether to retake the test

If you're not satisfied with your GMAT score, retaking the test may be advantageous, especially as most selective MBA programs prioritize high scores. Fortunately, the GMAT administrators let you take the test up to five times during a 12-month period and up to eight total times over the course of your life. Having multiple opportunities to take the test increases your chances of improving your score, thereby enhancing your prospect of getting accepted into your desired program.

Block 2
Vanquishing the Verbal Section

The Verbal section of the GMAT mixes reading comprehension questions with critical reasoning questions — about half and half. In this block, we explain how to approach a variety of questions in both categories and present you with plenty of sample reading passages and questions to help you gain valuable practice.

Acing the Reading Comprehension Questions

Reading comprehension questions are designed to test how well you understand unfamiliar reading material. But you're probably less concerned with the reason these passages are included on the GMAT than you are with getting through all that reading and question-answering with enough time remaining to confront those pesky critical reasoning questions. What you need is a proven strategy. And in this section, we deliver by introducing you to the types of passages and questions you'll encounter and telling you how to deal with them.

Knowing what reading comprehension questions look like

When the GMAT presents you with a reading comprehension question, you'll see a split screen with an article passage on the left and a question with five answer choices on the right. Although every passage has more than one question (usually, passages have about three to four questions), only one question pops up at a time. You read the passage (which contains about 350 words), click on the choice that best answers the question, and confirm your answer. As soon as you confirm your answer, another question pops up on the right side of the screen. The passage remains on the left. Sometimes a question refers to a particular part of the passage. For these questions, the GMAT highlights the portion of the passage you need to focus on to answer the question.

Approaching reading passages

Reading comprehension questions don't ask you to do anything particularly unfamiliar. You've probably been reading passages and answering multiple-choice questions about them since you were in elementary school. If you're having difficulty answering reading comprehension questions correctly, don't worry: Your reading skills are likely fine. You're probably just not familiar with the specific way you have to read for the GMAT.

REMEMBER

You have about two minutes to answer each reading comprehension question, and that includes the time for reading the passage. Generally, you shouldn't spend more than five minutes reading a passage before you answer its questions, so you have to read as efficiently as you can. You need a plan for getting through the passage in a way that allows you to answer questions correctly and quickly. When you read a passage, focus on the following elements:

>> The passage's general theme

>> The author's tone

>> The way the author organizes the passage

TIP

Don't try to figure out the passage's minutiae while you're reading it. If you encounter a question about a tiny detail, you can go back and reread the relevant section.

Mastering the message: The main point

Generally, people write passages to inform or persuade. Most of the passages on the GMAT are informative rather than argumentative, and even the argumentative ones are pretty tame.

REMEMBER

The main point of GMAT passages is often *to discuss a topic, to inform the reader about a phenomenon,* or *to compare one idea to another.* Rarely does a GMAT passage seek to condemn, criticize, or enthusiastically advocate a particular idea or position.

Because most authors present the main theme in the first paragraph or two, you'll probably figure it out in the first few seconds of your reading. If it's not clear in the first paragraphs, it probably appears in the last paragraph, where the author sums up the ideas. After you've figured out the author's overall theme, quickly jot down on your note board a word or two to help you remember the theme.

Absorbing the ambiance: Author's tone

In addition to understanding the author's main point, you need to know how the author feels about the issue. You get clues to the authors' tone or mood by the words they use. GMAT passages either inform the reader about something or try to persuade the reader to adopt the author's viewpoint. Informative passages are often more objective than persuasive ones, so the author's tone is usually neutral. Authors of persuasive passages may exhibit more emotion. You may sense that an author is critical, sarcastic, pessimistic, optimistic, or supportive. When you figure out how the author feels about the topic, write a short description on your note board, like *objective, hopeful,* or *mildly critical.* Knowing the tone of a passage helps you choose answers that exhibit the same tone or level of bias.

WARNING

Don't let your personal opinions about a passage's subject matter influence your answer. Remind yourself that correct answers are true *according to the passage* or *according to the author.*

Finding the framework: The passage's outline

Knowing the structure of a passage is much more important than understanding its details. Instead of trying to comprehend everything the author says, focus on how the author lays out the information. Standard essay format includes an introduction with a thesis, two or three supporting paragraphs, and a conclusion. Many GMAT passages are excerpts from larger works, so they may not exhibit exact standard essay form, but they'll contain evidence of all three elements. As you read, determine the passage's overall point and the main points of each paragraph.

TIP

You may find it helpful to construct a mini-outline of the passage as you read it. Underneath the main theme, jot down a word or two on your note board that describes the type of information contained in each paragraph. Building an outline in your head or on your note board helps you know where in the passage you can find answers to questions about particular details. Doing so also helps you answer any questions that ask you *how* authors develop their points.

WARNING

Even though you don't need to read and understand every detail of a passage before you answer its questions, we highly recommend that you scan the entire passage before you attempt the questions.

Sticking to the subject: Types of passages

You may think that because the GMAT measures your aptitude for MBA programs, its reading passages deal with subjects like marketing and economics. You're wrong. Although some of the passages do concern business matters, you'll also read about topics from the natural and social sciences. The GMAT wants to see how well you analyze a variety of topics, unfamiliar and familiar. In the following sections, we explore the types of reading passages found on the GMAT.

Experimenting with natural science passages

Physical and biological sciences mean big business. Some of the areas of commerce that depend on science include pharmaceuticals, computers, agriculture, the defense industry, household products, and materials manufacturing (such as plastics and polymers). These industries, taken together, exert a huge influence on people's lives and the nation's economy. Just think of this country without computers and pharmaceuticals, not to mention modern agriculture!

Note that reading comprehension questions don't assume that you have any previous knowledge in the subject. If you do come across a reading passage on chemistry and it's been 20 years since you've studied the periodic table, relax. The answer to every question is located somewhere in the passage.

WARNING

When you come across a passage on a subject that you're familiar with, don't rely on your outside knowledge to answer the question! Make sure the answers you choose can be justified by information contained in the passage.

REMEMBER

Natural science passages tend to be more objective and neutral than persuasive in tone. So usually the main theme of a natural science topic is *to explain, describe,* or *inform* about a scientific event.

Gathering in social circles: Social science passages

In addition to natural science passages, the GMAT presents passages about a different kind of science: social science, which includes topics like law, philosophy, history, political science, archeology, sociology, and psychology. The good news about social science passages is that their topics tend to crop up more in the news and in daily conversation than does, for example, physics! So you're more likely to be comfortable, if not necessarily familiar, with them.

Although passages about the social sciences are still mostly descriptive and informative, they're more likely to be persuasive than natural science passages, so you may see more variety in the kinds of tones these passages display.

Getting down to business passages

Business passages may be objective or persuasive and are generated from fields like economics, marketing, resource management, and accounting, among others. Finally, topics you're familiar with! You'll probably breeze right through most of these passages. But don't let familiarity with the topic serve as an excuse to slack off. You need your powers of concentration for every passage regardless of the topic.

WARNING

If the passage is on a familiar subject, don't fall into the trap of using your own information to answer questions. The correct answer is based on information in the passage and not on what you studied last semester in your marketing courses or discussed last week in your sales meeting.

Approaching reading comprehension questions

The GMAT Verbal section has 23 questions, and you're allotted 45 minutes to answer them. That comes out to about two minutes per question. If you spend too much time answering reading comprehension questions, you'll have less time to answer the critical reasoning questions that also comprise the Verbal section. So having a system for tackling reading comprehension questions is just as important as knowing how to read through the passages. Your approach should include

>> Recognizing the type of question

>> Quickly eliminating incorrect answer choices

>> Managing questions that ask for the answer that *isn't* supported by the passage

We show you how to apply all three of these techniques in the following sections and provide a few examples of what to look for so you know how to answer the questions correctly.

Identifying the question type

The first step in answering a reading comprehension question correctly is identifying the type of question. Most reading comprehension questions fall into one of these five categories:

>> Summarizing the main idea

>> Finding supporting information

>> Making inferences and applications

>> Evaluating logic and structure

>> Assessing the author's tone

Each of the question types requires a slightly different approach. Main idea and tone questions ask you to make determinations about the passage as a whole. Supporting information and inference questions usually ask you to home in on particular parts of the passage. For example, when you know that a question is about specific details in the passage, you can focus your attention on the portion of the passage that's relevant to the information in the question.

We share all the details about each of the five categories of reading comprehension questions in the following sections.

GETTING TO THE POINT: MAIN-IDEA QUESTIONS

Main-idea questions ask you to identify the primary purpose of the whole passage. Almost every passage has at least one question that asks you to identify the thesis of the passage, and often it's the first question you answer for a particular reading passage.

TIP

You can identify main-idea questions by the language they contain. Here are some examples of the ways main-idea questions may be worded:

>> The author of the passage is primarily concerned with which of the following?

>> The author's primary goal (or purpose) in the passage is to do which of the following?

>> An appropriate title that best summarizes this passage is . . .

While you read the passage, look for its main idea because you know you'll probably be asked about it. You may even want to write a sentence that briefly states the passage's primary purpose. Then, if you're asked a question about the passage's main theme, you'll look for an answer that conveys an idea similar to your statement of the author's purpose.

TIP

The best answer to a main-idea question is general rather than specific. If an answer choice concerns information that's discussed in only one part of the passage, it probably isn't the correct answer to a main-idea question. Here are some other ways to narrow down your options for main-idea questions:

>> Eliminate answer choices that contain information that comes from only the middle paragraphs of the passage. These paragraphs probably deal with specific points rather than the main theme.

>> Eliminate any answer choices that contain information that you can't find in the passage. These choices are irrelevant.

>> Look at the first words of the answer choices to see whether you can eliminate any answer choices based on the first words only. For example, if you're trying to find the best answer to the author's purpose in an objectively written natural science passage, you can eliminate answers that begin with less objective terms, such as *to argue that . . .*, *to criticize . . .*, and *to refute the opposition's position that . . . .*

FINDING THE DETAILS: SUPPORTING INFORMATION QUESTIONS

Some GMAT reading comprehension questions ask you about specific statements in the passage. These questions are potentially the easiest type of reading comprehension question because the information you need to answer them is stated in the passage. You just need to find it. This information may be quantitative, such as years, figures, or numbers, or it may be qualitative, like ideas, emotions, or thoughts.

Supporting information questions are worded in many different ways, but they almost always contain some reference to the passage. For example,

>> The passage states that . . .

>> According to the passage, . . .

>> In the passage, the author indicates that . . .

TIP

To succeed on supporting information questions, read the question carefully and refer to the outline of the passage you've written on your note board to remind yourself where the passage addresses certain types of information. And keep in mind that the correct answer may paraphrase the passage rather than repeat it word for word.

READING BETWEEN AND BEYOND THE LINES: INFERENCE AND APPLICATION QUESTIONS

Inference and application questions ask you about information that's *implied* by the passage rather than directly stated in it. These questions test your ability to draw conclusions, using evidence that appears in the passage. For inference questions, you're normally required to do one of these three things:

>> Identify a different interpretation of an author's statement.

>> Infer the intended meaning of a word that's used figuratively in the passage.

>> Interpret the author's statements one step beyond what is actually written.

For example, suppose you read a passage that compares the rapidity of wing beats between houseflies and horseflies. Information in the second paragraph may state that the wings of horseflies beat at 96 bps (beats per second). Information in the fourth paragraph may state that a Purple Winger is a type of horsefly. From this information, you can infer that the wings of the Purple Winger beat at a rate of 96 bps.

TIP

When you're answering an application question, look for the choice that slightly extends the meaning of the passage. Choices that go beyond the scope of the passage are usually incorrect. Don't choose an answer that requires you to come up with information that isn't somehow addressed by the passage.

The GMAT loves inference questions, so expect to see a lot of them. They're easily recognizable because they usually contain either *infer* or *imply* in the question, like these examples:

>> It can be inferred from the passage that . . .

>> The passage implies (or suggests) that . . .

>> In which of the following is the role played by the cichlid most like the role played by the algae raptor discussed in the passage?

>> The author brings up . . . to suggest which of the following?

Sometimes, the GMAT highlights in yellow the portion of the passage that discusses the material in question. If the test highlights information for you, it's likely an inference question rather than a supporting information type.

EVALUATING PASSAGE FLOW

Some reading questions focus more on the passage's structure than its contents. For these questions you analyze the passage's organization and note how information flows from one idea to another. Questions that call on your ability to follow the author's logic include wording similar to the following:

>> Which of the following best describes the organization of the passage?

>> What purpose does the third paragraph serve?

>> Which of the following would best support the scientist's theory in the second paragraph?

Some of these logic questions may resemble the wording of and require the approach to critical reasoning questions, so following the techniques presented in the later section "Sharpening Your Critical Reasoning Skills" may help you answer these reading questions.

FEELING MOODY: QUESTIONS ABOUT THE AUTHOR'S TONE

As you read the passage, be sure to look for clues to the author's tone as well as purpose. You're bound to see questions that ask you to gauge how the author feels about the topic. Tone questions commonly ask you to figure out the author's attitude or complete the logical flow of the author's ideas. The author may be neutral, negative, or positive and may have different attitudes about different types of information within the same passage. It's up to you to determine the nature and degree of the author's feeling from the language used in the passage. With practice, you'll figure out how to distinguish between an enthusiastic author and one who's faking enthusiasm to mock the subject of the passage.

You can recognize questions about tone by the way they're worded. Here are some examples of how tone questions may appear on the GMAT:

>> The author's attitude appears to be one of . . .

>> With which of the following statements would the author most likely agree?

>> The tone of the passage suggests that the author is most skeptical about which of the following?

When making determinations about the author's tone, consider the passage as a whole. You may find one or two examples of negative comments in an article that is otherwise overwhelmingly positive about a subject. Don't make the mistake of quickly categorizing the passage from a few words that happen to catch your attention. Instead, determine the main idea of the passage and the author's purpose (you need to do this to answer other questions, anyway) and use that information to help you discern the author's tone.

Eliminating answer choices

One of the most effective ways of moving through reading comprehension questions is to eliminate incorrect answer choices. That's because you're looking for the best answer choice, not necessarily the perfect answer choice. Sometimes, you'll have to choose the best choice out of five pretty great choices, and other times you'll choose from five really crummy ones. Because the definitive answer usually won't pop right out at you, eliminate obviously wrong choices first. In this section, we show you how.

Much of the time, you can eliminate wrong choices without having to refer back to the passage. As long as you carefully read the passage and have a good idea of the main theme, the author's purpose in writing the selection, and the author's tone, you should be able to recognize some wrong answers immediately.

Some common wrong answers include the following:

>> **Choices that concern information that isn't found in the passage:** Some answer choices contain information that's beyond the scope of the passage. Even if the information in these choices is true, you can't choose them. You have to choose answers based on what's stated or implied in the passage. Eliminate these choices, no matter how tempting they may be.

>> **Choices that contradict the main theme, author's tone, or specific information in the passage:** After you've read through the passage, you should be able to quickly eliminate most of the choices that contradict what you know about the passage.

WARNING

WARNING

>> **Choices that counter the wording of the question:** You can also eliminate some answer choices by paying careful attention to the wording of the question. For example, a question may ask about a *disadvantage* of something discussed in the passage. If one of the answer choices lists an advantage instead of a disadvantage, you can eliminate that choice without thinking too much about it. Or a question may ask you to choose which answer the author is most optimistic about. If one of the things listed is something the author is negative about, you can eliminate that choice.

The GMAT may try to entice you with answer choices that deal with information directly stated in the passage but don't relate to the actual question at hand. Don't choose an answer just because it looks familiar. Make sure it actually answers the question.

>> **Choices that contain *debatable* words:** Question any answer choice that uses absolutes. Examples are *all, always, only, complete, first, never, every,* and *none.* An answer choice that contains a word that leaves no room for exception is probably wrong. The GMAT makers don't want you calling them up complaining that you know of a circumstance where, say, not all fire engines are red. Beware: Usually the rest of an answer choice that includes a debatable word sounds pretty good, so you may be tempted to choose it.

Don't automatically eliminate an answer choice that contains a debatable word. If information in the passage justifies the presence of *all* or *none* in an answer choice, it may be right. For example, if a passage tells you that all horseflies beat their wings at a rate of 96 bps, the choice with *all* in it may be accurate.

Dealing with exception questions

Most questions ask you to choose the one correct answer, but some questions are cleverly disguised to ask for the *one* false answer. We call these gems *exception questions.* You'll recognize these questions by the presence of a negative word, usually *except* or *not.* When you see these words capitalized in a question, you know you're looking for the one answer choice that *doesn't* satisfy the requirements of the question.

REMEMBER

You won't see many exception questions on the GMAT, but when you do see that negative word, take a moment to make sure you know exactly what the question is asking. Don't get confused or rush and automatically select the first choice that looks good. *Remember:* The question is asking for the *one* answer out of five that's false or not part of the information stated or implied in the passage.

Exception questions aren't that difficult if you approach them systematically. Determining that an answer definitely isn't discussed in the passage takes time. You have to carefully look through the passage for the choice and *not* find it — then check again just to be sure. But a better way does exist: Instead of determining that an answer isn't discussed, eliminate the four true answers, which leaves you with the one false (and, therefore, correct) answer.

Identifying those choices that *do* appear in the passage is much easier than determining the one choice that isn't in the passage. After you've identified the four correct answers (remember to use your erasable note board to keep track), you can click on the one false answer as the choice for that question.

Take a look at two exception questions based on a fairly difficult natural science passage.

This passage is excerpted from *The Earth Through Time*, 7th Edition, by Harold L. Levin (John Wiley & Sons, Inc.):

Geologists have proposed the term *eon* for the largest divisions of the geologic time scale. In chronologic succession, the eons of geologic time are the Hadean, Archean, Proterozoic, and Phanerozoic. The beginning of the Archean corresponds approximately to the ages of the oldest known rocks on Earth. Although not universally used, the term *Hadean* refers to that period of time for which we have no rock record, which began with the origin of the planet 4.6 billion years ago. The Proterozoic Eon refers to the time interval from 2,500 to 544 million years ago.

The rocks of the Archean and Proterozoic are informally referred to as Precambrian. The antiquity of Precambrian rocks was recognized in the mid-1700s by Johann G. Lehman, a professor of mineralogy in Berlin, who referred to them as the "Primary Series." One frequently finds this term in the writing of French and Italian geologists who were contemporaries of Lehman. In 1833, the term appeared again when Lyell used it in his formation of a surprisingly modern geologic time scale. Lyell and his predecessors recognized these "primary" rocks by their crystalline character and took their uppermost boundary to be an unconformity that separated them from the overlying — and therefore younger — fossiliferous strata.

The remainder of geologic time is included in the Phanerozoic Eon. As a result of careful study of the superposition of rock bodies accompanied by correlations based on the abundant fossil record of the Phanerozoic, geologists have divided it into three major subdivisions, termed eras. The oldest is the Paleozoic Era, which we now know lasted about 300 million years. Following the Paleozoic is the Mesozoic Era, which continued for about 179 million years. The Cenozoic Era, in which we are now living, began about 65 million years ago.

EXAMPLE

The passage uses all the following terms to describe *eons* or *eras*, except

(A) Archean

(B) Paleozoic

(C) Holocene

(D) Phanerozoic

(E) Cenozoic

The terms in this passage may be unfamiliar to you, but if you read the passage carefully, you should be able to get a general sense of what it's talking about. For this exception question, which tests you on unfamiliar terms, the best way to approach the question is to consult the text and eliminate the four terms that it uses to describe eons or eras.

TIP

First, scan the answer choices so you have an idea of the words you're looking for. Then begin at the top of the passage and look for words that resemble the answer choices. You should be especially aware of any lists that occur in the text, because exception questions often focus on lists. It's very difficult for test-makers to come up with a good exception question without a list.

The passage contains three lists. The first one appears in the first paragraph. It names eons of geologic time. The question refers to eons and uses four terms that certainly resemble the answer choices. Consult this first list and eliminate any choices that appear on it. The terms *Archean* and *Phanerozoic* appear, so you can eliminate Choices (A) and (D). In the second paragraph, you see the term *Precambrian* (which isn't an answer choice) and a list of geologists who have mentioned Precambrian rocks. The second paragraph doesn't help with this question, so move quickly to the third paragraph.

The third paragraph also provides a list of eras that are part of the Phanerozoic eon. In this list, you see the terms *Paleozoic, Mesozoic,* and *Cenozoic. Paleozoic* is Choice (B), and *Cenozoic* is Choice (E), so you can eliminate both of these terms. Therefore, the correct answer to this exception question is Choice (C), *Holocene*, which isn't mentioned in the passage and, in fact, is neither an eon nor an era but the epoch in which you're living!

You can definitely skip the elimination process if you happen to stumble onto the right information, but that haphazard method won't work for all exception questions. You're better off approaching the question by eliminating the four answers that you find in the passage or that satisfy the criteria and locating the exception by process of elimination.

Exception questions can take some time, but they're among the easier reading comprehension questions because often the answers are right there in the text! So don't get in a hurry and make a mistake. Relax and use the proper approach, and you'll do exceptionally well.

Reading comprehension practice questions with answer explanations

To practice the approach to answering reading comprehension questions, try your hand at these practice questions. Read the passages and answer the questions, using the techniques we've discussed earlier in this block. When you're finished, read through the answer explanations that follow.

Reading comprehension practice questions

In this practice section, we provide you with two passages — one history and one science. Try to answer the following five questions within 9 minutes and 45 seconds (slightly less than two minutes per question). For each question, choose the best answer from the five options.

The GMAT won't label answer choices with letters as we have here to make our explanations easier to follow. To choose an answer on the computerized test, you'll simply click on the radio button next to the choice.

Answer Questions 1–3 based on the following passage.

For most Americans and Europeans, this should be the best time in all of human history to live. Survival — the very purpose of all life — is nearly guaranteed for large parts of the world, especially in the "West." This should allow people a sense of security and contentment. If life is no longer as Thomas Hobbes famously wrote, "nasty, brutish, and short," then should it not be pleasant, dignified, and long? To know that tomorrow is nearly guaranteed, along with thousands of additional tomorrows, should be enough to render hundreds of millions of people awe-struck with happiness. And modern humans, especially in the West, have every opportunity to be free, even as they enjoy ever-longer lives. Why is it, then, that so many people feel unhappy and trapped? The answer lies in the constant pressure of trying to meet needs that don't actually exist.

The term "need" has been used with less and less precision in modern life. Today, many things are described as needs, including fashion items, SUVs, vacations, and other luxuries. People say, "I need a new car," when their current vehicle continues to function. People with many pairs of shoes may still say they "need" a new pair. Clearly, this careless usage is inaccurate; neither the new car nor the additional shoes are truly "needed."

What is a need then? The *Oxford English Dictionary* defines the condition of "need" as "lack of means of subsistence." This definition points the way toward an understanding of what a need truly is: A need is something required for survival. Therefore, the true needs of life are air, food, water, and, in cold climates, shelter. Taken together, this is the stuff of survival. Because the purpose of life is to survive — or more broadly, to live — then these few modest requirements are all that a modern human truly needs. Other things make life exciting or enjoyable, and these are often referred to as "the purpose of life" — but this is surely an exaggeration. These additional trappings are mere wants and not true needs.

1. Which of the following most accurately states the main idea of the passage?

   (A) Modern Americans and Europeans feel unhappy and trapped because they don't distinguish true needs from mere wants.

   (B) There are no human needs, and all so-called needs are merely wants.

   (C) Human needs can never be satisfied in this life and, therefore, people will always be unhappy.

   (D) The satisfaction of human needs has resulted in nearly universal happiness for people in the United States and Europe.

   (E) There is no difference between needs and wants; the desire for wealth and power is just as real as the need for food and shelter.

2. According to the author, which of the following is an example of a fulfillment of a need?

   (A) Adding a roof to block moonlight from shining on a rudimentary sleeping structure built on a tropical island

   (B) Creating a pair of slippers from deer hide to protect one's bare feet from being cut by sharp rocks and stones

   (C) Traveling several miles through dense foliage to obtain a particular berry, known for its sweetness and antioxidant properties, to accompany one's regular bland diet of rice and beans

   (D) Climbing a steep rock face for the exhilaration and sense of accomplishment

   (E) Digging a hole to locate a new water supply after one's prior single source of refreshment has run out

3. Which of the following best defines the way the first paragraph of the passage is organized?

   (A) The author poses a question and provides context and then suggests an answer to the question.

   (B) The author presents an argument and develops that argument by referencing a famous quote that reiterates the point that precedes it.

   (C) The author presents an argument and then supports that argument by defining an essential term.

   (D) The author compares life in one area of the world to life in another area of the world and shows how one way of thinking about life is better than the other.

   (E) The author poses a rhetorical question and explains why modern humans are incapable of answering that question.

Answer Questions 4–5 based on the following passage.

A logarithmic unit known as the decibel (dB) is used to represent the intensity of sound. The decibel scale is similar to the Richter scale used to measure earthquakes. On the Richter scale, a 7.0 earthquake is ten times stronger than a 6.0 earthquake. On the decibel scale, an increase of 10 dB is equivalent to a tenfold increase in intensity or power. Thus, a sound registering 80 dB is ten times louder than a 70 dB sound. In the range of sounds audible to humans, a whisper has an intensity of 20 dB; 140 dB (a jet aircraft taking off nearby) is the threshold of immediate pain.

The perceived intensity of sound is not simply a function of volume; certain frequencies of sound appear louder to the human ear than do other frequencies, even at the same volume. Decibel measurements of noise are, therefore, often "A-weighted" to take into account the fact that some sound wavelengths are perceived as being particularly loud. A soft whisper is 20 dB, but on the A-weighted scale, the whisper is 30 dBA. This is because human ears are particularly attuned to human speech. Quiet conversation has a sound level of about 60 dBA.

Continuous exposure to sounds over 80 dBA can eventually result in mild hearing loss, while exposure to louder sounds can cause much greater damage in a very short period of time. Emergency sirens, motorcycles, chainsaws, construction activities, and other mechanical or amplified noises are often in the 80 to 120 dBA range. Sound levels above 120 dBA begin to be felt inside the human ear as discomfort and eventually as pain.

Unfortunately, the greatest damage to hearing is done voluntarily. Music, especially when played through headphones, can grow to be deceptively loud. The ear becomes numbed by the loud noise, and the listener often turns up the volume until the music approaches 120 dBA. This level of noise can cause permanent hearing loss in a short period of time, and in fact, many young Americans now have a degree of hearing loss once seen only in much older persons.

4. The primary purpose of the passage is to

   (A) argue for government mandates that decibel levels produced by headphones be reduced.

   (B) compare the scale used to measure intensity of sound to the scale used to measure the strength of earthquakes.

   (C) describe the way that sound intensity is measured and explain its effect on human hearing.

   (D) define which volume levels and sound exposure times are safe for humans and which are harmful.

   (E) warn readers about the harmful effects of continuous exposure to sounds over 80 dBA.

5. The author mentions that "emergency sirens, motorcycles, chainsaws, construction activities, and other mechanical or amplified noises" fall in the 80 to 120 dBA range. It can be inferred from this statement that these noises

   (A) are unwanted, outside intrusions common in urban life.

   (B) can cause hearing loss with constant exposure.

   (C) are more dangerous to hearing than sounds of the same dBA level from headphones.

   (D) are loud enough to cause immediate pain.

   (E) have no negative impacts.

Answer Explanations

1. **A.** First, identify the question type. This one's pretty easy because it contains the phrase *main idea* right in the question. You're dealing with a main-idea question, so the answer concerns the general idea and purpose of the passage and is probably found in the first or last paragraphs of the passage.

   Eliminate any choices that go beyond the scope of the information discussed in the passage. You recall that the passage distinguished *true needs* from *mere wants*. Choice (C) says, "Human needs can never be satisfied in this life. . . ." The reading passage never mentions anything about needs not being satisfied in this life. You may or may not agree with the statement in Choice (C), but you can eliminate it because it discusses ideas that aren't covered in the passage.

   Next, look for choices that contradict what you remember from reading through the passage. Choice (B) states that "there are no human needs." The passage specifically lists human needs of food, water, shelter, and so on. So, Choice (B) has to be wrong. You may also recall that this list of needs is included in a section in which the author distinguishes between needs and wants. Choice (E) says that there's "no difference between needs and wants." You know that the passage says otherwise, so you can eliminate that option.

   You're left with Choices (A) and (D). If you have trouble choosing between them, consult the passage. Concentrate on the first paragraph, which says that although Americans and

Europeans should be happy, many are "unhappy and trapped." You can, therefore, eliminate Choice (D).

Choice (A) should be the correct answer. But take a moment to reread Choice (A) to make sure it makes sense as the main idea of the passage. Choice (A) says, "Modern Americans and Europeans feel unhappy and trapped because they don't distinguish true needs from mere wants." This statement agrees with the author's questioning of the reasons behind modern unhappiness found in the first paragraph and the author's distinguishing of needs from wants in the last paragraph.

2. **E.** The author describes a need as "something required for survival" and lists the true needs as "air, food, water, and, in cold climates, shelter." Eliminate answer choices that don't have something to do with air, food, water, and shelter. Climbing a rock face for the fun of it likely falls within the author's definition of a want because it makes life "exciting or enjoyable." So, you can eliminate Choice (D). As nice as it would be to maintain your pedicure with a nice pair of soft deer-hide slippers, foot apparel doesn't fall within the author's criteria for survival. (Apparently, in the author's world, clothing is optional!) Cross off Choice (B).

You're left with Choice (A), which concerns shelter; Choice (C), which deals with food; and Choice (E), which regards water. Each of the remaining answer choices addresses one of the author's categories of needs, so it's up to you to determine which is required for survival. Although it would be nice to sleep peacefully without the interruption of pesky moonlight, the roof in Choice (A) is more likely a want than a need. The author clarifies that shelter is a need in cold climates, not tropical islands. Because Choice (C) tells you that the berry seekers already have a regular diet of rice and beans, you know they're not searching for the berry for survival purposes. The berry isn't necessary for survival, so it's unlikely that it fits the author's idea of a need.

By process of elimination, you settle on Choice (E) as the best answer. The purpose of the hole excavation is to find one of the author's required elements for survival: water. And you know that the exercise is urgent because the hole-digger has no other source for water.

Don't be fooled by the reference to *refreshment* in Choice (E). You may think that refreshment pertains to a want rather than a need, but the author tells you that water is necessary. Therefore, you can conclude that refreshment that refers to water is also necessary.

WARNING

3. **A.** Examine the way the author introduces the point in the first paragraph of the passage. The first several sentences explain that modern humans should be happy because their daily survival is virtually guaranteed. The author inserts the Hobbes quote about how rough life used to be to show that modern life has improved considerably. The author then wonders, given how good we have it, why modern humans are unhappy. The paragraph's ending statement is the author's answer to this question. Find the answer that best describes this organization.

Choice (D) and Choice (E) are pretty easy to eliminate. The author provides an answer to the question, so modern humans aren't incapable of answering it, and Choice (E) can't be right. The author references the "West" but doesn't compare western thinking to the way people think about life in other parts of the world. Choice (D) is wrong.

You may be tempted by Choice (B). The first paragraph has a famous quote, but that quote about the nastiness of life doesn't restate the prior point that people should feel secure and content. Choice (C) may also sound good at first, but it describes the organization of the entire passage rather than just the first paragraph. The author doesn't define a need until the last paragraph.

When you're asked to evaluate the organization of reading content, make sure you know the parameters of the portion you're supposed to consider.

WARNING

The best answer has to be Choice (A). The first several sentences provide background for the author's question about why modern humans aren't happy. Then the author answers the question by stating that humans aren't happy because they don't know what a need is.

4. **C.** This passage is almost exactly 350 words, so it's as long as any passage on the GMAT is going to get. Don't let the unfamiliar scientific concepts worry you. You're probably familiar with the term *decibel*, but you may have never encountered the *A-weighted decibel* or *dBA*, as it's abbreviated. Focus on the main point of the passage, which is to describe dBAs and how human ears perceive them, and what type of information appears in each paragraph so that you can approach this main-idea question systematically:

- First, check out the first word of each answer choice to find obvious incorrect answers. The tone of the passage is primarily objective and descriptive, so an answer that begins with *argue* is likely wrong. If you read Choice (A) further, you know you can eliminate it. The author doesn't mention anything about government mandates.

  Natural science passages are usually objective and informative. Their primary purpose is rarely to argue in favor of or against a particular position.

- Next, eliminate answer choices that deal with information found in only one area of the passage. The scales mentioned in Choice (B) appear only in the first paragraph, so a comparison of them can't be the purpose of the passage. The author discusses the harmful effects of exposure to sound only in the last two paragraphs, so Choice (E) isn't the primary purpose. For the same reason, you can likely eliminate Choice (D). While the author does indeed define the sound exposure levels and times that are safe for humans and does warn readers about the harmful effects of sound exposure, neither Choice (E) nor Choice (D) provides the overall reason for the passage.

- Finally, choose the answer that incorporates information from the passage as a whole. Choice (C) brings together the information in the first two paragraphs (how sound intensity is measured) and the information in the last two (how sound intensity affects humans). Therefore, it's the best answer.

5. **B.** The word *infer* in the question gives you a fairly obvious clue to the type of question you're dealing with. Again, you can rely on the process of elimination to answer it.

Begin by eliminating those choices that rely on outside information. This passage focuses on noise levels and health effects. The passage doesn't mention societal concerns, such as the intrusive impacts of a plethora of noise in urban life. Therefore, you can cross out Choice (A). All the other choices have something to do with noise levels and health, so don't eliminate them yet.

Next, look for choices that contradict what you know about the passage. One of the author's purposes in writing the passage is to warn young people of the hearing loss associated with headphone use (or abuse). To say that the noises mentioned in the question are *more* dangerous than noises at the same decibel level from headphones would be contradictory. Because Choice (C) is inconsistent with what you find out from the passage, you can eliminate it.

You can use the information in the question to narrow down your choices. The question indicates that the noises mentioned are in the 80 to 120 dBA range. Even if you don't remember all the specifics of the passage, you probably remember that noises over 100 dBA are very loud. You may even remember that 120 dBA is the threshold for feeling discomfort in the ear. It's, therefore, not logical to say, as Choice (E) does, that noises in this range would have *no* health effects. Noises that loud have some impact on the ear!

You can also eliminate Choice (E) because it contains an implicit debatable word. *No impacts* in this answer choice suggests *none*, and answer choices that contain the word *none* are almost always wrong because *none* doesn't allow for any exceptions. If the answer were worded a little differently to say "may have no negative impacts," it could be correct. Short exposure to noise may, in fact, have no impact.

You're left with just two answer choices. If you happen to remember that 140 dB is the threshold for immediate pain, you can answer the question without having to refer back to the text. However, if you have any doubt, take a few seconds to be sure.

The last sentence of the first paragraph indicates that 140 dB is the threshold of immediate pain, and in the third paragraph, you read that 120 dBA can "eventually lead to pain." Therefore, you can eliminate Choice (D), so Choice (B) is probably the answer. Glancing at the passage confirms that it indicates that constant exposure to sounds over 80 dBA can result in hearing loss.

Sharpening Your Critical Reasoning Skills

About half of the 23 questions in the GMAT Verbal section are critical reasoning questions. This question type tests your ability to analyze an argument. The good news is that you analyze arguments all the time, even though you may not know you're doing so. When you see a commercial advertising a new product that claims it'll make your life better, you probably question that claim. If a weight-loss drug helped someone lose 50 pounds, you ask, "Is that a typical result?" If four out of five dentists recommend a chewing gum, you say, "Did they ask only five dentists?" When a mutual fund boasts of its performance, you ask, "Is that better than the market average?" You'll use this same kind of thinking to ace the critical reasoning questions on the GMAT.

Focusing on "critical" concepts: An overview

Critical reasoning questions consist of an argument, a question, and five answer choices, of which only one is correct. You'll encounter short passages from a variety of sources, such as speeches, advertisements, newspapers, and scholarly articles. You may see an argument like this: "The local sales tax must be raised to fund city services. Admittedly, this increased sales tax will impose a greater hardship on the poorest citizens. But if the sales tax is not increased, all city services for the poor will have to be cut." The paragraph reflects the type of arguments you encounter in the news every day.

In the following sections, we clue you in on what to expect when you approach a critical reasoning question on the GMAT — from the length and format of the argument to the type of questions you'll be asked, to how to figure out the correct answer.

Understanding the structure of the questions

Each critical reasoning question has essentially the same structure. The question usually begins with a two- to five-sentence paragraph that contains the argument. The question contains all the information you need to answer the question. Don't rely on any outside information! Even if you happen to be an expert in the area a question covers, don't rely on your expertise to answer the question.

The short argument paragraph is followed by a question. The questions usually fall conveniently into one of a few types. The question may ask that you weaken or strengthen an argument, draw a conclusion, analyze the structure of an argument, or identify an unstated assumption the author makes. We examine each of these question types in the section, "Getting from Point A to Point B: Types of reasoning," later in this block.

Each question has five possible answer choices, which are often long, sometimes even longer than the argument or question. For this reason, you'll spend most of your time for each question examining the answer choices.

As with most GMAT questions, you can quickly eliminate one or two of the answers that are obviously wrong. The remaining answers will be more difficult to eliminate, so spend your time analyzing these better answer choices.

Figuring out how to answer the questions

To break down a critical reasoning question, follow these three steps:

1. **Read the question.**

2. **Read the argument paragraph, focusing on the specific information you need to know to answer the question.**

3. **As you read the argument, look for inconsistencies and/or assumptions in the logic.**

The best way to tackle a critical reasoning question is to read the question first to determine its type. The later section, "Thinking inside the box: Question types," shows you how to distinguish critical reasoning question types. When you first read the question, don't read all the answer choices; doing so takes way too much time and clutters your thinking. You need to concentrate on only the information you need to find to answer the question.

After you figure out what kind of question you're dealing with, you can read the paragraph very carefully. Be sure to locate the conclusion of the argument. The conclusion may come at the beginning, middle, or end of the paragraph. When you've identified the conclusion, you can better understand the rest of the paragraph. As you read the paragraph, look for inconsistencies or gaps in the argument that may help you answer the question. Isolating the argument's premises, assumptions, and conclusion helps you determine the method of reasoning.

The argument paragraph usually isn't too complicated, and therefore you may be tempted to read it too quickly. Force yourself to read slowly and carefully so you don't skim over the word or words that provide the keys to the argument. If you read thoroughly enough, you'll be able to eliminate some — or even most — of the answer choices. When you're down to two possible answers, you can then easily refer back to the text to make sure you choose the correct answer.

Making a case: Essentials of informal logic

You can score well on the GMAT critical reasoning questions without knowing the elements of informal logic, but if you understand a few terms and concepts, you can score even higher. You really just need to know the two basic components of a logical argument and a few methods of coming up with a conclusion, which we outline in the following sections.

Fighting fair: The elements of an argument

A logical argument consists of premises and a conclusion, and when you're analyzing arguments, identifying what parts are premises and what makes up the conclusion can help. The *premises* give the supporting evidence that you can draw a conclusion from. You can usually find the *conclusion* in the argument because it's the statement that you can preface with *therefore*. The conclusion is often but not always the last sentence of the argument. For example, take a look at this simple argument:

All runners are fast. John is a runner. Therefore, John is fast.

SURE SOUNDS GREEK TO ME: ORIGINS OF LOGICAL THOUGHT

Legend has it that a Greek philosopher named Parmenides in the 5th century BC had plenty of time on his hands while living in a Greek colony off the west coast of Italy. So he whiled away the hours contemplating logical thought and became one of the first Westerners to record his findings. He penned a philosophical poem in which an unnamed goddess instructs him in the ways of determining truth about the universe. His poem explored the contrast between truth and appearance and portrayed truth to be firm and steadfast, whereas appearance (the way mortals usually think) was unstable and wavering. Parmenides's work influenced other great Greek thinkers, including Plato, Aristotle, and Plotinus.

Unfortunately, you won't have a goddess to guide you through the critical reasoning questions of the GMAT, but you can rely on Aristotle's method of developing syllogisms to examine GMAT arguments. He is credited as the father of formal logic, which is the basis for this famous syllogism: "All humans are mortal; Socrates is human; therefore, Socrates is mortal."

The premises in the argument are "All runners are fast" and "John is a runner." They provide the supporting evidence for the conclusion that John is fast, which is the sentence that begins with *therefore.* Not all conclusions in the GMAT critical reasoning arguments will begin with *therefore* or other words like it (such as *thus* and *so*), but you can try adding *therefore* to any statement you believe is the conclusion to see whether the argument makes sense. We give you plenty of sample arguments in this block so you can use them to practice identifying premises and conclusions.

Getting from Point A to Point B: Types of reasoning

Each logical argument has premises and a conclusion, but not every argument leads to a conclusion in the same way. For the purposes of the GMAT, you should be familiar with two basic types of logical reasoning: deductive and inductive (which we explain further in the next sections). You use both types of reasoning all the time, but now you can apply definitions to your logical genius.

ELEMENTARY, MY DEAR WATSON: DEDUCTIVE REASONING

In *deductive reasoning*, you come up with a specific conclusion from more general premises. The great thing about deductive reasoning is that if the premises are true, the conclusion must be true! The following is an example of a deductive reasoning argument:

> All horses have hooves. (General premise)
>
> Bella is a horse. (More specific premise)
>
> Therefore, Bella has hooves. (Very specific conclusion)

If the premise that all horses have hooves is true, and if Bella is, in fact, a horse, then it must be true that Bella has hooves. The same holds true for all examples of deductive reasoning. Here's another example:

> All who take the GMAT must work through a Quantitative section. (General premise)
>
> You're taking the GMAT. (More specific premise)
>
> Therefore, you have to work through a Quantitative section. (Very specific conclusion)

This example shows the relationship between the truth of the premises and that of the conclusion. The first premise is categorically true: The GMAT requires you to work through a Quantitative section. The second premise, however, may not be true. Certainly, you're thinking of taking the GMAT or you wouldn't be reading this book, but you may still decide not to take the test. This possibility doesn't affect the logic of the argument. Remember, in deductive reasoning, the conclusion must be true *if* the premises are true. If you take the test, you have to work through a Quantitative section, so this argument is valid.

REMEMBER

When you analyze deductive reasoning arguments for the GMAT, the only way you can prove that a conclusion is true is by showing that all premises are true. The only way to prove that a deductive reasoning conclusion is false is to show that at least one of the premises is false.

PERHAPS I'M JUST GENERALIZING: INDUCTIVE REASONING

In deductive reasoning, you draw a specific conclusion from general premises. With *inductive reasoning*, you do just the opposite; you develop a general conclusion from specific premises or observations. Inductive reasoning differs from deductive reasoning in that the conclusion in an inductive reasoning argument could be false even if all the premises are true. With inductive reasoning, the conclusion is essentially your best guess. That's because an inductive reasoning argument relies on less complete information than deductive reasoning does. Consider this example of an inductive argument:

> Bella is a horse and has hooves. (Specific premise)
>
> Smoky is a horse and has hooves. (Specific premise)
>
> Nutmeg is a horse and has hooves. (Specific premise)
>
> Shadow is a horse and has hooves. (Specific premise)
>
> Therefore, it is likely that all horses have hooves. (General conclusion)

Because inductive reasoning derives general conclusions from specific examples, you can't come up with a statement that "must be true." The best you can say, even if all the premises are true, is that the conclusion can be or is likely to be true.

TIP

Inductive reasoning arguments come in all sorts of flavors, but the folks who create the GMAT tend to favor three types: analogy, cause and effect, and statistical. To excel on the GMAT, you want to get very familiar with these three methods of inductive reasoning:

>> **Analogy arguments:** An analogy argument tries to show that two or more concepts are similar so that what holds true for one is true for the other. The strength of the argument depends on the degree of similarity between the persons, objects, or ideas being compared. For example, in drawing a conclusion about Beth's likes, you may compare her to Alex: "Alex is a student, and he likes rap music. Beth is also a student, so she probably likes rap music, too." Your argument would be stronger if you could show that Alex and Beth have other similar interests that apply to rap music, like hip-hop dancing or fashion. If, on the other hand, you show that Alex likes to go to dance clubs while Beth prefers practicing her violin at home, your original conclusion may be less likely.

>> **Cause-and-effect arguments:** A cause-and-effect argument concludes that one event is the result of another. These types of arguments are strongest when the premises indicate that the alleged cause of an event is the most likely one and that no other probable causes exist. For example, after years of football watching, you may conclude the following: "Every time I wear my lucky shirt, my favorite team wins; therefore, wearing my lucky shirt causes the team to win." This example is weak because it doesn't take into consideration other, more-probable reasons (like the team's talent) for the wins.

» **Statistical arguments:** Arguments based on statistical evidence rely on numbers to reach a conclusion. These types of arguments claim that what's true for the statistical majority is also true for the individual. But because these are inductive-reasoning arguments, you can't prove that the conclusions are absolutely true. When you analyze statistical arguments on the GMAT, focus on how well the given statistics apply to the circumstances of the conclusion. For example, if you wanted people to buy clothing through your website, you might make this argument: "In a recent study of the preferences of consumers, 80 percent of shoppers surveyed spent more than six hours a day on the Internet; therefore, you'll probably prefer to buy clothes online." You'd support your conclusion if you could show that a positive correlation occurs between the amount of time people spend on the Internet and a preference for buying clothing online. If you can't demonstrate that correlation, the statistics regarding time spent on the Internet have little to do with predicting one's preference for online shopping.

TIP

To do well on the critical reasoning questions, you need to recognize premises and conclusions in arguments, determine whether the argument applies deductive or inductive reasoning (most will be inductive), and, if the argument is inductive, figure out the method the author uses to reach the conclusion. As you can induce, knowing a little about logical reasoning is essential to scoring well on the GMAT!

Thinking inside the box: Question types

When you were growing up, you probably experienced social groups or cliques. These groups were often defined by shared interests, behaviors, or backgrounds. Some of the common groups included those who enjoyed sports, those who were more laid-back, those who excelled academically (that was your group!), and various other categories. These labels were helpful because they gave you clues that allowed you to better understand how to interact with someone who was a member of a particular group. For instance, you likely knew better than to pick a fight with a talented athlete, and you might have found it easy to bond with an individual who was laid-back. Well, we categorize GMAT questions for the same reason. After you figure out a critical reasoning question's type, you know just how to deal with it. Most of the critical reasoning questions you'll encounter on the GMAT fit into one of the following five categories:

» **Strengthening or weakening arguments:** The argument presents premises and a conclusion and asks you to evaluate the answer choices to determine which one would best strengthen or weaken the author's conclusion.

» **Drawing conclusions from premises:** The argument paragraph consists of a bunch of premises but doesn't provide a conclusion. Your job is to choose the best conclusion for the argument.

» **Seeking assumptions:** This more-subtle type of question requires you to discover an essential premise of the argument that the author doesn't state directly.

» **Making inferences:** For these less-common question types, you have to surmise information that isn't directly stated, usually about one of the premises rather than the conclusion.

» **Finding the method of reasoning:** In these questions, you'll be asked to find an argument in the answer choices that uses the same method of reasoning as the original given argument.

Because each question type has a best way to handle it, recognizing what type of question you're dealing with before you try to answer it is important. That's why you read the question before you tackle the argument. You'll immediately know what you need to look for when you read the argument from the wording of the question.

Stalking your prey: How to approach each question type

Knowing the types of questions you'll face is valuable only if you know the specialized strategies for dealing with each one. The following sections give you the tips you need to make approaching each of the question types second nature. You get some practice questions, too, so you'll know just what to expect when you take the actual GMAT.

Strengthening or weakening arguments

Critical reasoning questions that ask you how to best support or damage an argument are some of the easiest to answer, which is a good thing because they appear the most frequently. You probably analyze ideas every day and think of evidence to attack or defend those ideas. Because you already have the skill to evaluate arguments, it doesn't take much work for you to modify that skill to fit this specific GMAT question format. This question category has two subtypes: One asks you to strengthen an argument, and the other asks you to weaken it. You'll recognize these questions because they include words that mean to strengthen or weaken (like *support*, *bolster*, or *impair*), and they almost always contain an "if true" qualifier.

Here are a couple samples of the ways the questions could be worded:

>> Which of the following statements, if true, would most seriously weaken the conclusion reached by the business owners?

>> Which of the following, if true, provides the most support for the conclusion?

WARNING

Nearly all these questions contain the words *if true*, but not all questions that have *if true* in them are strengthening- or weakening-the-argument types. To make sure an "if true" question is really a strengthening or weakening question, look for the identifying language that asks you to either strengthen or weaken the argument.

Here are three simple steps to follow when approaching strengthening- or weakening-the-argument questions:

1. **Read the question carefully so you know exactly what you'll be strengthening or weakening.**

   In most cases, you'll be asked to strengthen or weaken the conclusion of the main argument. But in less-frequent cases, you may be asked to support or impair a different conclusion, like the view of the author's opponent.

2. **Examine the argument to find the premises and conclusion and to determine what method of reasoning the author uses to reach the conclusion.**

   Usually the author uses inductive reasoning, so you'll need to figure out whether the argument relies on analogy, statistics, or cause and effect to arrive at the conclusion. In the following sections, we tell you what to look for in each type of reasoning.

3. **Evaluate the answer choices to determine which choice best fits with the author's conclusion and method of reasoning.**

   Assume all the answer choices are true and then determine which one best either supports or undermines the specific conclusion addressed in the question.

Always assume that all the answers to strengthening- or weakening-the-argument questions are true. Almost all these questions include the words *if true* in them to remind you that you're supposed to assume that each answer choice presents a true statement. Don't fall into the trap of trying to evaluate whether answer choices are true or false! Your only job is to determine whether the choices help or hurt the argument, not whether they're true or false.

ANALYZING ANALOGY ARGUMENTS

Analogy arguments rely on the similarity of the two persons, things, or ideas being compared. Therefore, if the author uses an analogy to reach a conclusion, answer choices that show similarities between the compared elements will support the conclusion, and choices that emphasize the differences between the elements will weaken the conclusion. Take a look at this example of an analogy argument.

Hundo is a Japanese car company, and Hundos run for many miles on a gallon of gas. Toyo is also a Japanese car company; therefore, Toyos should get good gas mileage, too.

The author's conclusion would be best supported by which of the following?

(A) All Japanese car manufacturers use the same types of engines in their cars.

(B) British cars run for as many miles on a tank of gas as Hundos do.

(C) The Toyo manufacturer focuses on producing large utility vehicles.

(D) Toyo has been manufacturing cars for more than 20 years.

(E) All Japanese cars have excellent service records.

Recognizing the premises and conclusion in this argument is simple. The author states directly that Hundo cars are Japanese and get good gas mileage and that Toyo cars are Japanese; therefore, Toyos also get good gas mileage. Your job is to find the answer that perpetuates the similarity between Hundos and Toyos.

You can generally eliminate answer choices that introduce irrelevant information, such as Choices (B), (D), and (E). The author compares Japanese cars, so what British cars do has nothing to do with the argument. The length of time that Toyo has been in business tells you nothing about how similar its cars are to Hundo's. And the question is talking about gas mileage, not service records, so don't spend too much time considering Choice (E).

Choice (C) tells you the focus of Toyo producers, but it doesn't give you any information about how that compares to Hundo, so the best answer is Choice (A). If all Japanese manufacturers supply their cars with the same engines and Hundo and Toyo are both Japanese manufacturers, it's more likely that Toyos will achieve a gas mileage similar to that experienced by Hundos.

CONSIDERING CAUSE-AND-EFFECT ARGUMENTS

Questions that ask you to evaluate arguments often apply cause-and-effect reasoning. If the argument uses cause and effect to make its point, focus on the causes. Almost always, the correct answer to a question that asks you to strengthen the conclusion is an answer choice that shows the cause mentioned is the most likely source of the effect. The best answer for a question for which you have to weaken the argument points to another probable cause of the effect. Here's how you'd apply this reasoning to a sample question.

Average hours of television viewing per American have rapidly increased for more than three decades. To fight the rise in obesity, Americans must limit their hours of television viewing.

Which of the following, if true, would most weaken the author's conclusion?

(A) A person burns more calories while watching television than while sleeping.

(B) Over the last 30 years, the number of fast-food restaurants in America has increased.

(C) Americans spend most of their television time watching sporting events rather than cooking shows.

(D) Television viewing in Japan has also increased over the past three decades.

(E) Studies show that the number of television commercials that promote junk food has risen over the past ten years.

To tackle this question, first identify the conclusion you're supposed to weaken and the premises the author states or implies to reach that conclusion. The conclusion is pretty easy to spot. The last thought of the argument is that Americans must limit their hours of television viewing to curb the rise in obesity. The author makes this judgment using the following evidence:

>> The author directly states that the number of television viewing hours has increased over the last 30 years.

>> According to the author, the number of obese Americans has also increased.

>> The author implies that television viewing causes obesity.

To weaken the argument that Americans have to reduce their television watching, you have to find the answer choice that shows that there's another cause for the rise in obesity.

You may have been tempted to select Choice (A) because it shows that television watching may be less fat-producing than another activity, sleeping. But it doesn't give you another reason for the rise in obesity. Choice (A) could be correct only if it showed that Americans were sleeping more than they were 30 years ago. It doesn't, so move on.

On the other hand, stating that during the same time period, the number of fast-food restaurants also increased introduces another possible cause of obesity and weakens the conclusion that Americans have to stop watching so much TV to get slimmer. Maybe it's the popularity of fast food that's the culprit! Choice (B) is a better answer than Choice (A), but read through all the possibilities before you commit. Choice (C) is wrong because there's nothing in the argument that suggests that the type of television Americans watch affects their obesity; nor does Choice (C) show that viewing patterns have changed over the last three decades. Choice (D) is also out because it doesn't correlate what's happening in Japan with what's happening in America. You don't know whether Japanese citizens weigh more now than they did 30 years ago, so the information in Choice (D) is useless.

If the question had asked you to strengthen the conclusion, Choice (E) would be a good option. It shows a reason that increased television watching could cause obesity. But the question asks you to weaken the conclusion, so Choice (B) is the best answer. It's the only one that shows that another cause could be to blame for the rise in obesity.

TAKING A STAB AT STATISTICAL ARGUMENTS

If you see statistics used to promote an argument, you're looking for an answer that shows whether the statistics actually relate to the topic of the conclusion. If they do, you'll strengthen the conclusion. On the other hand, an answer choice that shows the statistics are unrelated to the conclusion significantly weakens that conclusion. The following is an example of a statistical argument critical reasoning question you could find on the GMAT.

EXAMPLE

In a survey of 100 pet owners, 80 percent said that they would buy a more expensive pet food if it contained vitamin supplements. Consequently, CatCo's new premium cat food should be a top-seller.

Which of the following best demonstrates a weakness in the author's conclusion?

(A) Some brands of cat food contain more vitamin supplements than CatCo's does.

(B) CatCo sells more cat food than any of its competitors.

(C) Some of the cat owners surveyed stated that they never buy expensive brands of cat food.

(D) Ninety-five of those pet owners surveyed did not own cats.

(E) Many veterinarians have stated that vitamin supplements in cat food do not greatly increase health benefits.

Because the argument hinges on statistics, eliminate answers that don't directly address the statistical evidence. Those surveyed stated that they'd pay more for pet food with vitamin supplements, but they didn't provide information on whether the amount of vitamin supplements was important. So even though Choice (A) may entice you, it isn't the best answer because it doesn't address the statistics used in the argument. Choice (B) doesn't regard the survey results, either, and it supports the conclusion rather than weakens it. The argument has nothing at all to do with veterinarians, so Choice (E) can't be right. Only Choices (C) and (D) deal with the survey the author uses to reach the conclusion that CatCo's premium cat food will be a big seller.

TIP

You can eliminate answer choices that show an exception to the statistical evidence. Exceptions don't significantly weaken a statistical argument.

Therefore, Choice (C) is wrong and Choice (D) is the best answer because it demonstrates a weakness in the statistics the author uses to support the conclusion. The preferences of dog or bird owners isn't a good indicator of the habits of cat owners.

DABBLING IN DEDUCTIVE-REASONING ARGUMENTS

Rarely will you see a strengthen- or weaken-the-argument question that uses deductive reasoning to reach a conclusion. It's just too hard to come up with challenging answer choices for weakening deductive arguments, because the only way to weaken them is to question the accuracy of the evidence, and correct answers are pretty easy to spot. The only way to strengthen a deductive argument is to reinforce the validity of the premises, which seems sort of silly. Even though GMAT creators don't want to make things too easy for you, one or two deductive arguments may crop up. To weaken an argument with a conclusion that must be true, look for an answer choice that shows that one of the premises is untrue. For example, you may see a question with the following argument:

All horses have tails. Nutmeg is a horse. Therefore, Nutmeg must have a tail.

The only way to weaken this argument is to question one of the two premises. Answer choices like "Scientists have recently developed a breed of horses that has no tail" or "Although Nutmeg looks like a horse, she's really a donkey" would weaken the conclusion.

Delving into drawing conclusions

Another common critical reasoning question type tests your ability to draw logical conclusions (or hypotheses). The GMAT gives you a series of premises (the evidence), and you choose an answer that best concludes the information. Questions that ask you to draw conclusions from premises may be worded like this:

>> Which of the following conclusions is best supported by the preceding information?

>> Assuming the preceding statements are true, which of the following must also be true?

>> The experimental results support which of the following hypotheses?

As you read through the premises, think of a logical conclusion of your own. Then look through the answer choices to see whether one listed comes close to what you've thought up.

TIP

The key to correctly answering drawing–conclusions questions is to look for an answer choice that addresses all the information contained in the premises. Eliminate any choices that are off topic or incomplete. A conclusion that addresses only part of the information may be plausible, but it probably isn't the best answer. For example, consider the following premises:

> Five hundred healthy adults were allowed to sleep no more than five hours a night for one month. Half of the group members were allowed 90-minute naps in the afternoon each day; the remaining subjects were allowed no naps. Throughout the month, the subjects of the experiment were tested to determine the impact of sleep deprivation on their performance of standard tasks. By the end of the month, the group that was not allowed to nap suffered significant declines in their performance, while the napping group suffered more moderate declines.

The best conclusion for these premises would have to address all the following:

>> The nightly sleep deprivation of healthy adults

>> The allowance for naps for half of the study group

>> The smaller decline in performance of standard tasks for the group who took naps

Any conclusion that fails to address all three points isn't the best conclusion. For example, the statement "Sleep deprivation causes accumulating declines in performance among healthy adults" wouldn't be the best conclusion because it fails to address the effect of naps. A better conclusion would be "Napping helps reduce the declines in performance caused by nightly sleep deprivation among healthy adults."

WARNING

You'll often see more than one plausible conclusion among the answer choices. Your task is to identify the best choice. Don't fall for the trap of choosing an answer that just restates one of the premises. Answer choices that restate a premise may entice you because they echo part of the information in the argument, but the best choice must contain an element of each of the pieces of information presented in the question.

The process is pretty simple, really. Try this sample question to see for yourself.

EXAMPLE

Over the last eight years, the Federal Reserve Bank has raised the prime interest rate by a quarter–point more than ten times. The Bank raises rates when its Board of Governors fears inflation and lowers rates when the economy is slowing down.

Which of the following is the most logical conclusion for the preceding paragraph?

(A) The Federal Reserve should be replaced with regional banks that can respond more quickly to changing economic conditions.

(B) The Federal Reserve has raised the prime rate in recent years to try to control inflation.

(C) The economy has entered a prolonged recession caused by Federal Reserve policies.

(D) The monetary policy of the United States is no longer controlled by the Federal Reserve.

(E) The Federal Reserve has consistently raised the prime rate over the last several years.

You know from the language that this is a drawing-conclusions question, so you don't have to look for a conclusion in the argument. Just read through the premises and formulate a quick conclusion, something like "Because the Federal Reserve has raised interest rates many times over the last eight years, it must fear inflation."

Eliminate answer choices that aren't relevant or that contain information not presented by the premises. The argument says nothing about regional banks or the termination of the Federal Reserve's control over U.S. monetary policy, so you can disregard Choices (A) and (D). Then get rid of any choices that don't take all premises into consideration. Choice (E) just reiterates the first premise, so it's wrong. You're left with Choices (B) and (C), but Choice (C) contradicts the information in the premises. The problem says the Federal Reserve responds to the economy, not the other way around, so it'd be wrong to say the Federal Reserve causes a recession. Choice (B) is clearly the best answer. It takes into consideration the information that the Federal Reserve has raised rates and that raising rates is its response to inflation.

WARNING

Be careful to avoid relying on outside knowledge or opinions when answering drawing-conclusions questions. You may have studied the Federal Reserve Bank and have opinions about monetary policy. Choices (A), (C), and (D) reflect some possible opinions about the Federal Reserve. Don't get trapped into choosing an answer because it supports your opinion.

Spotting those sneaky assumptions

Some GMAT critical reasoning questions ask you to identify a premise that isn't there. For these types of questions, the author directly states a series of premises and provides a clear conclusion, but in getting to that conclusion, the author assumes information. Your job is to figure out what the author assumes to be true but doesn't state directly in drawing the conclusion to the argument. Seeking-assumptions questions may look like these:

>> The argument in the preceding passage depends on which of the following assumptions?

>> The conclusion reached by the author of the preceding passage is a questionable one. On which of the following assumptions did the author rely?

>> The preceding paragraph presupposes which of the following?

TIP

Words like *assume, rely, presuppose, depend on,* and their derivatives usually indicate seeking-assumptions questions. Remember, these questions ask you to look for the ideas the author relies on but doesn't state.

As you read seeking-assumptions questions, look for information that's necessary to the argument but isn't stated by the author. In these questions, the author always takes for granted something on which the entire argument depends. You just need to identify what that is. To do so effectively, choose an answer that links the existing premises to the conclusion. The assumption you're seeking always bears directly on the conclusion and ties in with one or more premises, often with the last premise. Therefore, the best answer often contains information from both the last premise and the conclusion.

EXAMPLE

Women receive fewer speeding tickets than men do. Women also have lower car insurance rates. It is clear that women are better drivers than men.

The preceding conclusion is based on which of the following assumptions?

I. Men and women drive cars equal distances and with equal frequency.

II. Having lower car insurance rates indicates that one is a better driver than those who have higher rates.

III. Speeding tickets are equally awarded for violations without any gender bias on the part of police officers.

(A) I only

(B) III only

(C) I and III only

(D) II and III only

(E) I, II, and III

As always, read the question first. Because it references assumptions, we bet you figured out pretty quickly that it's a seeking-assumptions question.

Next, read through the argument and try to figure out the assumption or assumptions the author makes in reaching the conclusion that women are better drivers. The author moves from the premises to the conclusion pretty quickly and assumes that fewer speeding tickets and lower car insurance rates indicate better driving skills. The author also assumes that men and women have equal driving experiences. Use this information to examine each of your options.

Look at Statement I first. It fits with your second observation that men and women experience equal driving situations, so eliminate any answer choices that *don't* include Statement I. This means that you can get rid of Choices (B) and (D), which leaves you with Choices (A), (C), and (E).

TIP

Before you continue reading through your options, examine the remaining answer choices. You'll see that it's best to examine Statement II next, because if it's true, you won't even have to read Statement III; you'll know the answer is Choice (E). You have to read Statement III only if you determine that Statement II isn't an assumption.

The information in Statement II links the author's last premise, that women have lower insurance rates, to the conclusion that women are better drivers. Thus, Statement II is also correct. You can eliminate Choices (A) and (C), and by process of elimination, the answer must be Choice (E). If you read through Statement III, you'll confirm that it, too, is an assumption the author makes about men and women having an equal playing field in the driving game.

TIP

If you find seeking-assumption questions to be tricky, try arguing the opposite position. For example, in the sample question, you could've taken the opposing view, that men are better drivers. This means you'll be looking for ways to undermine the conclusion. If you assume the premises to be true, the best way to attack the conclusion is to show that the author assumes things that aren't true. For example, you may argue that men have more accidents because they drive more, they get more tickets because police are less forgiving with male speeders, and they have higher car insurance rates because they drive more-expensive cars. Those counterarguments expose the author's assumptions!

Using your noggin to make inferences

Critical reasoning inference questions ask you to make an inference (using inductive reasoning) based on the argument in the passage. Making-inferences questions are pretty easy to recognize because they usually include the word *infer*, such as the following examples:

>> Which of the following statements can be correctly inferred from the preceding passage?

>> Which of the following can be inferred from the preceding statements?

The key to answering these questions correctly is to know that they usually ask you to make an inference about one of the premises in the argument rather than about the entire argument or the conclusion. Because these questions usually deal with the premises and not the conclusion, you should choose an answer that makes a plausible inference about one or more of the premises. Like the correct answer choices for the drawing-conclusions questions, the best answers to this type of question don't go beyond the scope of the information provided in the paragraph. Here's what one looks like.

EXAMPLE

The highest-rated television shows do not always command the most advertising dollars. Ads that run during shows with lower overall ratings are often more expensive because the audience for those shows includes a high proportion of males between the ages of 19 and 34. Therefore, ads that run during sporting events are often more expensive than ads running during other types of programs.

Which of the following can properly be inferred from the preceding passage?

(A) Advertisers have done little research into the typical consumer and are not using their advertising dollars wisely.

(B) Sports programs have higher overall ratings than prime-time network programs.

(C) Advertisers believe males between the ages of 19 and 34 are more likely to be influenced by advertisers than are other categories of viewers.

(D) Advertising executives prefer sports programs and assume that other Americans do as well.

(E) Ads that run during the biggest sporting events are the most expensive of all ads.

You know you're dealing with an inference question before you read through the argument because you've read the question first and it contains the word *inferred*. Focus on the premises of the argument as you read it. Then look through the answer choices and eliminate any that don't address one of the premises or that present inferences that require additional information.

The argument says nothing about advertising research or whether the particular advertising practice is wise, so you can eliminate Choice (A) immediately. You're stretching beyond the scope of the information if you infer that advertisers are unwise. Likewise, Choice (D) mentions the preferences and assumptions of advertisers, but none of the premises discuss advertisers, so you can get rid of Choice (D). The inference in Choice (E) relates to the conclusion rather than any of the premises, so you can probably eliminate it right away. Furthermore, just because sporting events ads are "often more expensive" than other ads doesn't necessarily mean that they're always the most expensive. This leaves you with Choices (B) and (C).

Choice (B) contradicts information in the argument. The author implies that some sporting events have lower overall ratings even though they have higher advertising rates. You're left with Choice (C). You need an explanation for the information in the second sentence that states that advertising is often more expensive for lower-rated shows viewed by males who are between 19 and 34 years old. This practice would be logical only if males of these ages were more susceptible to advertising than other groups. It makes sense that Choice (C) is the correct answer.

WARNING

Remember to check your outside knowledge about the critical reasoning subjects at the door! You may know that Super Bowl ads are the most expensive ads, which may tempt you to pick Choice (E). Using your own knowledge rather than what's expressly stated in the test questions will cause you to miss questions that someone with less knowledge may answer correctly.

Pondering the paradox

A few critical reasoning questions test your ability to resolve paradoxes or apparent inconsistencies. They present a potential conflict and ask you to choose the answer that contains the piece of information that helps explain why the apparent conflict is not in fact a conflict at all.

The following list includes some examples of questions that test apparent inconsistencies:

>> Which of the following, if true, most helps to resolve the apparent paradox?

>> Which of the following, if true, most helps to explain the apparent inconsistency in the school's policy?

>> Which of the following, if true, explains why the birds do not fly away from their predators?

>> Which of the following, if true, most helps to resolve the apparent conflict described above?

>> Which of the following, if true, most helps to reconcile the experts' belief with the apparently contrary evidence described above?

You answer these questions by reading the passage to figure out which facts seem to be at odds. Then try to come up with an idea that would reconcile the inconsistency and make the paradox disappear. You probably won't be able to envision the exact answer before reading the choices, but you can come up with something in the ballpark.

Here's an example of a question that asks you to resolve an apparent inconsistency.

EXAMPLE

Skydiving experts have noted that improvements in gear and training techniques have led to fewer fatalities than occurred in the sport's earlier years. However, fatalities among very experienced skydivers, who use the most modern gear equipped with a device that automatically opens the reserve parachute if the skydiver has not opened the main parachute by a certain altitude, have held steady for the last 12 years.

Which one of the following, if true, most helps to resolve the apparent inconsistency in this passage?

(A) Most skydivers prefer not to buy improved gear because it costs too much.

(B) Experienced skydivers favor tiny parachutes that fly at high velocities and that must be landed precisely, which makes them more likely to hit the ground at an uncontrolled high speed, even under an open parachute.

(C) Not all jumpers choose to use the device that automatically opens their reserve parachute for them.

(D) The U.S. Parachute Association's recommended minimum opening altitude for reserve parachutes has increased over the last 12 years.

(E) Most inexperienced skydivers rent gear from drop zones instead of owning their own gear.

Read the question. The passage contains an apparent inconsistency. Despite advancements in safety, skydiving fatalities have not decreased among experienced skydivers. This fact is surprising because experienced skydivers use modern gear that guarantees that their parachutes will open. An open parachute must not be the only guarantee of a safe landing. If experienced skydivers are dying despite open parachutes, their fatalities must result from another cause. Snipers aren't picking them off from the ground, so they must be dying on landing. Perhaps experienced skydivers land differently from novices. See what the answer choices have to offer.

>> Choice (A) doesn't explain the specific paradox related to the fates of experienced skydivers. The buying habits of other, less experienced skydivers are irrelevant.

>> Choice (B) does explain the results; experienced skydivers land differently and more dangerously than novices do, which could explain why the safer parachutes aren't leading to fewer deaths.

>> Choice (C) is also irrelevant because it doesn't pertain specifically to the experienced skydivers who are at the heart of the paradox.

>> Choice (D) makes the inconsistency even more apparent. If the reserve parachutes activate at higher altitudes, fewer fatalities should result.

>> Choice (E) doesn't explain anything about fatalities. It may explain why inexperienced and experienced skydivers use different gear, but it doesn't explain why experienced skydivers die despite having good, high-tech, perfectly functioning equipment.

Choice (B) is the correct answer.

Making your way through method-of-reasoning questions

Method-of-reasoning questions are the rarest form of GMAT critical reasoning question types. This type of question either directly asks you what type of reasoning the author uses to make an argument or, more often, asks you to choose an answer that uses the same method of reasoning as the argument. You may see method-of-reasoning questions phrased like these:

>> Which of the following employs the same method of reasoning as the preceding argument?

>> The author's point is made by which method of reasoning?

>> David's argument is similar to Ari's in which of the following ways?

The two types of method-of-reasoning questions may seem different, but each of them asks you to do the same thing: to recognize the type of reasoning used in the argument.

REMEMBER

For the purposes of the GMAT, the methods of reasoning are as follows:

>> Deductive, which is reaching a specific conclusion from general premises

>> Inductive, which is drawing a general conclusion from specific premises and includes the following methods:

• Analogy, which shows that one thing is sufficiently similar to another thing such that what holds true for one is true for the other

• Cause and effect, which shows that one event resulted from another

• Statistics, which uses population samples (surveys) to reach conclusions about the population as a whole

Questions that ask you to specifically choose what kind of reasoning the author uses are straightforward, so we focus on the other type of question, which asks you to choose an answer that mimics the reasoning method of the given argument. When you know you're dealing with this type of question, you just need to focus on the way the author makes the argument to make sure you choose an answer that follows the logic most exactly.

Don't choose an answer just because it deals with the same subject matter as the given argument. These choices are often traps to lure you away from the answer that more exactly duplicates the author's logic but addresses another topic.

It doesn't matter whether the argument makes sense. If the given argument isn't logical, pick an answer choice that isn't logical in the same way.

You may focus on the method of reasoning better if you substitute letters for ideas in the argument. For example, say you're presented with this argument: "Balloons that contain helium float. Jerry's balloon doesn't float, so it contains oxygen rather than helium." You could state this logic with letters like this: "All A (helium balloons) are B (floaters). C (Jerry's balloon) isn't B (a floater), so C isn't A." Then you can apply that formula to your answer choices to see which one matches best.

Some of the reasoning methods may be as obscure as the one in this sample question.

A teacher told the students in class, "The information that you read in your history book is correct because I chose the history book and I will be creating the test and assigning your grades."

The reasoning in which of the following statements most closely resembles that of the preceding argument?

(A) The decisions made by the Supreme Court are just because the Court has the authority to administer justice.

(B) The people who have fame are famous because they deserve to be famous.

(C) Those who play sports get better grades because of the link between the health of the body and the health of the mind.

(D) Because my favorite teacher chooses to drive this kind of car, I should as well.

(E) Of 100 professors surveyed, 99 agree with the conclusions reached by the scientist in his paper on global warming.

Reading the question first tells you that you'll have to analyze the way the author reaches the conclusion in the argument. As you read, you find that this illogical cause-and-effect argument states that information is correct because someone in a position of authority (the teacher) says so, so you need to find an equally illogical argument based on power and authority.

Because this is a cause-and-effect argument, you can eliminate any choices that don't use cause and effect to reach a conclusion. All choices contain an element of cause and effect except Choice (D), which presumes an analogy between a favorite teacher and the writer, and Choice (E), which uses statistical evidence. (Note that just because Choice [D] also concerns a teacher doesn't automatically make it the correct answer.) Disregard Choices (D) and (E) and examine the other three choices.

Among Choices (A), (B), and (C), the only choice that uses power to justify a cause-and-effect relationship is Choice (A). Choice (B) is faulty because it uses circular reasoning, which means it uses its conclusion as a premise, instead of using power to advance its position. Choice (C) doesn't work because its logic isn't necessarily faulty. Instead, it relies on a logical correlation between physical health and intellectual prowess. Therefore, Choice (A) is the answer that most nearly matches the kind of reasoning in the original argument.

Critical reasoning practice questions and answer explanations

With practice, you'll probably find that critical reasoning questions become some of the easiest question types to master in the GMAT Verbal section. To master your approach, work through these practice questions and read through the answer explanations.

Critical reasoning practice questions

This set of five critical reasoning practice questions offers a preview of what to expect from this verbal reasoning question type, which assesses your ability to analyze arguments. To mimic the approximate amount of time you'll have to answer critical reasoning questions on the actual exam, try to answer these five questions in about 9 minutes and 45 seconds. Answer each question based on the passage that precedes it and choose the best answer from the five answer choices provided.

REMEMBER

Don't expect to see letters before the answer choices on the computerized GMAT. Each answer will have a radio button next to it that you select by clicking on it. We've put letters next to the answer choices in this practice section to make it easier to discuss the choices in the explanations that follow the questions.

1. It seems that Americans are smarter than they were 50 years ago. Many more Americans are attending college now than in the past, and the typical entry-level job in business now requires a college degree.

   Which of the following statements, if true, would most seriously weaken the argument in the preceding paragraph?

   (A) High school courses are more rigorous now than they were in the past.

   (B) Tuition at colleges and universities has more than tripled in the past 25 years.

   (C) High school class sizes have gotten smaller, and computers have introduced a more individualized curriculum.

   (D) Businesses are not requiring as high a level of writing or math skills as they did in past decades.

   (E) Many of the skills and concepts taught in high school 50 years ago are now taught in college.

Questions 2 and 3 are based on the following argument.

Rachel: The legal drinking age in America should remain at 21, because teens have not yet reached an age where they are able to consume alcohol responsibly. Additionally, the actions of 18-year-olds are more likely to be imitated by teens aged 15 to 17 than are the actions of those who are significantly older, so lowering the drinking age to 18 would also result in increased alcohol consumption by younger teens trying to emulate the actions of their older peers.

Mackenzie: The drinking age in America should be lowered to 18, because keeping it at 21 has not only failed to curb teen drinking but has encouraged those teens who *do* drink to do so in private, uncontrolled environments where they are more prone to life-endangering behavior. Many youths in European countries drink from an early age, and those countries have substantially fewer alcohol-related problems than we do in America.

2. Which of the following, if true, would most significantly weaken Mackenzie's argument?

   (A) The idea that Europeans and other nations with low or no minimum drinking ages do not have alcohol-related problems is a myth.

   (B) If Americans are allowed to give their lives for this country at age 18, then they should be considered old enough to make the proper decision as to what to put in their bodies.

   (C) More American high school students drink now than they did decades ago, when the drinking age was lower.

   (D) In European culture, youths are taught at an early age that it is acceptable to either abstain from alcohol entirely or drink in moderation and that it is never acceptable for them to abuse alcohol, regardless of their age.

   (E) European youths are just as likely as American youths to drink in private, uncontrolled environments.

3. Rachel's argument is based on which of the following assumptions?

   (A) Those who have reached the age of 21 are able to consume alcohol more responsibly than those who are 18.

   (B) When European teenagers consume alcohol, they do so in public, controlled environments.

   (C) Teens who are 15 to 17 years old are more impressionable than those who are aged 18 or older.

   (D) The impressionability of one's actions on others should not be a consideration when deciding the legal age to consume alcohol.

   (E) Consuming alcohol in private, uncontrolled environments is not more dangerous than consuming alcohol in more public environments, such as bars or restaurants.

4. A recent census of all American females revealed that the current average age that females in America marry is 27. The average age that females have their first child is also 27. According to a census taken 20 years ago, the average ages that females married and had their first child were 23 and 25 years, respectively.

   If the information recorded in the two censuses is true, which of the following must also be true about American females?

   (A) Currently, more females are having their first child before they marry than they did 20 years ago.

   (B) On average, females are currently waiting longer to have their first child than they did 20 years ago.

   (C) Females today are more likely to complete their education before getting married and having children than they were 20 years ago.

   (D) On average, females had larger families 20 years ago than they have today.

   (E) Twenty years ago, most females waited at least two years after they were married to have their first child.

5. Continuous technological advances are critical to many types of business, because they allow machines to do the work previously done by humans — and they don't have to be compensated. Banking executives are always looking for ways to cut costs, so they support a heavy emphasis on automated technology in the workplace. Yet what customers look for most in their banks is to be recognized by their teller and feel a sense of familiarity and friendliness upon entering, so the reliance of banks on machines should be minimized, rather than exacerbated.

Which of the following best outlines the main idea of the argument?

(A) Banks should reduce their dependence on technology.

(B) Bank patrons desire personal attention.

(C) Machines can work faster than humans.

(D) Bank executives are a greedy bunch.

(E) Bank automation is inevitable.

Answer explanations

1. **E.** Read the question first so you know what to focus on in the passage. Because this question asks you to weaken the argument, you know you need to figure out what the conclusion is and what kind of reasoning the author uses in moving from the premises to the conclusion.

   When you examine the argument, you may notice that the conclusion actually comes first. The author concludes that Americans are smarter than they were 50 years ago and does so by contrasting current college participation and entry-level job requirements with those of the past. The method of reasoning is similar to analogy, except instead of showing similarities between Americans now and 50 years ago, the author shows the differences. To weaken the conclusion that Americans are smarter today, you need to find the answer choice that shows that things really aren't all that different today than they were 50 years ago.

   First, eliminate answer choices with irrelevant information. Neither college tuition rates nor class size and curriculum have anything to do with levels of intelligence, so Choices (B) and (C) are wrong. Plus, you're looking for an answer that shows that things aren't much different between now and yesterday, and Choices (B) and (C) accentuate the difference.

   Then, get rid of any answer that tends to strengthen rather than weaken the conclusion that Americans are smarter. More-difficult high school courses seem to indicate that Americans may indeed be smarter, so disregard Choice (A). This leaves you with Choices (D) and (E), and your job is to choose the one that shows that now and then aren't all that different. Not only does Choice (D) demonstrate a difference between the eras, but it also refutes the premise that businesses are looking for the higher skill levels of a college education.

   The correct answer must be Choice (E). If skills that were part of the high school curriculum 50 years ago are now offered in college, actual education hasn't changed all that much from then to now. Americans must now attend college to acquire the high school skills of earlier times, and businesses need to require college degrees to make sure their employees have the same skills that high school students had in the past. If the skill levels are the same, Americans aren't really any smarter than they were 50 years ago.

REMEMBER

   You must know precisely what point a paragraph is arguing before you can strengthen or weaken that argument. Take the time to understand the premises, conclusion, and method of reasoning so you can quickly eliminate answer choices and accurately select the best answer. When you really understand the argument, attacking or defending it is fairly easy.

2. **E.** First, a quick review of Mackenzie's argument indicates that she is in *favor* of lowering the drinking age, not opposed, so you can quickly eliminate any answer choices that include support for doing so, such as Choices (B) and (C), because those choices actually strengthen Mackenzie's argument.

Now, determine which of the remaining options *best* weakens Mackenzie's argument that the legal drinking age should be lowered. The remaining answers focus on Mackenzie's premise that because European countries have lower drinking ages and fewer problems with alcohol, lowering the drinking age in America would likewise lead to fewer alcohol-related problems. She makes her argument based on an analogy between Europe and America, so weaken her contention by showing that Europe and America are substantially similar in their approach to teenage drinking. It may sound surprising to weaken an analogy with a similarity, but in this case Mackenzie's analogy seeks to liken the alleged present state of affairs in Europe to the supposed future state of affairs in America if the American drinking age is lowered. Showing a similarity between present-day Europe and present-day America can therefore weaken the argument that a change in the drinking age will reduce alcohol-related problems in America.

Mackenzie doesn't say that European countries have *no* alcohol-related problems, just that there are fewer, so Choice (A) is irrelevant to her argument. Choice (D) provides a concrete difference between European and American culture that reveals why European teens tend to be more responsible than American teens when it comes to alcohol consumption, so this is an answer choice that seems to lend support to Mackenzie's argument that a lower drinking age won't result in less-responsible drinking among American teens. On the other hand, Choice (E) reveals a similarity between European and American youth, which best serves to weaken Mackenzie's analogy between the lower drinking age in Europe and the proposed lower drinking age in America. If both European and American youths drink in private, uncontrolled environments despite the difference in the drinking ages of the two cultures, it's unlikely that changing the drinking age in America will affect the behavior that Mackenzie claims is dangerous (drinking in private). Choice (E) is correct.

3. **A.** Rachel argues for retaining the current legal drinking age of 21. She bases her conclusion on the premises that younger drinkers are more likely to influence the behavior of 15- to 17-year-olds and that teens haven't reached an age where they can drink alcohol responsibly.

REMEMBER

To find the correct answer to questions that ask for an assumption, look for the answer choice that links one or more of the premises to the conclusion. Eliminate answer choices that don't relate to at least one of the premises of the argument.

Choices (B) and (E) relate to one of Mackenzie's premises, so it's unlikely that they would reveal one of Rachel's assumptions. Cross out those two answers on your note board.

You can also check off Choice (D) because it contradicts Rachel's premise that the effect an 18-year-old's alcohol consumption can have on younger peers is an important consideration in determining the legal drinking age. It's also unlikely that Choice (C) is correct because Rachel doesn't make comparisons regarding the impressionability of teens based on their ages. Her premise is that younger teens are more likely to be influenced by 18-year-olds than 21-year-olds. Furthermore, Choice (C) doesn't link one of Rachel's premises to her conclusion in the way that Choice (A) does.

If Rachel concludes that the legal drinking age must remain at 21 because younger drinkers don't consume alcohol responsibly, she must think that 21-year-olds have achieved some level of responsibility that's greater than those who are younger. Choice (A) links the relevance of one of Rachel's premises (a lower level of responsible drinking) to her conclusion that people who are younger than 21 shouldn't be able to legally consume alcohol. So the correct answer is Choice (A).

4. B. This question asks you to come up with a conclusion based on the information in the paragraph.

TIP

Notice that the question asks you for what *must* be true rather than what *could* be true. So you can cross out any answers that aren't absolutely true given the data in the paragraph.

All you know from the paragraph is the average marrying age for females today and 20 years ago and the average age that females have their first child today compared to 20 years ago. The paragraph says nothing about the number of children females have or had, so you can easily wipe Choice (D) out of contention. Furthermore, the paragraph provides no explanation for why the data has changed over the years, so you can't know the reason that the average age has increased. So Choice (C) can't be right.

WARNING

Don't choose an answer based on an assumption or your own experience. The paragraph merely reports data instead of commenting on it, and it treats the age of marrying and having one's first child as two separate statistics. You can't make assumptions about how the two sets of data are related.

That means that Choice (A) doesn't have to be true. Just because the average age for marrying and having a first child are currently the same doesn't mean that more American females are having their first child before they marry. For example, the increased marrying age could be the result of females who marry when they're older and have no children. Eliminate Choice (E) for the same reason. You can't assume from these limited statistics that the females who are 23 when they marry are the ones who are having their first child at 25. There are too many other variables in the population.

The only thing you know for sure is that, because the average age for having a first child has risen over the last 20 years, on average, females are having their first child at a later age than they did 20 years ago. Choice (B) is the only answer that must be true.

5. A. Asking for the main point of an argument is another sneaky way of getting you to pick out the conclusion. This paragraph makes it easy for you because the conclusion follows the *so* in the last sentence: Banks should rely less on machines. The first sentence of the argument equates machines with technological advances, which means that you can say that the main point is that banks should rely less on technology, Choice (A).

Choices (C), (D), and (E) require you to make assumptions that aren't supported by the argument. Because you read newspaper headlines, you may think that Choice (D)'s assertion about the avarice of bank executives is a foregone conclusion, but, alas, it isn't mentioned in the argument. (You should also have been alerted by the debatable word *inevitable* in Choice [E].) The paragraph does suggest that bank patrons want personal attention (Choice [B]), but this statement is a premise rather than the conclusion. So the correct answer is Choice (A).

Block **3**

Conquering the Quantitative Section

I f you majored in math in college, you probably look at the math section of the GMAT like an old friend. If you haven't stepped into a math class since high school, you're more likely dreading it. Don't worry, this block takes you back to the beginning with a review of the concepts you have learned through the years but may have forgotten and need to know for the test — numbers and operations, algebra, statistics, and sets.

Juggling Numbers and Operations

Numbers and operations comprise concepts that form the foundation of mathematics — concepts such as number types, basic operations, exponents, radicals, fractions, and ratios. Whether you're working with simple equations, complex algebraic expressions, or statistical analysis, having a solid understanding of these fundamental concepts is essential for success. In this section, we bring you up to speed on these fundamental concepts.

Just your type: Kinds of numbers

The GMAT requires familiarity with common number types, such as integers, rational numbers, real numbers, and prime numbers, along with a couple of the less common types, such as irrational and imaginary numbers:

>> **Integers:** Numbers that belong to the set of all positive and negative whole numbers with 0 included. Integers can't be fractions or decimals or portions of a number. Integers include –5, –4, –3, –2, –1, 0, 1, 2, 3, 4, and 5 and continue infinitely on either side of 0. Integers greater than 0 are the *natural numbers* or *positive integers*. Integers less than 0 are the *negative integers*. 0 is neither positive nor negative.

>> **Rational numbers:** Numbers that can be expressed as quotients (or fractions) of two integers, where no divisor (or denominator) is zero. Rational numbers comprise all positive and negative

integers, zero, fractions, and decimal numbers that either end or repeat. For example, the fraction $\frac{1}{3}$ can be expressed as $0.3\overline{33}$. Rational numbers don't include numbers like π or radicals like $\sqrt{2}$ because the decimal equivalents of these numbers don't end or repeat. They're *irrational numbers*.

» **Real numbers:** Real numbers encompass all integers, rational numbers, and irrational numbers. They correspond to points on a number line — positive, negative, or zero; and all points on the number line correspond to real numbers. Real numbers are used for measurements such as the weight of an object or the temperature recorded on a given day. So, when the GMAT asks you to give an answer expressed in terms of real numbers, just solve the problem as you normally would.

» **Imaginary numbers:** Numbers that aren't real numbers. An imaginary number represented as *i* is a number like $\sqrt{-1}$. Think about it: When you square any positive or negative real number, the result is a positive number. This means you can't find the square root of a negative number unless the root is simply not a real number.

» **Consecutive integers:** A sequence of two or more integers, such as 25, 26, and 27, in which each integer is one unit greater than the previous one. Consecutive integers can be positive, negative, or a mix of both, depending on the starting point. You can represent consecutive integers by n, $n+1$, $n+2$, and so on, where n is an integer.

» **Prime numbers:** A *prime number* is any positive integer greater than one that has only two factors — the number one and itself. Prime numbers include 2, 3, 5, 7, 11, 13, 17, 19, 23, 29, and so on.

TIP

Positive integers other than 1 that aren't prime numbers are *composite numbers*. A composite number has more than two different positive factors, so it's the product of more than simply itself and the number 1. Zero (like the number 1) is neither prime nor composite.

It's not brain surgery: Basic operations

Now that you're a bit more comfortable with some terms, it's time to take a stab at manipulating numbers.

Adding, subtracting, multiplying, and dividing

You're probably familiar with the standard operations of addition, subtraction, multiplication, and division. But even these math basics have some tricky elements that you may need to refresh your memory on.

PUTTING TWO AND TWO TOGETHER: ADDITION

Adding is pretty simple. Addition is just the operation of combining two or more numbers to get an end result called the *sum*. For example, here's a simple addition problem: $3+4+5=12$

Addition also has two important properties that you may remember from elementary school: the associative property and the commutative property. Understanding these simple concepts for the GMAT math questions is important:

» **Associative property:** The *associative property* states that the order in which you choose to add three or more numbers doesn't change the result. It shows how numbers can group differently with one another and still produce the same answer. So regardless of whether you add 3 and 4 together first and then add 5 or add 4 and 5 together followed by 3, you still get an answer of 12.

> **» Commutative property:** The *commutative property* states that it doesn't matter what order you use to add the same numbers. Regardless of what number you list first in a set of numbers, they always produce the same sum. So $2 + 3 = 5$ is the same as $3 + 2 = 5$.

DEPLETING THE SUPPLY: SUBTRACTION

Subtraction, as you probably know, is the inverse of addition. You take away a value from another value and end up with the *difference*. So, if $3 + 4 = 7$, then $7 - 3 = 4$. In subtraction, order *does* matter, so neither the associative property nor the commutative property applies. You get completely different answers for $3 - 4 - 5$, depending on what method you use to associate the values; for example, $(3 - 4) - 5 = -6$ but $3 - (4 - 5) = 4$. The order of the values counts in subtraction, too; for example, $3 - 4 = -1$ but $4 - 3 = 1$.

INCREASING BY LEAPS AND BOUNDS: MULTIPLICATION

Think of multiplication as repeated addition with an end result called the *product:* 3×5 is the same as $5 + 5 + 5$. They both equal 15.

On the GMAT, you may see several signs that represent the multiplication operation. A multiplication sign can be designated by $\times$ or simply with a dot, like this: $\cdot$. And in many instances, especially when variables are involved (for more about variables, see the later section "Considering All the Variables: Algebra"), multiplication can be indicated by just putting the factors right next to each other. So, *ab* means the same thing as $a \times b$, and *2a* is the same as $2 \times a$. One or more of these back-to-back factors may appear in parentheses: 2(3) means 2×3, and so does (2)(3).

Multiplication is like addition, in that the order of the values doesn't matter. So, it obeys both of the following properties:

> **» Commutative property:** $a \times b = b \times a$
>
> **» Associative property:** $(a \times b) \times c = a \times (b \times c)$

Another property associated both with multiplication and addition is the *distributive property*. It basically means that *multiplication distributes over addition*. So, you may encounter this problem: $a(b + c) =$. You solve it by distributing the *a* to *b* and *c*, which means that you multiply *a* and *b* to get *ab* and then *a* and *c* to get *ac*, and then you add the results together like this: $a(b + c) = ab + ac$.

SHARING THE WEALTH: DIVISION

With division, you split one value, the *dividend*, into equal parts determined by another number, the *divisor*. The end result is the *quotient*. So, whereas $3 \times 5 = 15$, $15 \div 5 = 3$, and $15 \div 3 = 5$. If the division is exact, meaning there is no remainder, then the dividend (15 in the last expression) is a *multiple* of the divisor (3 in the last expression), and the dividend is said to be *divisible* by the divisor. If the dividend cannot be divided evenly by the divisor, there will be a *remainder*. For example, when 35 is divided by 8, the quotient is 4 and the remainder is 3.

Division Algorithm: If an integer *m* is divided by a positive integer *d*, the result is a unique integer *q* (the *quotient*) and unique integer r (the *remainder*), where $0 \leq r < d$ and $m = dq + r$. In addition, $r = 0$ if and only if *m* is a multiple of *d*.

REMEMBER

As in subtraction, order matters, so division doesn't follow either the commutative or associative properties. Division by 0 is undefined; so, 0 as a divisor is not allowed. The division sign may be represented by a fraction bar (/). For more info on fractions, see the later section "Splitting up: Fractions, decimals, and percents."

A balancing act: Operations with even and odd numbers

We're pretty sure you know that *even numbers* are integers divisible by 2: . . . −4, −2, 0, 2, 4, 6, 8, 10, and so on. And *odd numbers* are those integers that aren't divisible by 2: . . . −3, −1, 1, 3, 5, 7, 9, 11, and so on. What's important to remember for the GMAT is what happens to even or odd numbers when you add, subtract, or multiply them by one another. Here are the rules regarding evens and odds for addition and subtraction:

>> If two integers are both even or both odd, then their sum and their difference is even.

>> If you add or subtract an even integer and an odd integer, your result is an odd integer.

Here's what you should know about multiplying even and odd integers:

>> If any of the factors in a product of integers is even, then the product itself is even.

>> If every factor in a product of integers is odd, then the product itself is odd.

Division rules are a little more complex because the quotients aren't always integers; sometimes they're fractions. Here are a few rules to know:

>> When you divide an even integer by an odd integer, you get an even integer or a fraction.

>> An odd integer divided by another odd integer results in an odd integer or a fraction.

>> An even integer divided by another even integer can result in either an odd or even quotient, so that's not very helpful.

>> When you divide an odd integer by an even one, you always get a fraction; because fractions aren't integers, the quotient for this scenario is neither odd nor even.

Checking out the real estate: Fundamental concepts of real numbers

In addition to basic operations, the GMAT expects you to have a solid grasp of fundamental concepts of real numbers. These include understanding comparative relationships such as less than and greater than, comprehending absolute value, and performing computations with positive and negative numbers.

NOT ALL THINGS ARE EQUAL: COMPARING REAL NUMBERS

On a number line, numbers that lie to the left of zero are negative and numbers that lie to the right of zero are positive. For any two numbers on the number line, the number to the left is less than the number to the right. For example, $-5 < -2 < -1.5 < 3$ and $3 < \pi < 4$.

To say that a number x is between −2 and 3 means that $x > -2$ and $x < 3$; that is, $-2 < x < 3$. If x is "between −2 and 3, inclusive," then $-2 \le x \le 3$.

ABSOLUTES DO EXIST: ABSOLUTE VALUE

To simplify things, just think of the absolute value of any known real number as that same number without a negative sign. It's the distance between the number and 0 on the number line. The absolute value is denoted by enclosing the number within absolute value bars ($|\ |$), so the absolute value of 3 is written mathematically as $|3|$. And because the number 3 sits three spaces from

0 on the number line, $|3| = 3$. Likewise, because -3 sits three spaces from 0 on the number line, its absolute value is also 3: $|-3| = 3$. Examples of absolute values of numbers are $|4| = |-4| = 4$, $\left|-\frac{5}{6}\right| = \left|\frac{5}{6}\right|$, and $|0| = 0$.

The absolute value of any nonzero number is positive. However, if a negative sign appears outside the absolute value, the value of the expression is negative; for example, $-|-3| = -3$.

When you're working with variables in absolute-value expressions, remember that there is likely more than one solution for the variable because the value within the absolute value bars may be positive or negative, as demonstrated by this sample problem.

Which of the following is the complete set of solutions for x when $|x - 3| = 6$?

(A) $\{9\}$

(B) $\{-9, 9\}$

(C) $\{-3, 9\}$

(D) $\{3, 9\}$

(E) $\{-9, -3, 3\}$

To find one solution for x, remove the absolute-value bars and then solve for x:

$$|x - 3| = 6$$
$$x - 3 = 6$$
$$x = 9$$

You know 9 is a solution for x, so you can eliminate Choice (E) because it doesn't contain 9. You can't end with Choice (A), though; you have to consider that the value within the absolute value bars could be negative. To accomplish this feat, multiply the terms between the bars by -1 and then solve for x:

$$|x - 3| = 6$$
$$-1(x - 3) = 6$$
$$-x + 3 = 6$$
$$-x = 3$$
$$x = -3$$

Because the value enclosed in the absolute-value bars may be either negative or positive, x may be either -3 or 9. Choice (C) is the complete set of solutions.

HALF EMPTY OR HALF FULL: POSITIVE AND NEGATIVE NUMBERS

Positive and negative numbers have their own set of rules regarding operations, and they're even more important to remember than those for even and odd integers. Here's what you need to know for multiplying and dividing:

>> When you multiply or divide two positive numbers, the result is positive.

>> When you multiply or divide two negative numbers, the result is also positive.

>> Multiplying or dividing a negative number by a positive number gives you a negative result (as does multiplying or dividing a positive number by a negative number).

As you may expect, you need to know some things about adding and subtracting positives and negatives:

>> When you add two positive numbers, your result is a positive number.

>> When you add two negative numbers, the resulting sum is negative.

>> When you add a positive number to a negative number, the result is positive when the number with the largest absolute value is positive and negative when the number with the largest absolute value is negative.

>> If you subtract a negative number from another number, you end up adding the positive version of the negative number to the other number. For example, $x - (-3)$ is the same thing as $x + 3$.

Working with bases and exponents

Because multiplication can be thought of as repeated addition, you can think of positive integer exponents as indicating repeated multiplication. This means that 4^3 is the same as $4 \times 4 \times 4$ or 64. In the example, you refer to 4 as the *base*, the superscript 3 as the *exponent*, and 4^3 as an *exponential expression*. If you include a variable into this mix, such as $4b^3$, the base becomes b and the 4 becomes the *coefficient*. In our example, b^3 is multiplied by the coefficient 4.

The exponent doesn't affect the coefficient. Only the base gets squared or cubed or whatever the exponent says to do. This rule brings up some fascinating properties regarding positive and negative bases and even and odd exponents:

>> A positive number taken to an even or odd power remains positive.

>> A negative number taken to an odd power remains negative.

>> A negative number taken to an even power becomes positive.

TIP

What all of this means is that any number taken to an even power either remains or becomes positive, and any number taken to an odd power keeps the sign it began with. Another interesting tidbit to digest is that any term with an odd power that results in a negative number will have a negative root, and this is the only possible root for the expression. For example, if $a^3 = -125$, then $a = -5$. That is, the cube root of -125 is -5.

On the other hand, anytime you have an exponent of 2, you have two potential roots, one positive and one negative, for the expression. For example, if $a^2 = 64$, then $a = 8$ or -8. So, 64 has two possible square roots: either 8 or -8.

In the following sections, we outline a few rules for adding, subtracting, multiplying, and dividing exponents. We also clue you in on how to figure out the powers of 0 and 1 and what to do with fractional and negative exponents.

Adding and subtracting with exponents

The only catch to adding or subtracting with exponents is that the base and exponent of each term must be the same. So, you can add and subtract like terms such as $4a^2$ and a^2 like this: $4a^2 + a^2 = 5a^2$ and $4a^2 - a^2 = 3a^2$. Notice that the base and exponent remain the same and that the coefficient is the only number that changes in the equation.

Multiplying and dividing with exponents

The rules regarding multiplying and dividing with exponents are pretty numerous, so to keep them straight, we've set up Table 3-1 for you. The table describes each rule and gives you an example or two.

TABLE 3-1 Rules for Multiplying and Dividing with Exponents

Rule	Examples
To multiply exponential expressions with the same bases, add the exponents and keep the same base.	$a^2 \times a^3 = a^5$
If the expressions contain coefficients, multiply the coefficients as you normally would.	$4a^2 \times 2a^3 = 8a^5$
When you divide two exponential expressions with the same bases, just subtract the exponent of the divisor term from the exponent of the dividend term and keep the same base.	$a^5 \div a^2 = a^3$
Any coefficients are also divided as usual.	$9a^5 \div 3a^3 = 3a^2$
To multiply exponential expressions with different bases, first make sure the exponents are the same. If they are, multiply the bases and maintain the same exponent.	$4^3 \times 5^3 = 20^3$; $a^5 \times b^5 = (ab)^5$
Follow the same procedure when you divide exponential expressions with different bases but the same exponents.	$20^3 \div 5^3 = 4^3$; $(ab)^5 \div a^5 = b^5$
When you raise a power to another power, multiply the exponents and keep the same base.	$\left(5^4\right)^5 = 5^{20}$; $\left(a^3\right)^5 = a^{15}$
If your expression includes a coefficient in parentheses, take it to the same power.	$\left(2a^2\right)^3 = 8a^6$

Figuring out the powers of 0 and 1

Exponents of 0 and 1 have special properties that you'll have to commit to memory:

>> The value of a base with an exponent of 0 (such as 7^0) is always 1 with the exception that 0^0 is undefined.

>> The value of a base with an exponent of 1 is the same value as the base ($3^1 = 3$).

Dealing with fractional exponents

If you see a problem with an exponent in fraction form, consider the top number of the fraction (the *numerator*) as indicating a power and the bottom number (the *denominator*) as indicating a root. So, to solve $256^{\frac{1}{4}}$, simply take 256 to the first power (because the numerator of the fraction is 1), which is 256. Then take the fourth root of 256 (because the denominator of the fraction is 4), which is 4, and that's your answer. (Find out more about roots in the later section "Checking out the ancestry: Roots.") Here's what it looks like mathematically:

$$256^{\frac{1}{4}} = \sqrt[4]{256^1} = \sqrt[4]{256} = 4$$

The GMAT may also present you with a variable base and a fractional exponent. You handle those the same way, like this:

$$a^{\frac{2}{3}} = \sqrt[3]{a^2}$$

This is what you get when you take a to the second power and then find its cube root.

Working with negative exponents

A negative exponent works like a positive exponent with a twist. A negative exponent takes the positive exponent and then flips the base and exponent around so that together they become the reciprocal (see the later section "Delving into fractions"), like this:

$$3^{-3} = \frac{1}{3^3} = \frac{1}{27}$$

When you work with negative exponents, don't fall for the trick of assuming that the negative exponent somehow turns the original number into a negative number. For example,

$$3^{-3} \neq -27 \text{ or } \frac{1}{-27}.$$

To see how the GMAT may test exponents, check out a sample problem.

If $8^{2x-3} = 1$, what is the value of x?

(A) 0

(B) 1.5

(C) 2

(D) 8

(E) 10.5

The trick to mastering this problem is to remember that a nonzero number to the power of 0 is equal to 1. So, for the expression to equal 1, 8^{2x-3} must equal 8^0. When you know that $8^{2x-3} = 8^0$, you know $2x - 3 = 0$. Solve for x.

$$2x - 3 = 0$$
$$2x = 3$$
$$x = \frac{3}{2}$$
$$x = 1.5$$

The simple answer to this perhaps initially confusing problem is Choice (B). If you picked Choice (C), you may have thought the exponent was equal to 1 instead of 0.

Checking out the ancestry: Roots

If you like exponents, you'll *love* roots, which are often presented as *radicals*. Roots are sort of the opposite of exponents. The square root of a number is a number that you square to get that number. So, because you can square 3 or -3 to get 9, the two square roots of 9 are 3 and -3. What could be simpler?

There are as many roots as there are powers. Most of the time, the GMAT has you work with square roots, but you may also see other roots. That won't intimidate you, though. If you come upon a cube root or fourth root, you'll recognize it by the radical sign, $\sqrt{}$. For even roots of positive numbers, the radical sign returns only the positive root of the number. Thus, $\sqrt{9} = 3$. For example, the cube root of 27 is expressed as $\sqrt[3]{27}$. This expression asks what number, when raised to the third power, equals 27. Of course, the answer is 3 because $3^3 = 27$.

TIP

Radicals, even the seemingly ugly ones, can often be simplified. For example, if you come up with an answer of $\sqrt{98}$, you're not done yet. Just think of the factors of 98 that are perfect squares. You know that $2 \times 49 = 98$, and 49 is a perfect square: $7^2 = 49$. Put these factors under the radical sign: $\sqrt{49 \times 2}$. Now you can extract the 49 from the square root sign because its positive square root is 7. The result is $7\sqrt{2}$.

Roots obey the same rules as exponents when it comes to performing operations. You can add and subtract roots as long as the roots are of the same order (that is, square root, cube root, and so on) and the same number. Here are a couple of examples:

$$5\sqrt{7} + 6\sqrt{7} = 11\sqrt{7}$$
$$11\sqrt{a} - 6\sqrt{a} = 5\sqrt{a}$$

When you need to multiply or divide radicals, make sure the roots are of the same order (such as all square or all cube roots) and you're good to go! For multiplication, just multiply what's under the radical signs, like this: $\sqrt{9} \times \sqrt{3} = \sqrt{27}$. Divide what's under the radical signs like this: $\sqrt{9} \div \sqrt{3} = \sqrt{3}$.

Following the order of operations

Basic arithmetic requires that you perform operations in a certain order. If you have an expression that contains addition, subtraction, multiplication, division, exponents (and roots), and parentheses to boot, it helps to know which operation you perform first, second, third, and so on. The acronym *PEMDAS* (Please Excuse My Dear Aunt Sally) can help you remember to perform operations in the following order:

» **P**arentheses (or other grouping symbol such as brackets, braces, and fraction bars)

» **E**xponents (and roots)

» **M**ultiplication and **D**ivision, from left to right

» **A**ddition and **S**ubtraction, from left to right

Here's an example:

$$20(4-7)^3 + 4\left(\frac{9}{3}\right)^2 = x$$

First, evaluate what's inside the parentheses:

$$20(-3)^3 + 4(3)^2 = x$$

Then evaluate the exponents:

$$20(-27) + 4(9) = x$$

Then multiply from left to right:

$$-540 + 36 = x$$

Finally, do the addition and subtraction from left to right:

$$-504 = x$$

Splitting up: Fractions, decimals, and percents

Fractions, decimals, and percents are interrelated concepts; they all represent parts of a whole. You'll likely need to convert from one form to the other to solve several problems on the GMAT math.

Fractions are really division problems. If you divide the value of a by the value of b, you get the fraction $\frac{a}{b}$. So $1 \div 4 = \frac{1}{4}$. To convert the fraction to a decimal, you simply perform the division indicated by the fraction bar: $\frac{1}{4} = 0.25$.

To convert a decimal back to a fraction, you first count the digits to the right of the decimal point; then divide the original number over a 1 followed by the same number of zeroes as there were digits to the right of the decimal. Then you simplify. So $0.25 = \frac{25}{100} = \frac{1}{4}$; $0.356 = \frac{356}{1,000} = \frac{89}{250}$.

Changing a decimal to a percent is really pretty easy. Percent simply means *out of one hundred*, or times $\frac{1}{100}$. To perform the conversion, you move the decimal two places to the right. Then you write the resulting number as a percent. For example, $0.25 = 25\%$, and $0.925 = 92.5\%$.

To turn a percent back into a decimal, you follow the procedure in reverse. You move the decimal point two spaces to the left and lose the percent sign, like this: $1\% = 0.01$.

Dealing with decimals

If you're a pro at computing with whole numbers, then you totally have the skills to handle decimals, too. In a nutshell, here's how:

>> To add or subtract decimals line up their decimal points, and then add or subtract as with whole numbers.

>> To multiply two decimals, ignore the decimal points and multiply as with whole numbers. The number of decimal places in the product is the total number of decimal places in the two numbers being multiplied.

>> To divide two decimals, first move the decimal points of the two numbers equally many digits to the right until the divisor is a whole number, and then divide as with whole numbers.

Delving into fractions

GMAT questions may refer to the parts of a fraction. The *numerator* is the number on top and represents the part of the whole. The *denominator* is the number on the bottom and represents the whole. The horizontal line that separates the numerator and denominator is the *fraction bar*. To better understand these terms, picture a cherry pie sliced into eight equal pieces (see Figure 3-1) and a hungry family of seven, each of whom has a slice after dinner (or before dinner if they're sneaky).

The shaded pieces of pie show how much of the dessert was gobbled up by the family; the unshaded piece shows what's left of the pie when the family is finished. To put this pie into terms of a fraction, the total number of equal pieces in the pie to begin with (the whole) represents the denominator, and the number of pieces that were eaten (the part of the whole) is represented by the numerator. In this case, the number of pieces that were eaten made up $\frac{7}{8}$ of the total pie, so 7 is the numerator and 8 is the denominator. To look at the scenario another way, you can say that the fraction of pie that was left is $\frac{1}{8}$ of what you started with.

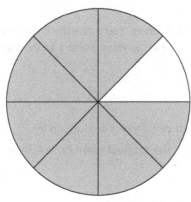

FIGURE 3-1:
Fraction of
a pie.

Here are a few other fraction definitions you should be familiar with:

>> **Proper fractions:** Fractions where the numerator is less than the denominator. Examples of proper fractions are $\frac{3}{4}$ and $\frac{13}{15}$.

>> **Improper fractions:** Fractions where the numerator is either greater than or equal to the denominator. An example is $\frac{15}{2}$.

>> **Mixed fractions:** Another way of formatting improper fractions is with a whole number and a proper fraction, such as $1\frac{2}{3}$, which is shorthand for $1 + \frac{2}{3}$.

>> **Reciprocal:** The flip-flop of a fraction. The numerator and denominator switch places. So, the reciprocal of $\frac{3}{5}$ is $\frac{5}{3}$. To get the reciprocal of a whole number, you simply divide 1 by your number. So, the reciprocal of 5 is $\frac{1}{5}$. The reciprocal of a variable a is $\frac{1}{a}$, just as long as $a \neq 0$.

>> **Equivalent fractions:** Two fractions that represent the same number. For example, $\frac{18}{24}$ and $\frac{21}{28}$ are equivalent because they both represent the number $\frac{3}{4}$. In each case, you reduce the fraction to its simplest terms by dividing both the numerator and denominator by their *greatest common factor* (gcf). The gcf of 18 and 24 is 6 and the gcf of 21 and 28 is 7.

TIP

To change a mixed fraction to an improper fraction, multiply the whole number by the denominator, add the numerator, and put that value over the original denominator, like this:

$$2\frac{2}{3} = \frac{8}{3}$$

You multiply the whole number (2) by the denominator (3) to get 6; add the numerator (2) to 6, which gives you 8; and place that value over the original denominator of 3.

To convert an improper fraction to a mixed number, you divide the numerator by the denominator and put the remainder over the denominator, like this:

$$\frac{31}{4} = 7\frac{3}{4}$$

First, you divide 31 by 4: 4 goes into 31 seven times with a remainder of 3 ($4 \times 7 = 28$ and $31 - 28 = 3$). Put the remainder over the original denominator, and place that fraction next to the whole number, 7.

TIP

Simplifying a fraction means reducing it to its simplest terms. You make the larger terms smaller by dividing both the numerator and denominator by the same value. Here's an example of reducing or simplifying a fraction:

$$\frac{12}{36} \div \frac{12}{12} = \frac{1}{3}$$

The greatest common factor of 12 and 36 is 12. When you divide the fraction by $\frac{12}{12}$, it's the same as dividing by 1. And any number divided by 1 equals the original number. You know that $\frac{1}{3}$ has the same value as $\frac{12}{36}$. It's just in simpler terms.

Adding and subtracting fractions

Because fractions involve parts of whole numbers, they're not as easy to add together as $2 + 2$. To add or subtract fractions with the same denominator, all you do is either add or subtract the numerators and put that value over the original denominator, like this: $\frac{2}{7} + \frac{4}{7} = \frac{6}{7}$; $\frac{6}{5} - \frac{4}{5} = \frac{2}{5}$.

WARNING

Be careful when you're asked to add or subtract fractions with different denominators. You can't just add or subtract the numerators and denominators. You have to change the fractions to equivalent fractions that have the same denominator. So, first, you determine the *least common denominator* (lcd). For example, if you see $\frac{2}{3} + \frac{1}{9}$, you know you have to change the denominators before you add.

To determine the lcd, consider values that are divisible by both 3 and 9. When you multiply 3 by 9, you get 27. So, both 3 and 9 go into 27, but that's not the smallest number that both 3 and 9 go into evenly. Both 3 and 9 are factors of 9, so the lcd is 9 rather than 27.

Convert $\frac{2}{3}$ to $\frac{6}{9}$ by multiplying the numerator and denominator by 3. The second fraction already has a denominator of 9, so you're ready to add:

$$\frac{6}{9} + \frac{1}{9} = \frac{7}{9}$$

Multiplying and dividing fractions

Multiplying fractions is easy. Just multiply the numerators to get the product's numerator, and multiply the denominators to get the product's denominator. Reduce if you have to:

$$\frac{4}{5} \times \frac{5}{7} = \frac{20}{35} = \frac{4}{7}$$

TIP

An easier and faster (and faster is better on the GMAT) way to perform this task is to simply cancel out the fives that appear in the denominator of the first fraction and the numerator of the second one, like so:

$$\frac{4}{\cancel{5}} \times \frac{\cancel{5}}{7} = \frac{4}{7}$$

Dividing fractions is pretty much the same as multiplying them except for one very important initial step. Here's what you do to divide two fractions:

1. **Find the reciprocal of the second fraction (that is, turn the second fraction upside down).**

2. **Multiply (yes, multiply) the numerators and denominators of the resulting fractions.**

Here's an example:

$$\frac{2}{7} \div \frac{3}{5} = \frac{2}{7} \times \frac{5}{3} = \frac{10}{21}$$

To test your knowledge of how to perform operations with fractions, the GMAT may present you with a straightforward computation, such as the following.

EXAMPLE

$$\frac{1}{2} + \left(\frac{3}{8} \div \frac{2}{5}\right) - \left(\frac{5}{6} \times \frac{7}{8}\right) =$$

(A) $\frac{1}{8}$

(B) $\frac{15}{16}$

(C) $\frac{17}{24}$

(D) $2\frac{1}{6}$

(E) $\frac{5}{6}$

To solve this problem, you need to know how to perform all four operations with fractions. Be sure to follow the order of operations. (See the earlier section, "Following the order of operations," for details.) First, compute the operations inside the first set of parentheses:

$$\left(\frac{3}{8} \div \frac{2}{5}\right) = \frac{3}{8} \times \frac{5}{2} = \frac{15}{16}$$

Then, figure out the value of the second set of parentheses:

$$\left(\frac{5}{6} \times \frac{7}{8}\right) = \frac{35}{48}$$

Now the equation looks like this:

$$\frac{1}{2} + \frac{15}{16} - \frac{35}{48} =$$

The least common denominator of 2, 16, and 48 is 48. To convert the denominator in the first fraction to 48, multiply the fraction by $\frac{24}{24}$:

$$\frac{1}{2} \times \frac{24}{24} = \frac{24}{48}$$

To convert the denominator in the second fraction to 48, multiply by $\frac{3}{3}$:

$$\frac{15}{16} \times \frac{3}{3} = \frac{45}{48}$$

Now you can compute the expression:

$$\frac{24}{48} + \frac{45}{48} - \frac{35}{48} = \frac{34}{48}$$

That's not one of your answer options, so you need to simplify the fraction. Divide both the numerator and denominator by 2 to get $\frac{17}{24}$, which is Choice (C).

Calculating percent change

Percent change is the amount a number increases or decreases expressed as a percent of the original number. For example, if a store normally sells tennis shoes for $75 and has them on sale for $60, what is the percent change of the markdown? To get the percent decrease, simply take the difference in price, which is $15, and divide that number by the original price:

$$15 \div 75 = 0.2 = 20\%$$

WARNING

Pay careful attention when figuring percent change. For example, if the store then increases the marked down price by 20%, you may think the price returns to its original value. But that's not right. If you increase the lower price of $60 by 20%, you get a $12 increase. The price goes from $60 to just $72: $\$60 \times 0.2 = \$12$; $\$60 + \$12 = \$72$. How can that be? The reason the numbers don't seem to add up is that when you drop the price the first time, you take 20% of $75, which is a bigger number to take a percent from than the lower sale price.

So, what percent of the marked-down price of $60 must you increase the price by in order to get the original price of $75? To find out, take the difference in price, $15, and determine what percent that is of the sale price of $60:

$$15 \div 60 = \frac{15}{60} = \frac{1}{4} = 0.25 = 25\%$$

So, it's a 25% increase from $60 to $75.

TIP

If you know what the percent increase or decrease of an original number is and want to find out how that increase or decrease changes the original number, keep these two important details in mind:

>> To find the result of a percent increase, multiply the original number by 1 plus the rate as a decimal.

>> To find the result of a percent decrease, multiply the original number by 1 minus the rate as a decimal.

So, if you increase 100 by 5%, you multiply 100 by $(1 + 0.05)$:

$$100 \times (1 + 0.05) = 100 \times 1.05 = 105$$

If you decrease 100 by 5%, you multiply 100 by $(1 - 0.05)$.

$$100 \times (1 - 0.05) = 100 \times 0.95 = 95$$

Taking it further: Repeated percent change

Now suppose you want to show a percent change repeated over a period of time, such as when you need to figure out how much interest accrues on a bank account after several years. To do so, you take the formula for percent change a step further. Suppose you have $100 in a bank account at the end of 2013, and you want to know how much money will be in that same account at the end of 2023 at an annual interest rate of 5 percent (if you make no withdrawals or additional deposits). No fair pulling it out when the stock market is making a bull run! One way to figure this out is by using the percentage increase formula. The first step looks something like this:

$$100 \times (1 + 0.05) = 105$$

Thus, you have $105 at the end of the first year.

WARNING

Don't make the mistake of thinking that all you have to do is multiply by 10 and you have $1,050 after 10 years. You wish! This type of question will trap anyone who isn't paying attention every time.

To get the correct answer, tweak the formula a bit by adding an exponent. The exponent will be the number of times the original number changes. The formula looks like this, where n is the number of changes:

$$\text{Final Amount} = \text{Original Number} \times (1 + \text{Rate})^n$$

Plug the numbers into the formula and solve:

$$100 \times (1 + 0.05)^{10} = x$$
$$100 \times 1.05^{10} = x$$
$$100 \times 1.6289 = x$$
$$162.89 = x$$

Therefore, after 10 years, you'd have $162.89 in the bank.

To show a repeated percent decrease over time, you'd use this similar formula:

$$\text{Final Amount} = \text{Original Number} \times (1 - \text{Rate})^n$$

Making comparisons: Ratios and proportions

A ratio is the relation between two like numbers or two like values. A ratio may be written as a fraction ($\frac{3}{4}$), as a division expression ($3 \div 4$), or with a colon ($3 : 4$), or it can be stated as "3 to 4."

Because a ratio can be regarded as a fraction, multiplying or dividing both terms of a ratio by the same number doesn't change the value of the ratio. So $1 : 4 = 2 : 8 = 4 : 16$. To reduce a ratio to its lowest terms, simplify the ratio as you would a fraction. (See the earlier section, "Delving into fractions.")

Ratios often crop up in word problems. Suppose an auto manufacturer ships a total of 160 cars to two dealerships at a ratio of 3 to 5. This means that for every three cars that go to Dealer 1, five cars ship to Dealer 2. To determine how many cars each dealership receives, add the terms of the ratio, or $3 + 5$, to get the total number of fractional parts each dealership will get: $3 + 5 = 8$. The first dealership will receive $\frac{3}{8}$ of 160 cars, or $\frac{3}{8} \times 160$, which equals 60. The second dealership receives $\frac{5}{8}$ of 160 cars, or 100.

TIP

As long as the total number of *items* in a ratio problem can be evenly divided by the total number of fractional parts, you can find the total number of items that are attributable to each part.

A *proportion* is a statement that two ratios are equal. It may be written as the proportion sign :: or with an equal sign. You can read 1:4 :: 2:8 or $\frac{1}{4} = \frac{2}{8}$ as "1 is to 4 as 2 is to 8."

The first and last terms in a proportion are the *extremes*, and the second and third terms are the *means*. If you multiply the means together and multiply the extremes together and then compare the products, you find that the products are the same:

$$1 \times 8 = 2 \times 4$$

Anytime you know three terms of a proportion, you can find the missing term: first, by multiplying either the two means or the two extremes (depending on which are known), and then dividing the product by the remaining term. This is commonly known as *cross-multiplying*. If you know 7:8 :: x:104, you can solve for x by using cross-multiplication:

$$\frac{7}{8} = \frac{x}{104}$$
$$8x = 7(104)$$
$$8x = 728$$
$$x = 91$$

Be sure to keep the order of the terms of your ratios and proportions consistent. For example, if your proportion is "3 is to 4 as 5 is to x," you must set up the problem like this:

$$\frac{3}{4} = \frac{5}{x}$$

rather than this:

$$\frac{3}{4} = \frac{x}{5}$$

Playing the numbers: Scientific notation

Scientific notation is a simple way to write out humongous (technical term) or teensy weensy (another technical term) numbers so they're more manageable. You express a number in scientific notation by writing it as the product of a number and a power of 10. Simply move the decimal point so all digits except one are to the right of the decimal point; then multiply that decimal number times 10 raised to an exponent that equals the number of places you moved the decimal point. If you're working with a large number and you moved the decimal point to the left, the exponent is positive:

$$1,234,567 = 1.234567 \times 10^6$$
$$20 \text{ million} (20,000,000) = 2.0 \times 10^7$$

To display very small numbers in scientific notation, you move the decimal point to the right so one value is to the left of the decimal point. When you move the decimal point to the right, the exponent is negative. In this example, the decimal point moved six places to the right:

$$0.0000037 = 3.7 \times 10^{-6}$$

Here's how the GMAT may test you on scientific notation.

The number of organisms in a liter of water is approximately 6.0×10^{23}. Assuming this number is correct, about how many organisms exist in a covered Petri dish that contains $\frac{1}{200}$ liters of water?

(A) 6.9

(B) 3.0×10^{21}

(C) 6.0×10^{22}

(D) 3.0×10^{23}

(E) 1.2×10^{26}

This question uses many words to ask you to the find the answer to $\frac{6.0 \times 10^{23}}{200}$. If a liter of water contains a certain number of organisms, $\frac{1}{200}$ liter of water would contain the same number of organisms divided by 200. Try not to let the wording of the question confuse you.

So, if 6.0 divided by 200 equals 0.03, the answer is 0.03×10^{23}, but that's not scientific notation because the decimal point is in the wrong place. Move the decimal point two places to the right and decrease the power by two (remember that when you move the decimal point to the right, the exponent is negative, so you subtract). The answer is Choice (B), 3.0×10^{21}.

Considering All the Variables: Algebra

Algebra is a branch of mathematics that uses variables (usually letters) to stand for unknown numbers. You use algebra to solve equations and find the numerical value of the variable. For example, a typical algebra question will provide an equation and ask you to "solve for x."

Many GMAT math problems involve basic algebra (expressions and equations you encountered in Algebra I), and this section provides what you should know to excel on all of them.

Defining the elements: Algebraic terminology

In the following sections, we provide some key definitions to know. Although the GMAT doesn't explicitly ask you to define certain terminologies such as *variable*, *constant*, or *coefficient*, it does expect you to know these concepts when they crop up in the questions.

Braving the unknowns: Variables and constants

You'll see a lot of *variables* in algebra problems. They're the symbols that stand for numbers. Usually, the symbols take the form of letters and represent specific numeric values. True to their name, variables' values can change depending on the equation they're in. Think of variables as symbols representing distinct entities. For example, if a store charges different prices for apples and peaches and you buy two apples and four peaches, the clerk can't ring them up together by simply adding $2 + 4$ to get 6. That strategy would be flawed because the two fruits are not the same price. So, to express the transaction in algebraic terms, you use variables to stand in for the price of apples and peaches, something like $2a$ and $4p$.

In contrast, *constants*, as their name implies, are numbers with values that don't change in a specific problem. All the real numbers are constants. Each has a definite, fixed value. Letters may also be used to refer to constants, but they don't change their value in an equation as variables do (for example, a, b, and c stand for fixed numbers in the formula $y = ax^2 + bx + c$).

Coming together: Terms and expressions

A *numerical expression* is any constant or combination of two or more constants joined by explicit or implied operational symbols. For example, 200, 4.5, $\frac{4 \times 25}{2 \times 5}$, $0.75(2{,}000) + 2{,}000$, $\frac{50\pi}{30\pi}$, and $\pi(4)^2$ are numerical expressions.

An *algebraic expression* is a meaningful combination of one or more variables joined by one or more ordinary operations of arithmetic, with or without constants (explicitly) included. It is a symbolic representation of a number. For example, $7x$, axy, $5x + 3$, $3abc$, $(x-3)^2 - 9$, $ax^2 + bx + c$, $\frac{10}{t-25}$, $8x^3 - 12x^2 + 6x - 1$, and $3xy - y^2 + x$ are algebraic expressions.

An algebraic expression can be *evaluated* by substituting values of the variables in the expression. For example, if $x = -2$ and $y = 3$, then $3xy - y^2 + x$ can be evaluated as $3(-2)(3) - (3)^2 + (-2) = -18 - 9 - 2 = -29$.

A *term* is any combination of one or more variables or constants that you can multiply or divide to form a single unit in an expression. In algebraic expressions, terms are separated by addition. For example, the algebraic expression $ax^2 + bx + c$ has three terms. The first term is ax^2, the second term is bx, and the third term is c. When subtraction is involved in an algebraic expression, be mindful that terms are separated by *addition*. Thus, the terms of the algebraic expression $8x^3 - 12x^2 + 6x - 1$ are $8x^3$, $-12x^2$, $6x$, and -1. This is the case because, by the definition of subtraction, $8x^3 - 12x^2 + 6x - 1 = 8x^3 + (-12x^2) + 6x + (-1)$. The terms $8x^3$, $-12x^2$, and $6x$ are variable terms, and -1 is the constant term in the expression.

Although an expression can contain just one term, it's more common to think of expressions as combinations of two or more terms. So, in the apples and peaches scenario presented earlier, you can write an expression for the cost of two apples and four peaches as $2a + 4p$.

In a term that is a product of two or more factors, the *numerical coefficient*, or simply *coefficient*, is the numerical factor, or the product of the numerical factors, in that term. In $2a + 4p$, the variables are a and p, and the numbers 2 and 4 are the coefficients of the variables. This means that the coefficient of the variable a is 2 and the coefficient of the variable p is 4. If no coefficient is explicitly written, then the numerical coefficient is understood to be 1. Thus, the coefficient of xy^2 is 1.

In an algebraic expression, terms involving the same variable, even if they have different coefficients, are *like terms*. For example, in the expression $3x + 4y - 2x + y$, $3x$ and $-2x$ are like terms because they both contain the single x variable; $4y$ and y are also like terms because they both contain the y variable and only the y variable. All constant terms are like terms.

REMEMBER

For like terms, the variables must be exact matches with the same powers; for example, $3x^3y$ and x^3y are like terms, but x and x^2 aren't like terms, and neither are $2x$ and $2xy$.

You can combine (add/subtract) like terms together, but you can't combine unlike terms. So, in the expression $3x + 4y - 2x + y$, you can subtract the terms with the common x variable: $3x - 2x = x$. And you can add the like terms with the common y variable: $4y + y = 5y$ (y is understood to be $1y$). All this combining results in the final expression of $x + 5y$, which is a much simpler expression to work with. We work with many more algebraic expressions in the later section "Mastering algebraic operations."

Knowing the nomials: Kinds of expressions

On the GMAT, you'll work with various monomials and polynomials. These algebraic expressions comprising single or multiple terms are an integral part of the exam.

A *monomial* consists of a single term, which when simplified is a constant, a variable, or a product of a numerical coefficient and one or more variables, where each variable is raised to a non-negative integer power, such as $4x$, $6x^2y$, and x^3z^2. The *degree of a monomial* is the sum of the exponents of its variables. Thus, the degree of $4x$ is 1, the degree of $6x^2y$ is 3, and the degree of x^3z^2 is 5.

Poly means many, so we bet you've already figured out that a *polynomial* is an algebraic expression that is the sum of monomials, such as $6x^2y + 2xy^2$, $x + 5y$, and $8x^3 - 12x^2 + 6x - 1$. Polynomials can have more specific designations, depending on how many terms they contain. For example, as previously noted, a *monomial* is a polynomial of exactly one term, such as $-12x^2$. A *binomial* is a polynomial of exactly two terms, such as $a+b$ or $2x+3$. And a *trinomial* is a polynomial of exactly three terms, like $4x^2 - 8x - 5$. Polynomials can have any number of terms, but for the GMAT, you don't need to know specific names to describe polynomials beyond three terms.

TIP

Often of interest are polynomials that are the sum of several terms that contain different powers of the same variable.

The *degree of a polynomial* is the same as the greatest of the degrees of its monomial terms after the polynomial has been simplified. The binomial $2x+3$ is a *first-degree* (or *linear*) *polynomial in x* since the highest power of x is 1. The trinomial $4x^2 - 8x - 5$ is a *second degree* (or *quadratic*) *polynomial in x* since the highest power of x is 2.

REMEMBER

A famous trinomial that you should be very familiar with for the GMAT is the expression known as a *quadratic polynomial*, which is the trinomial expression $ax^2 + bx + c$, where *a, b,* and *c* are constants with $a \neq 0$. We discuss this very important expression in the later section "Solving quadratic equations."

Mastering algebraic operations

Symbols like $+$, $-$, $\times$, and $\div$ are common to arithmetic and algebra. They symbolize the operations you perform on numbers. Arithmetic uses numbers with known values, such as $5+7=12$, in its operations (see the earlier section "Juggling Numbers and Operations" for more on basic arithmetic operations), but algebraic operations deal with unknowns, like $x+y=z$. This algebraic equation can't produce an exact numerical value because you don't know what x and y represent, let alone z. But that doesn't stop you from solving algebra problems as best you can with the given information. In the following sections, we show you how to add, subtract, multiply, and divide expressions with unknowns.

Adding to and taking away

From arithmetic, you know that 3 dozen plus 6 dozen is 9 dozen, or

$$(3 \times 12) + (6 \times 12) = (9 \times 12)$$

In algebra, you can write a somewhat similar equation by using a variable to stand in for the dozen: $3x + 6x = 9x$. And you can subtract to get the opposite result: $9x - 6x = 3x$.

TIP

Remember to combine positive and negative numbers according to the rules of arithmetic (see the earlier section "Juggling Numbers and Operations" if you need a refresher). For example, to tackle the expression $7x + (-10x) + 22x$, find the sum of the two positive numbers ($7x$ and $22x$) and then subtract the value of the negative number (because adding a negative is the same as subtracting a positive), like this:

$$7x + (-10x) + 22x =$$
$$29x - 10x =$$
$$19x$$

That's fine for adding and subtracting like terms, you may say, but what about working with unlike terms? You can't combine terms with different symbols or variables the same way you can when the symbols are the same. For instance, look at this example:

$$7x + 10y + 15x - 3y$$

If you were to simply combine the whole expression by adding and subtracting without accounting for the different variables, you'd come up with a wrong answer, something like 29xy. (And you can bet the GMAT will offer this incorrect expression as one of the answer choices to try to trap you.) Instead, you first separate the x terms from the y terms and add and subtract to get something more manageable, like this:

$$7x + 15x = 22x$$
$$10y - 3y = 7y$$

which gives you this final expression:

$$22x + 7y$$

If you want to get tricky and add two or more expressions, you can set them up just as you would an addition problem in arithmetic. Remember, only like terms can be combined this way.

$$3x + 4y - 7z$$
$$2x - 2y + 8z$$
$$\underline{-x + 3y + 6z}$$
$$4x + 5y + 7z$$

Here's how an algebra problem may look on the GMAT.

For all x and y, $\left(4x^2 - 6xy - 12y^2\right) - \left(8x^2 - 12xy + 4y^2\right) = ?$

(A) $-4x^2 - 18xy - 16y^2$

(B) $-4x^2 + 6xy - 16y^2$

(C) $-4x^2 - 6xy - 8y^2$

(D) $4x^2 - 6xy + 16y^2$

(E) $12x^2 - 18xy - 8y^2$

The easiest way to approach this problem is to distribute the negative sign to the second expression (see the later section, "Distributing terms") and combine the two expressions with like terms by following these steps:

1. **Distribute the negative sign (multiply each term in the second expression by –1).**

    Remember that subtracting is the same as adding the opposite of a number. So, your problem is really $\left(4x^2 - 6xy - 12y^2\right) + -1\left(8x^2 - 12xy + 4y^2\right)$. Distributing the negative sign changes the second expression to $-8x^2 + 12xy - 4y^2$, because a negative times a positive makes a negative and two negatives make a positive.

2. **Combine the expressions with like terms together:**
    $$4x^2 - 8x^2 - 6xy + 12xy - 12y^2 - 4y^2$$

3. **Add and subtract like terms:**
    $$4x^2 - 8x^2 = -4x^2$$
    $$-6xy + 12xy = 6xy$$
    $$-12y^2 - 4y^2 = -16y^2$$

4. **Put the terms back into the polynomial:**
    $$-4x^2 + 6xy - 16y^2$$

So, the answer is $-4x^2 + 6xy - 16y^2$, which is Choice (B). If you chose any of the other answers, you either distributed the negative sign improperly or you added and subtracted the like terms incorrectly. Eliminate wrong answers as you combine terms. For instance, once you determine that the first term is $-4x^2$, you can eliminate Choices (D) and (E).

WARNING

After you've combined like terms, double-check that you've used the correct signs, particularly when you change all the signs like you did in the second expression. The other answer choices for the sample problem are similar to the correct choice. They're designed to trap you in case you make an addition or subtraction error. Add and subtract carefully, and you won't fall for these tricks.

Multiplying and dividing expressions

Multiplying and dividing two or more variables works just as though you were performing these same operations on numbers with known values. So, if $2^3 = 2 \times 2 \times 2$, then $x^3 = x \times x \times x$. Likewise, if $2^2 \times 2^3 = 2^5$, then $x^2 \times x^3 = x^5$. Similarly, if $2^6 \div 2^4 = 2^2$, then $y^6 \div y^4 = y^2$.

The process is pretty simple for monomials, but polynomials may be a little more complicated. In the next sections, we explore the different methods for multiplying and dividing polynomials.

DISTRIBUTING TERMS

You can distribute terms in algebra just like you do in arithmetic. For example, when you multiply a binomial by a number, you multiply each term in the binomial by the number. In this example, you multiply each term inside the parentheses by $4x$:

$$4x(x-3) = 4x^2 - 12x$$

With division, you do the same operation in reverse. It's important to mention that, in algebra, division is commonly indicated by the fraction bar. To perform the division, divide each term in the numerator by $4x$:

$$\frac{16x^2 + 4x}{4x} = \frac{16x^2}{4x} + \frac{4x}{4x} = 4x + 1$$

Here's an example of a GMAT question in which you use distribution to answer.

EXAMPLE

For all x, $12x - (-10x) - 3x(-x + 10) =$

(A) $10x$

(B) $-3x^2 - 10x$

(C) $3x^2 - 52x$

(D) $3x^2 + 8x$

(E) $3x^2 - 8x$

This question tests your ability to add, subtract, and multiply terms in an algebraic expression.

1. **Use distribution to multiply $(-x + 10)$ by $-3x$:** $-3x(-x + 10) = 3x^2 - 30x$

Now the equation looks like this: $12x - (-10x) + 3x^2 - 30x$

2. **Combine the terms that contain just x:** $12x + 10x - 30x = -8x$

Now you have: $3x^2 - 8x$

So, the answer is Choice (E): $3x^2 - 8x$.

STACKING TERMS

One easy way to multiply two polynomials is to stack them on top of one another. Suppose you have this problem: $(x^2 + 2xy + y^2)(x - y)$.

You can stack this expression just like an old-fashioned multiplication problem. Just remember to multiply each of the terms in the first line by each term in the second line.

$$
\begin{array}{r}
x^2 + 2xy + y^2 \\
x - y \\
\hline
x^3 + 2x^2y + xy^2 \\
-x^2y - 2xy^2 - y^3 \\
\hline
x^3 + x^2y - xy^2 - y^3
\end{array}
$$

Line up like terms during the first round of multiplication so they match up before you add the partial products.

The GMAT may ask you to divide a polynomial by a monomial. Simply divide each term of the polynomial by the monomial. Here's how you'd divide in the expression $\dfrac{60x^4 - 20x^3}{5x}$:

$$
\frac{60x^4 - 20x^3}{5x} = \frac{60x^4}{5x} - \frac{20x^3}{5x} = \left(12x^{4-1}\right) - \left(4x^{3-1}\right) = 12x^3 - 4x^2
$$

TAKING A SHINE TO THE FOIL METHOD

You can multiply two binomials by using the *FOIL* method. FOIL is an acronym for *first, outer, inner, last,* which indicates the order that you multiply the terms from one binomial by the terms of the second binomial before adding their products. Look at this example:

$$
(4x - 5)(3x + 8) =
$$

1. **Multiply the first terms (4x and 3x) of each binomial:** $4x \times 3x = 12x^2$

2. **Multiply the outer terms (4x and 8):** $4x \times 8 = 32x$

3. **Multiply the inner terms (3x and –5):** $3x \times -5 = -15x$

4. **Add these two products at this point because they're like terms:** $32x - 15x = 17x$

5. **Multiply the last terms (–5 and 8) of each binomial:** $-5 \times 8 = -40$

6. **Combine all the results to form the final product:** $12x^2 + 17x - 40$

You may recognize this expression as a quadratic polynomial, which we discussed in the earlier section, "Knowing the nomials: Kinds of expressions."

Commit the following factors and their special products to memory:

$$
(x + y)^2 = x^2 + 2xy + y^2
$$
$$
(x - y)^2 = x^2 - 2xy + y^2
$$
$$
(x + y)(x - y) = x^2 - y^2
$$

So, if you're asked to multiply $(x + 3)(x + 3)$, you know without using FOIL that the answer is $x^2 + 2(3x) + 9$ or $x^2 + 6x + 9$. Also, $(x - 3)(x - 3) = x^2 + -6x + 9$ or $x^2 - 6x + 9$. And $(x + 3)(x - 3) = x^2 - 9$.

If you're able to keep track of the terms, you can use FOIL to multiply terms in the proper order without taking the time to stack them. The FOIL method comes in handy for solving GMAT problems like the next one.

EXAMPLE

When the polynomials $3x + 4$ and $x - 5$ are multiplied together and written in the form $3x^2 + kx - 20$, what is the value of k?

(A) 2

(B) 3

(C) −5

(D) −11

(E) −20

This question asks you for the coefficient of the middle term of the quadratic expression formed by multiplying $3x + 4$ and $x - 5$. Remember with FOIL, you multiply the first, outer, inner, and last. The problem gives you the product of the first terms: $3x^2$. The product of the last terms is also there: −20. Because the problem provides the products of the first terms and last terms, all you have to do to get the middle term is to multiply the outer and inner terms of the two expressions and then add them together.

1. Multiply the outer terms: $3x \times -5 = -15x$

2. Multiply the inner terms: $4 \times x = 4x$

So, the middle term of the quadratic is $-15x + 4x = -11x$. The coefficient k must equal −11, which is Choice (D).

Knowing binomial factors with variables and their special products can help you solve similar problems that have the same form, but no variables, such as this one:

EXAMPLE

What is the value of $\left(2 + \sqrt{3}\right)\left(2 - \sqrt{3}\right)$?

(A) −1

(B) 0

(C) 1

(D) $2\sqrt{3}$

(E) $4\sqrt{3}$

You may look at this question and think "Gee, I wish I had a calculator to help me add and subtract the stuff in the parentheses." But then you may notice that this problem looks a lot like $(x + y)(x - y)$, which yields the difference of x^2 and y^2, or $x^2 - y^2$, as the product when multiplied. In this problem, x is the constant 2 and y is the constant $\sqrt{3}$; but that shouldn't be a worry. It all works out fast and easy as shown here:

1. Square 2: $(2)^2 = 2 \times 2 = 4$

2. Square $\sqrt{3}$: $\left(\sqrt{3}\right)^2 = \sqrt{3} \times \sqrt{3} = 3$

3. Write the difference of the two squares and simplify the result: $4 - 3 = 1$

Thus, $\left(2 + \sqrt{3}\right)\left(2 - \sqrt{3}\right) = 4 - 3 = 1$. The answer is Choice (C) — no calculator needed.

Extracting information: Factoring polynomials

Factors are the numbers you multiply together to get a product. So, factoring a value means you write that value as a product of its factors. For the GMAT, you should know how to pull out the common factors in expressions and the two binomial factors in a quadratic polynomial. We show you how to do both in the following sections.

Something in common: Finding common factors

To simplify polynomials for complex problems, extract their common factors by dividing each term by the factors that are common to every term. You can think of the process as the inverse of distributing terms. For example, to find the common factors of the terms in the expression $-14x^3 - 35x^6$, follow these steps:

1. **Consider the coefficients.**

   Because –7 is common to both –14 and –35, take this factor out of the expression by dividing both terms by –7. Then put the remaining expression in parentheses next to the common factor: $-7\left(2x^3 + 5x^6\right)$.

2. **Now look at the variables.**

   Because x^3 or a multiple of it is common to both terms, divide both terms in parentheses by x^3, multiply x^3 by the other common factor (–7), and put the remaining expression in parentheses: $-7x^3\left(2 + 5x^3\right)$.

   Hence, $-14x^3 - 35x^6 = -7x^3\left(2 + 5x^3\right)$.

Two by two: Factoring quadratic polynomials

The GMAT also expects you to know how to factor quadratic polynomials. To accomplish this task, you must perform the FOIL operations in reverse to come up with a couple of binomial factors that look something like this: $(x \pm a)(x \pm b)$.

For example, look at the following quadratic polynomial:

$$x^2 + 5x + 6$$

To find its factors, draw two pairs of parentheses: ( )( ). The first terms of the two factors must be x and x because x^2 is the product of x and x. So, you can insert x as the first term in each pair of parentheses. You know that the operation in both terms must be addition because both the middle and last terms of the quadratic expression are positive:

$$(x+\ \ )(x+\ \ )$$

To find the second terms for the two factors, ask yourself which two numbers have a product of 6 (the third term of the quadratic) and add up to the number 5 (the coefficient of the quadratic's second term). The only two factors that meet these two criteria are 2 and 3. The other pairs of factors of 6 (6 and 1, –6 and –1, –2 and –3) don't add up to 5. So, the binomial factors of the quadratic equation are $(x+2)$ and $(x+3)$. Thus, $x^2 + 5x + 6 = (x+2)(x+3)$.

TIP

Because you do just the reverse of what you do when you multiply binomials using the FOIL method, you can use the FOIL method to make sure the binomial factors result in the original quadratic when you multiply them together.

There's a timesaving way to factor binomials that are made up of a difference of two squares, such as $x^2 - 4$. Factors for these types of quadratic polynomials (known as the difference of two squares) result in the following form: $(x + a)(x - a)$. The variable x is the square root of the first term, and a is the positive square root of the second term. So, $x^2 - 4 = (x + 2)(x - 2)$.

This factoring technique is quite easy to memorize and can help you answer some algebra questions much more quickly than if you were to take the time to carry out long calculations. For example, if you're asked to perform the multiplication $(x + 5)(x - 5)$, you could use the FOIL method to figure out the answer, but spotting that the correct answer will be the difference of two squares is much faster. You know the correct answer is $x^2 - 25$ without performing time-consuming calculations.

Likewise, if you need to factor $x^2 - 25$, all you do is determine the square root of x^2 and the positive square root of 25 and enter those results into the factoring form for the difference of two squares. You know right away that the factorization is $(x + 5)(x - 5)$.

When you can break down quadratic polynomials into factors, you'll be able to solve numerous quadratic equations. For more about how to do this, see the later section "Solving quadratic equations."

Knowing how to factor quadratic polynomials can help you more efficiently factor similar polynomials of higher degree, such as this one:

EXAMPLE

Factor $9x^6 - 25y^4$.

(A) $\left(3x^3 + 5y^2\right)^2$

(B) $\left(3x^3 - 5y^2\right)^2$

(C) $\left(4.5x^3 + 12.5y^2\right)^2$

(D) $\left(4.5x^3 + 12.5y^2\right)\left(4.5x^3 - 12.5y^2\right)$

(E) $\left(3x^3 + 5y^2\right)\left(3x^3 - 5y^2\right)$

Notice that this problem looks a lot like the difference of two squares. So, all you do is determine the square root of $9x^6$ and the square root of $25y^4$ and enter those values into the factoring form for the difference of two squares:

1. Determine the square root of $9x^6$: $\left(9x^6\right)^{\frac{1}{2}} = 3x^3$

2. Determine the square root of $25y^4$: $\left(25y^4\right)^{\frac{1}{2}} = 5y^2$

3. Enter the results into the factoring form for the difference of two squares:
$$9x^6 - 25y^4 = \left(3x^3 + 5y^2\right)\left(3x^3 - 5y^2\right)$$

Thus, the answer is Choice (E).

Minding your Ps and Qs: Functions

Some of the GMAT math questions involve functions. Simply put, functions are relationships between two sets of numbers; each number you put into the formula gives you only one possible answer. Functions may sound complicated, but they're really pretty simple. A function problem looks something like this:

Given $f(x) = 2x^2 + 3$. What is $f(2)$?

We explore the terminology of functions and how to find the domain and range of functions in the following sections.

Standing in: Understanding function terminology

Before we show you how to solve function problems, you need to know a few definitions. Table 3-2 gives you the terms we use when we discuss functions.

TABLE 3-2 **Defining Terms for Functions**

Term	Definition
Function	A rule that assigns each member of one set of numbers to a corresponding *unique* member of another set.
Independent variable (input)	In the function $y = f(x)$, x is the independent variable.
Dependent variable (output)	In the function $y = f(x)$, y is the dependent variable.
Domain	The set of all possible values of the independent variable.
Range	The set of all possible values of the dependent variable.

Functions on the GMAT are usually (but, not always) displayed with lowercase letters such as f, g, or h. For example, $f(x)$ indicates the function of x, and it simply means "f of x." Don't let this technical language confuse you. Think of a function as a process f that takes an input number x and produces from it an output number, which is found by substituting the input value into $f(x)$. In simple terms: $f(\text{input}) = \text{output}$. In any function, there can be no more than one output for any given input. However, more than one input can produce the same output. For example, if $h(x) = |x + 5|$, then $h(-6) = |-6 + 5| = |-1| = 1$ and, also, $h(-4) = |-4 + 5| = |1| = 1$.

Basically, to *evaluate a function*, all you must do is substitute the indicated value for x into the function.

WARNING

Don't think that the parentheses in the function notation mean multiplication like they do in algebraic operations. The expression $f(x)$ doesn't mean $f \times x$.

To see how functions work, consider the earlier example:

Given $f(x) = 2x^2 + 3$. What is $f(2)$?

The initial expression means that the f function rule is "Square x, multiply the result by 2, and then add 3." To evaluate $f(2)$, you just substitute 2 for x in the expression and solve.

$$f(2) = 2(2)^2 + 3 = 2(4) + 3 = 8 + 3 = 11$$

So, when x is 2, $f(x)$ is 11. The substitution of 2 for x in the expression can be written as $f(2) = 11$. Then $f(2)$ is called the "value of f at $x = 2$." That's all there is to it! The function notation is just a fancy way of telling you to perform a substitution.

Taking it to the limit: Domain and range of functions

The *domain of a function* is the set of all numbers that can possibly be an input of the function, the x in $f(x)$. The *range of a function* is the set of all numbers that can possibly be an output of the function, the value for $f(x)$. In other words, if you think of the domain of a function as the set of all input values that you can put into that function, the range is the set of all possible output values that can come out of it. Domain and range questions aren't difficult, but you need to be aware of some basic rules to determine the proper limits of the domain and range.

MASTERING THE TERRITORY: DOMAIN

Unless a problem specifies otherwise, the domain of a function includes all real numbers for which the function is defined and can produce meaningful outputs. Here are some reasons for exclusion of a number from the domain of a function:

>> The output would result in division by zero, such as in a fraction with a denominator of 0, because then the output would be undefined.

>> The output would result in an even-numbered root of a negative number. Even-numbered roots of negatives aren't real numbers because any number that's squared or has an even-numbered power can't result in a negative number.

For example, there's no real number such as $\sqrt{-4}$ because there's no one real number whose square is a negative 4. No matter whether you calculate $(-2)(-2)$ or $(2)(2)$ the product always equals positive 4. This occurs because squaring a positive number or a negative number always yields a positive product.

To see how the first rule affects domain, look at this function:

$$f(x) = \frac{x+4}{x-2}$$

Normally, the domain of a function can contain an unlimited number of x values. In the preceding example, though, the function rule is a fractional expression with the variable x in the denominator. Because your denominator can't add up to 0, the denominator, $x-2$, can't equal 0, which implies that x can't equal 2. Therefore, the domain of $f(x) = \frac{x+4}{x-2}$ is all real numbers except 2, which you can shorten to $\{x \neq 2\}$. That's all there is to it!

Here's a function that relates to the second rule: $g(n) = 3\sqrt[4]{n+2}$. In this function, you have an even-numbered radical sign with the variable n within it. You know that the root of an even-numbered radical, in this case, the 4th root, can't be a negative number. Otherwise, you wouldn't have a real number as your final answer. Therefore, the number under the radical sign can't be less than 0. So, this means $n \geq -2$. The result is that the domain of the function $g(n)$ is $\{n \geq -2\}$.

The GMAT may test your knowledge of domain with a problem such as the following.

EXAMPLE

Determine the domain of the function $f(x) = \frac{4}{x^2 - x - 2}$.

(A) $\{x \neq -1, 2\}$

(B) $\{x \neq 1, -2\}$

(C) $\{x = -1, 2\}$

(D) $\{x = -4, 2\}$

(E) $\{x \neq -4, 2\}$

This problem involves simple algebra. You know the denominator can't equal 0, so set the trinomial in the denominator equal to 0 and solve for x to find out what x can't be. We show you how to solve trinomials later in the "Solving quadratic equations" section.

$$x^2 - x - 2 = 0$$
$$(x+1)(x-2) = 0$$
$$x + 1 = 0; x = -1$$
$$x - 2 = 0; x = 2$$

WARNING

You're not finished! If you picked Choice (C) as your answer, your factoring would have been absolutely right, but your answer would be absolutely wrong. Answer Choice (C) gives you only the values for x that make the denominator equal to 0. You're trying to find the values that make the denominator *not* equal to 0.

So, the correct answer is Choice (A); x can be any real number other than −1 and 2 because if x were equal to −1 or 2, the denominator would be 0, and the value would be undefined. If you chose Choice (B), you switched the signs of the factors. If you chose Choices (D) or (E), you found the correct factors of the denominator but mistakenly divided the numerator by each root of the denominator.

ROAMING THE LAND: RANGE

Just as the domain of a function is limited by certain laws of mathematics, so, too, is the range. Here are the rules to remember when you're determining the range of a function:

>> An absolute value of a real number can't be a negative number.

>> An even exponent or power can't produce a negative number.

>> A square root radical can't return a negative number.

Check out some situations where these rules come into play. Look at the following functions:

$$f(x) = |x|$$
$$g(x) = x^2$$
$$h(x) = \sqrt{x}$$

Each of these functions can result only in an output that's a positive number or 0. So in each case, the range of the function is greater than or equal to 0. Here's a question that puts the range rules to work.

EXAMPLE

What is the range of the function $g(x) = 1 - \sqrt{x-2}$?

(A) $g(x) \geq -2$

(B) $g(x) \leq -2$

(C) $g(x) \geq 2$

(D) $g(x) \geq -1$

(E) $g(x) \leq 1$

TIP

First, make sure the square root radical represents a real number. The value inside the square root radical symbol has to be equal to or greater than 0. So, x must be equal to or greater than 2, because any value less than 2 would make the value inside the radical a negative value. And, as you know, square roots of negative numbers are not real numbers. To check the possible outputs, consider that no matter what value of x is the input from the restricted domain (which includes only values that are greater than or equal to 2), $\sqrt{x-2}$ is nonnegative. Therefore, the output of $g(x) = 1 - \sqrt{x-2}$ always equals $1 - ($a nonnegative number$)$, which is always less than or equal to 1. So, the correct answer is Choice (E).

WARNING

Getting confused and looking for the domain when you should be finding the range is very easy. If you chose Choice (C), you solved for the domain of x. If you chose Choices (A) or (B), you're hung up trying to make the number under the radical a positive number. If you chose Choice (D), you simply don't know how to solve for range, so be sure to review this section.

Getting in line: Sequences and series

A *sequence* is a function whose domain consists of only positive integers. For example, $a(n) = n^2$ for $n = 1, 2, 3, \ldots$ is an *infinite sequence*, whose domain is all positive integers. The sequence $a(n)$ is denoted a_n. The value of this sequence at $n = 3$ is $a_3 = 3^2 = 9$. It is customary to describe a sequence by listing its terms in the order in which they correspond to the positive integers as $a_1, a_2, a_3, \ldots, a_n, \ldots$ as follows: $1, 4, 9, \ldots, n^2, \ldots$. This sequence has *initial term* $a_1 = 1$ and its nth term is $a_n = n^2$. A *finite sequence of length k* is the function whose domain is the set of the first k positive integers.

Here is a typical GMAT question that asks you to find the next term in a sequence. For questions like these, your best approach is to look for a pattern.

EXAMPLE

What is the next number in the sequence 2, 5, 10, 17, 26, . . . ?

(A) 34

(B) 37

(C) 38

(D) 40

(E) 42

To find the pattern look for differences between consecutive terms:

$$5 - 2 = 3; 10 - 5 = 5, 17 - 10 = 7; 26 - 17 = 9$$

The differences are 3, 5, 7, and 9. Notice that these differences between consecutive terms are increasing by 2 each time. Apply this pattern to find the next difference: $9 + 2 = 11$. To find the next number in the sequence, add the difference (11) to the last number (26):

$$26 + 11 = 37, \text{Choice (B)}.$$

A series is the sum of the terms of a sequence. The sum of the first k terms of a sequence is a partial sum. It is written as $\sum_{i=1}^{k} a_i = a_1 + a_2 + \ldots + a_k$, where the letter i is the index, the lower limit is 1, and the upper limit is k. For example, the partial sum of the first three terms of the sequence based on the function $a(n) = n^2$ is $(1)^2 + (2)^2 + (3)^2 = 1 + 4 + 9 = 14$.

Putting on your thinking cap: Problem solving

You may be wondering how the GMAT tests your knowledge of algebra concepts. Well, wonder no more. The following sections present you with many of the ways you'll use algebra to solve GMAT math problems.

Isolating the variable: Linear equations with one unknown

A *linear equation* with one unknown is a first-degree, one-variable equation, meaning that it contains one variable whose highest power is 1. Plainly, these equations are fairly basic. In its simplest form, a linear equation with one variable x is expressed as $ax + b = c$, where x is the variable and a, b, and c are constants with $a \neq 0$. Linear equations, each with one variable, that share a common solution, are *equivalent equations*. For example, the equations $2x - 5 = 3$ and $2x = 8$ have the same unique solution: $x = 4$.

To solve a linear equation with one unknown means to find the value of the unknown that *satisfies the equation* (that is, that makes the equation true when substituted for the unknown in the equation). To solve a linear equation with one unknown, isolate the variable in the equation you're trying to solve, which means getting the variable all by itself on one side of the equation. To accomplish this task, perform identical mathematical operations to each side of the equation. It's important to keep in mind the following two rules:

>> Adding or subtracting the same number from each side of the equation does not change the equality.

>> Multiplying or dividing each side of the equation by the same *nonzero* number does not change the equality.

Decide what operation to do based on what has been done to the variable. Basically, your goal is to undo what's been done. As you proceed, exploit the fact that addition and subtraction undo each other; and, similarly, multiplication and division undo each other.

TIP

This process essentially transforms the original equation into an equivalent equation that has the form: variable = solution (or solution = variable).

This easy question asks you to solve a linear equation: If $4x + 10 = -38$, what is the value of x? Solve for x by isolating prep the variable on one side of the equation:

1. **Eliminate 10 from the left side of the equation by subtracting it from each side.**

   (Remember that if you do something to one side of the equation, you need to do the same thing to the other side. Otherwise, your math teacher is liable to rap you on the knuckles with a slide rule.) Here's what happens when you subtract 10 from each side:

   $$4x + 10 - 10 = -38 - 10$$
   $$4x = -48$$

2. **Divide each side by 4, and you have your answer.**

   $$\frac{4x}{4} = \frac{-48}{4}$$
   $$x = -12$$

   Hence, the value of x is –12.

You tackle division problems the same way. So, if you're asked to solve for x in the problem $\frac{x}{4} = -5$, you know what to do. Isolate x to the left side of the equation by multiplying each side of the equation by 4:

$$\frac{x}{4} \times 4 = -5 \times 4$$
$$x = -20$$

Being absolutely positive: Absolute value equations

To solve an equation involving an absolute value, be mindful that the expression inside the absolute value bars can be positive or negative. This situation results in two equations, each of which you must solve independently.

Suppose you are asked to solve the equation $|x - 3| = 5$.

This equation results in the two equations: $x - 3 = 5$ and $-(x - 3) = 5$

Solving $x - 3 = 5$ yields $x = 8$ as a solution, and solving $-(x - 3) = 5$ (which implies $-x + 3 = 5$) yields $x = -2$ as a solution. Thus, the original equation has two solutions: $x = 8$ and $x = -2$.

TIP

When setting up the negative possibility, use parentheses around the whole expression inside the absolute value bars.

Getting in sync: Simultaneous equations

Solving for x is simple when it's the only variable in a linear equation, but what if your equation has more than one variable, say x and y? When you have another linear equation that contains at least one of the variables, you can solve for either variable. These two equations are *simultaneous equations*. The *solution* is a pair of values, one for x with one for y that makes both equations true when substituted for x and y, respectively.

TIP

If two equations are to be solved together, the solution must satisfy both equations simultaneously.

For two linear equations with two variables, if the equations are equivalent, there are infinitely many solutions to the equations. For example, $x - 3y = 2$ and $2x - 6y = 4$ are equivalent. (Note that the second equation is 2 times the first equation.) Thus, there are infinitely many solutions to these two equations such as these pairs: $x = 2$ with $y = 0$, $x = 0$ with $y = -\frac{2}{3}$, and $x = 5$ with $y = 1$.

If the equations are not equivalent but one *contradicts* the other (both cannot be true at the same time), there is no solution. For example, $x - 3y = 2$ and $2x - 6y = 10$ have no simultaneous solution because $x - 3y = 2$ implies that $2x - 6y = 4$, which contradicts the second equation. Thus, no values of x and y can simultaneously satisfy both equations. (Note that the coefficients of the second equation are 2 times the corresponding coefficients of the first equation.)

If the equations are neither equivalent nor contradictory, you can determine exact values for the two variables.

REMEMBER

For either equivalent or contradictory equations, the ratios of corresponding coefficients of the variables are equal.

There are several methods of solving two linear equations with two variables. One way is to solve by substitution: You just solve one of the equations for one of the variables and then plug the answer into the other equation and solve. Here's a simple example:

If $4x + 5y = 30$ and $y = 2$, what is the value of x?

Because the second equation tells you that y is 2, just substitute 2 for the value of y in the first equation and you're on your way:

$$4x + 5y = 30$$
$$4x + 5(2) = 30$$
$$4x + 10 = 30$$
$$4x = 20$$
$$x = 5$$

That's all there is to it! Thus, the solution is $x = 5$ with $y = 2$.

TIP

You also can solve simultaneous linear equations by stacking them. This method works when you have as many equations as you have possible variables to solve for. So, you can stack these two equations because they each contain the same two variables:

$$6x + 4y = 66$$
$$-2x + 2y = 8$$

Your goal is to find a way to remove one of the variables. Here's how:

1. **Examine the equations to determine what variable you can eliminate through addition or subtraction.**

If you multiply the entire second equation by 3, you can eliminate the x variable terms in both equations because $3(-2x) = -6$, and $6x - 6x = 0$. Just be sure to multiply each term in the second equation by the same value. So, the second equation becomes $-6x + 6y = 24$.

2. **Stack the equations, combine like terms, and solve for y.**

$$6x + 4y = 66$$
$$\underline{-6x + 6y = 24}$$
$$0 + 10y = 90$$
$$y = 9$$

3. **Plug the value of one variable into one of the equations and solve for the other value.**

You've found that $y = 9$, so substitute 9 for the value of y into one of the equations to solve for x.

$$-2x + 2y = 8$$
$$-2x + 2(9) = 8$$
$$-2x + 18 = 8$$
$$-2x = -10$$
$$x = 5$$

Therefore, the solution to the simultaneous equations is $x = 5$ with $y = 9$.

For linear equations that are neither equivalent nor contradictory, you can determine a unique simultaneous solution provided the number of separate linear equations is the same as the number of distinct variables they contain. This certitude can help you efficiently answer certain data sufficiency questions, such as this example.

EXAMPLE

What is the value of x?

1. $2x - 9y = 28$

2. $4y - 3x = 42 + y$

(A) Statement (1) *alone* is sufficient, but Statement (2) alone is not sufficient.

(B) Statement (2) *alone* is sufficient, but Statement (1) alone is not sufficient.

(C) *Both* statements *together* are sufficient, but *neither* statement *alone* is sufficient.

(D) *Each* statement *alone* is sufficient.

(E) Statements (1) and (2) *together* are *not* sufficient.

You can't solve for x using either of the statements by itself. The best you can do is solve for x in terms of y in either case. So, the answer is either Choice (C) or (E). Without lifting a pencil, you know that the answer is Choice (C); the statements are sufficient together. The two distinct equations each contain the same two variables and are neither equivalent nor contradictory, which you can quickly confirm by checking the ratios of corresponding x and y coefficients — so, the conditions are met to reach an exact value for x. You shouldn't use your limited time to actually solve for x during the exam, but we'll take you through the process in case you aren't convinced.

1. **Combine like terms in Statement (2):**

$$4y - 3x = 42 + y$$
$$-3x + 3y = 42$$

2. **Multiply all terms in the resulting equation by 3 so you can eliminate the y terms when you stack the two equations:**

$$3(-3x + 3y = 42)$$
$$-9x + 9y = 126$$

3. **Stack the equations and solve:**

$$2x - 9y = 28$$
$$\underline{-9x + 9y = 126}$$
$$-7x = 154$$
$$x = -22$$

REMEMBER

For two linear equations with two variables:

» If the two equations have a unique solution, their graphs are two lines which intersect at the point that is their common solution.

» If the two equations are equivalent, their graphs coincide and there are infinitely many solutions.

» If the two equations are contradictory, their graphs are two parallel lines that don't intersect and there is no solution.

See the later section "Seeing is believing: The coordinate plane" for a discussion of graphing linear equations as lines in the coordinate plane.

Not playing fair: Inequalities

An *inequality* is a statement such as "x is less than y" or "x is greater than or equal to y." In addition to the symbols for add, subtract, multiply, and divide, mathematics also applies standard symbols to show how the two sides of an equation are related. You're probably pretty familiar with these symbols, but a little review never hurts. Table 3-3 gives you a rundown of the symbols you'll deal with on the GMAT.

TABLE 3-3 ## Mathematical Symbols for Equality and Inequality

Symbol	Meaning
=	Is equal to
≠	Is not equal to
≈	Is approximately equal to
>	Is greater than
<	Is less than
≥	Is greater than or equal to
≤	Is less than or equal to

These are some of the more common symbols used in algebra to signify equality and inequality.

PERFORMING OPERATIONS WITH LINEAR INEQUALITIES

You treat linear inequalities in one variable a lot like linear equations in one variable. Isolate the variable to one side and perform the same operations on each side of the inequality. The only difference is that if you multiply or divide by a negative number, you need to reverse the direction of the inequality sign. The set of all real numbers that are solutions of an inequality is its *solution set*. So, here's how you solve this simple inequality:

$$-2x \leq 10$$
$$x \geq -5$$

Here is a GMAT candidate:

Solve $3x + 9 < 5x - 7$.

(A) $x < -8$

(B) $x < -4$

(C) $x > -8$

(D) $x > 4$

(E) $x > 8$

Here's how to solve it.

1. **Write the original equation:** $3x + 9 < 5x - 7$

2. **Subtract 9 from each side:** $3x < 5x - 16$

3. **Subtract 5x from each side:** $-2x < -16$

4. **Divide each side by −2 and reverse the inequality symbol:** $x > 8$, Choice (E).

WORKING WITH INTERVALS OF NUMBERS

A (*finite*) *interval* is a range of numbers between two given endpoints, where one, both, or neither of the endpoints may be included in the interval. You can use inequalities to show an interval of numbers. For example, the GMAT may show the interval of numbers between −6 and 12 as a *double inequality*, like this: $-6 < x < 12$. This double inequality means that x must simultaneously be greater than −6 and less than 12.

To show the interval between −6 and 12 including −6 and 12, you use the ≤ sign, like this: $-6 \leq x \leq 12$. You can add or subtract values within an interval. For example, you can add 5 to each part of $-6 < x < 12$ to get this double inequality:

$$-6 + 5 < x + 5 < 12 + 5$$
$$-1 < x + 5 < 17$$

And you can perform operations between different intervals, such as $4 < x < 15$ and $-2 < y < 20$. To find the sum of these two intervals, follow these steps:

1. **Add the least values of each interval:** $4 + (-2) = 2$

2. **Add the greatest values of each interval:** $15 + 20 = 35$

3. **Create a new interval with the sums:** $2 < x + y < 35$

This result means that the sum $x + y$ is between 2 and 35.

Here's an example of how the GMAT may ask you to deal with inequalities.

EXAMPLE

If $x^2 - 1 \leq 8$, what is the smallest real value x can assume?

(A) −9

(B) −6

(C) −3

(D) 0

(E) 3

This problem asks you to determine the least real value of x if $x^2 - 1$ is less than or equal to 8.

REMEMBER

Before you begin, it is essential that you know that $\sqrt{x^2} = |x|$. This is the case because the *square root radical* ($\sqrt{}$) always returns the nonnegative *principal square root* of a number. Since you don't know whether x is positive or negative, you use the absolute value bars to guarantee a nonnegative result. For example, $\sqrt{3^2} = |3| = 3$ and $\sqrt{(-3)^2} = |-3| = 3$.

Now, for the problem at hand. Solve the inequality for x.

1. Write the original inequality: $x^2 - 1 \leq 8$

2. Isolate x^2 by adding 1 to each side of the inequality: $x^2 \leq 9$

3. Take the square root of each side of the inequality: $\sqrt{x^2} \leq \sqrt{9}$

4. Simplify: $|x| \leq 3$

Which indicates that $-3 \leq x \leq 3$ (See "Solving absolute value inequalities" in the section that follows for a rule that applies.) Thus, the least real value of x is −3, Choice (C). To make sure you're right, you can eliminate answer choices by using common sense. For example, −9 in Choice (A) would make $x^2 - 1$ equal 80, and −6 in Choice (B) would make $x^2 - 1$ equal 35. So, neither Choices (A) nor (B) can be a solution for x. In Choice (D), 0 is a possible value for x, but it isn't the least solution, because you know that −3 is less than 0. Choice (E) can't be right because it's greater than two other possible solutions, −3 and 0. So Choice (C) is the correct answer.

SOLVING ABSOLUTE VALUE INEQUALITIES

Solving absolute value inequalities requires that you remember a couple of rules:

Given a variable x (or a linear expression in x) and a real number $a \geq 0$,

If $|x| < a$, then $-a < x < a$; and

If $|x| > a$, then $x < -a$ or $x > a$.

REMEMBER

These two rules remain valid if you replace < with ≤ and > with ≥ throughout. Okay, give this one a whirl!

Solve $|x - 5| < 7$.

Here's how to do it.

1. Write the original equation: $|x - 5| < 7$

2. Write the equivalent double inequality: $-7 < x - 5 < 7$

3. Add 5 to each part to isolate x: $-7+5 < x-5+5 < 7+5$

4. Simplify: $-2 < x < 12$

Solving quadratic equations

A *quadratic equation* in the variable x is one that you can write in the standard quadratic form $ax^2 + bx + c = 0$, where a, b, and c are constants with $a \neq 0$ and x is a variable that you have to solve for. Specifically, a is the numerical coefficient of x^2, b is the numerical coefficient of x, and c is the constant term. Notice that all nonzero terms are on one side of the equation, and 0 is the only term on the other side. For example, $2x^2 = 0$, $x^2 - 4 = 0$, and $3x^2 - 6x + 5 = 0$ are quadratic equations in standard form.

If a quadratic equation is not in standard form, you can use algebraic manipulation to get all non-zero terms on one side and 0 on the other side. For example, in standard form $x^2 + x = 6 + 2x$ is $x^2 - x - 6 = 0$, $-4x + 4 = -x^2$ is $x^2 - 4x + 4 = 0$, and $(x+4)(2x-3) = 0$ is $2x^2 + 5x - 12 = 0$.

The *solution set* of a quadratic equation is the set containing its *roots*. A quadratic equation has at most two distinct real roots; and, in some cases, it has no real root.

FACTORING TO FIND *X*

The procedure for solving a quadratic equation by factoring relies on the *zero product property* of real numbers: If the product of two quantities is zero, then at least one of the quantities is zero.

To solve a quadratic equation by factoring do the following: First, make sure it's in standard form; next, factor the nonzero side into two binomials just like you did earlier in the section, "Two by two: Factoring quadratic polynomials"; then set each factor containing the variable equal to zero; finally, solve each of the resulting linear equations. The solutions to these simpler equations are the *solutions* of the original equation.

The GMAT may give you a quadratic equation like this one, and ask you to solve for x:

$x^2 - 6x + 5 = 0$

To factor the trinomial on the left side, identify a pair of numbers with a product of 5 and a sum of -6. The two pairs of factors of 5 are 1 and 5 and -1 and -5. To get a sum of -6, you need to go with the negative values. Doing so gives these two binomial factors: $(x-1)$ and $(x-5)$. So, the resulting equation is $(x-1)(x-5) = 0$.

Now set each of the binomial factors equal to 0. You can do so because, by the zero product property, you know that at least one of the factors must equal 0 if their product is 0: $x-1=0$ or $x-5=0$. Solve the resulting linear equations: The solutions are $x=1$ and $x=5$; or the solution set is $\{1, 5\}$. Voilà! The roots of the equation are now evident: 1 and 5. Substituting either 1 or 5 for x into the original equation, makes the equation true.

REMEMBER

Quadratic equations always have two roots (where, sometimes, a single root is repeated). On the GMAT the roots will be real numbers.

DETERMINING SOLUTIONS FOR THE DIFFERENCE OF TWO SQUARES

Solving a quadratic equation consisting of the difference of two squares (like $x^2 - a^2 = 0$) is a straightforward process if you remember that $x^2 - a^2 = (x+a)(x-a)$. Suppose the GMAT presents you with the task of solving a quadratic equation in which the difference of two squares is equal to 0. You know that all you need to do is find the square root of the first square and the positive square root of the second square, and then enter those results into the factoring form for the difference of two squares.

Suppose you are told to find the solution set for $x^2 - 49 = 0$. To solve by factoring, all you do is determine the square root of x^2 and the positive square root of 49 and enter those results into the factoring form for the difference of two squares to obtain $(x + 7)(x - 7) = 0$. Next, setting each factor equal to zero and solving the resulting linear equations yields $\{-7, 7\}$ as the solution set for the equation. It couldn't be easier!

USING THE QUADRATIC FORMULA

Solving quadratic equations is easy when the solutions contain nice, round numbers. But what if the ultimate solutions have harsh-looking radicals or perhaps unwieldy fractions? For the rare GMAT occasions when you can't simply solve a quadratic equation by factoring, you may have to use the *quadratic formula*, which is a rearrangement of the standard equation: $ax^2 + bx + c = 0$. It looks like this:

$$x = \frac{-b \pm \sqrt{b^2 - 4ac}}{2a}$$

REMEMBER

Although this formula may look mighty unmanageable, it may be the only sensible way to find the solutions for quadratic equations that aren't easily factored. Here's how you'd apply the formula when asked to solve $3x^2 + 7x - 6 = 0$ for x. In this equation, $a = 3$, $b = 7$, and $c = -6$. Plug these numbers into the quadratic formula and evaluate:

$$x = \frac{-7 \pm \sqrt{7^2 - 4(3)(-6)}}{2(3)}$$

$$x = \frac{-7 \pm \sqrt{49 + 72}}{6}$$

$$x = \frac{-7 \pm \sqrt{121}}{6}$$

$$x = \frac{-7 \pm 11}{6}$$

$$x = -\frac{18}{6} \text{ or } \frac{4}{6}$$

$$x = -3 \text{ or } \frac{2}{3}$$

The solution set is $\left\{-3, \frac{2}{3}\right\}$. Whew!

Reading between the lines: Word problems

The GMAT tests algebra and arithmetic concepts in word problems as well as mathematical equations. In fact, word problems are more common on the GMAT than straightforward equation-solving. So you have to know how to translate the English language into mathematical expressions.

REMEMBER

To help you with the translation, Table 3-4 provides some of the more common words you'll encounter in word problems and tells you what they look like in math symbols.

TABLE 3-4 Common Words and Their Math Equivalents

Plain English	Math Equivalent
Added to, more than, plus, increased by, combined with, total of, sum of	Plus (+)
Minus, less than, fewer than, decreased by, diminished by, reduced by, difference between, taken away from	Minus (–)
Multiplied by, of, times, product of, twice, double, triple	Multiply (×)
Divided by, ratio of, per, out of, quotient, for every, for each, half of	Divide (÷ or /)
x percent of y	$(x \div 100) \times y$
Is, are, was, were, becomes, results in	Equals (=)
How much, how many, a certain number	Variable (x, y)

Here's an example of how you play foreign language interpreter on GMAT word problems.

EXAMPLE

On the first day of an alpine slalom competition, the total combined time of Grace's two runs was 1 minute and 57 seconds. If twice the number of seconds in her first run was 30 seconds more than the number of seconds in her second run, what was her time in seconds for the first run?

(A) 15

(B) 30

(C) 49

(D) 68

(E) 147

Focus on what you're supposed to figure out. The question asks for the time of Grace's first run in seconds. So, you know you must convert her total time to seconds so you're working in the correct units. A minute has 60 seconds, which means that Grace's total time was $60 + 57$, or 117 seconds.

TIP

You can immediately eliminate Choice (E) because Grace's first run couldn't have been longer than the sum of her two runs. Now apply your math translation skills. You have two unknowns: the time of Grace's first run and the time of her second run. Let x stand for the first unknown and y for the second.

REMEMBER

You can solve a problem with two variables when you know two different equations that involve those two variables. So, search the problem for two equations.

For the first equation, the problem tells you that the total time of the two runs is 117 seconds. According to the English-to-math-translation dictionary, that means $x + y = 117$. You've got one equation!

You also know that 2 times (×) the number of seconds in her first run (x) was (=) 30 seconds more (+) than her time for the second run (y). Translation please? $2x = 30 + y$.

After you have the two equations, you can use substitution or stacking to solve for x. For this problem, stacking is faster. Notice that $2x = 30 + y$ is the same as $2x - y = 30$. When you stack and add the two equations, you can eliminate the y variable because $y - y = 0$.

$$x + y = 117$$
$$\underline{2x - y = 30}$$
$$3x = 147$$
$$x = 49$$

So, Grace ran her first race in 49 seconds, which is Choice (C). If you chose Choice (D), you solved for *y* instead of *x*. Grace's second run was 68 seconds.

Burning the midnight oil: Work problems

Work problems ask you to find out how much work gets done in a certain amount of time. Use this formula for doing algebra work problems: Production = (Rate of Work) × Time

Production means the amount of work that gets done. Because you get that quantity by multiplying two other numbers, you can say that production is the product of the rate times the time. Here's how you'd apply the formula in a GMAT work problem.

EXAMPLE

There are two dock workers, Alf and Kendric. Alf can load 16 tons of steel per day, and Kendric can load 20 tons per day. If they each work eight-hour days, how many tons of steel can the two of them load in one hour, assuming they maintain a steady rate?

(A) 2.5

(B) 4.5

(C) 36

(D) 160

(E) 320

This question asks you to find the amount of production and gives you the rate and the time. But to calculate the rate properly, you must state the hours in terms of days. Because a workday is eight hours, one hour is $\frac{1}{8}$ of a day. Figure out how much Alf loads in one hour ($\frac{1}{8}$ of a day) and add it to what Kendric loads in one hour.

$$\text{Total Production} = \text{Alf's Production} + \text{Kendric's Production}$$
$$\text{Total Production} = \left(16 \times \frac{1}{8}\right) + \left(20 \times \frac{1}{8}\right)$$
$$\text{Total Production} = 2 + 2.5$$
$$\text{Total Production} = 4.5$$

So, Alf and Kendric load 4.5 tons of steel in one hour ($\frac{1}{8}$ of a day), which is Choice (B). If you chose Choice (C), you figured out the total production for one day rather than one hour.

Going the distance: Distance problems

Distance problems are a lot like work problems. The formula for computing distance or speed problems is this: Distance = Rate × Time. Any problem involving distance, speed, or time spent traveling can be boiled down to this equation. The important thing is for you to have your variables and numbers plugged in properly. Here's an example.

EXAMPLE

Lucia can run a mile in seven minutes. How long, in seconds, does it take her to run $\frac{1}{10}$ of a mile at the same speed?

(A) 30

(B) 42

(C) 60

(D) 360

(E) 420

Before you do any calculating, you can eliminate Choice (E) because 420 seconds is 7 minutes, and you know it takes Lucia less time to run $\frac{1}{10}$ of a mile than it does for her to run a mile.

The problem tells you that Lucia's distance is $\frac{1}{10}$ of a mile. You can figure her rate to be $\frac{1}{7}$ mile per minute because she runs 1 mile in 7 minutes. The problem is asking how long she runs, so you need to solve for time. Plug the numbers into the distance formula:

$$\text{Distance} = \text{Rate} \times \text{Time}$$
$$\frac{1}{10} = \frac{1}{7} \times t$$

You need to isolate t on one side of the equation, so multiply each side by 7:

$$\frac{1}{10} \times 7 = t$$
$$\frac{7}{10} = t$$

So, Lucia runs $\frac{1}{10}$ of a mile in $\frac{7}{10}$ of a minute. Convert minutes to seconds. There are 60 seconds in a minute, and $\frac{7}{10} \times 60 = 42$ seconds. The correct answer is Choice (B).

Mixing it up: Mixture problems

In a mixture problem, the amount (or value) of an ingredient in a substance before mixing equals the amount (or value) of that ingredient in the substance after mixing: Amount of Ingredient Before Mixing = Amount of Ingredient After Mixing. Here's how you'd apply this concept in a GMAT mixture problem.

What amount (in milliliters) of a 1% hydrogen peroxide solution must be added to 60 milliliters of a 6% hydrogen peroxide solution to yield a 5% hydrogen peroxide solution?

(A) 12

(B) 15

(C) 18

(D) 20

(E) 45

Let x = the amount (in milliliters) of the 1% hydrogen peroxide solution that must be added. Then $x + 60$ = the amount (in milliliters) in the final hydrogen peroxide solution.

1. **Determine the amount of hydrogen peroxide before mixing:** $1\%x + 6\%(60)$

2. **Determine the amount of hydrogen peroxide after mixing:** $5\%(x + 60)$

3. **Set the two amounts equal and solve the resulting equation:**

$$\text{Amount of Ingredient Before Mixing} = \text{Amount of Ingredient After Mixing}$$
$$1\%x + 6\%(60) = 5\%(x + 60)$$
$$0.01x + 0.06(60) = 0.05(x + 60)$$
$$0.01x + 3.6 = 0.05x + 3$$
$$0.6 = 0.04x$$
$$15 = x$$

Choice (B) is the correct answer.

Catching a break: Break-even problems

In break-even problems, you determine the point at which revenue equals cost: Revenue = Cost. Here's how you'd apply this idea on the GMAT.

EXAMPLE

A company manufactures and sells a certain product. The total cost, in dollars, to produce x units of the product is given by $C(x) = 3x^2 + 50x + 100$. The selling price in dollars, for each unit of the product is given by $S(x) = 6x + 30$. The company wants to determine the break-even point, which is the number of units they need to sell to cover their costs. What is the break-even point?

(A) 10

(B) 15

(C) 20

(D) 25

(E) 30

The break-even point occurs when the total revenue $(6x + 30)x$ — which is the product of the selling price per unit and the number of units sold — equals the total cost $3x^2 + 50x + 100$. To find the break-even point, set the total revenue equal to the total cost and solve for x.

$$(6x + 30)x = 3x^2 + 50x + 100$$
$$6x^2 + 30x = 3x^2 + 50x + 100$$
$$3x^2 - 20x - 100 = 0$$
$$(3x + 10)(x - 10) = 0$$
$$3x + 10 = 0; \; x = -\frac{10}{3}$$
$$x - 10 = 0; \; x = 10$$

The break-even point represents the number of units sold, so reject the negative solution. Therefore, the break-even point is 10 units, Choice (A).

Seeing is believing: The coordinate plane

The coordinate plane is a two-dimensional system used to represent points and graphically depict relationships between them. In this section, you will revisit the definitions and formulas necessary for excelling in problem solving related to the coordinate plane.

Getting the plane truth: Coordinate plane terminology

Before you get too excited about graphical depictions, prepare yourself with an understanding of these essential terms.

>> **Coordinate plane:** The coordinate plane consists of two perpendicular real number lines intersecting at a point, called the *origin*, where points can be identified by their positions using *ordered pairs* of numbers.

>> ***x*-axis:** The horizontal axis in a coordinate plane. From the origin, the numbers on the axis increase in value to the right of the origin and decrease in value to the left.

>> ***y*-axis:** The vertical axis in a coordinate plane. From the origin, the numbers on the axis increase in value going up from the origin and decrease in value going down.

>> **Origin:** The point (0, 0) in the coordinate plane. It's where the *x*- and *y*-axes intersect.

» **Quadrants:** The four regions formed by the intersection of the *x*- and *y*-axes.

» **Ordered pair:** The pair of values (*x, y*), called *coordinates*, arranged in a specific order to represent points in the coordinate plane. The horizontal (*x*) coordinate is always listed first, and the vertical (*y*) coordinate is listed second.

» **x-coordinate of a point:** The directed distance from the *y*-axis to the point (positive to the right and negative to the left). If it's 0, the point is on the *y*-axis.

» **y-coordinate of a point:** The directed distance from the *x*-axis to the point (positive upward and negative downward). If it's 0, the point is on the *x*-axis.

» **x-intercept:** The value of *x* where a line, curve, or some other function crosses the *x*-axis. The value of *y* is 0 at the *x*-intercept.

» **y-intercept:** The value of *y* where a line, curve, or some other function crosses the *y*-axis. The value of *x* is 0 at the *y*-intercept.

» **Slope:** The measure of a line's steepness or incline.

» **Graph of a two-variable linear equation:** The line in the coordinate plane that consists of all the ordered pairs that are elements of the solution set of the equation.

Getting to the point? Finding the coordinates

You can identify any point in the coordinate plane by its coordinates, which designate the point's location in the plane. For example, to plot the ordered pair (2, 3) go two units to the right of the origin along the *x*-axis and from there go up three units. In Figure 3-2, point A is at (2, 3). The *x*-coordinate appears first, and the *y*-coordinate shows up second. Pretty simple so far, huh?

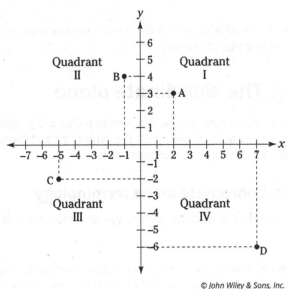

FIGURE 3-2:
Points in the coordinate plane.

© John Wiley & Sons, Inc.

Dividing the territory: Identifying quadrants

The intersection of the *x*- and *y*-axes forms four quadrants in the coordinate plane, which just happen to be labeled Quadrants I, II, III, and IV in a counterclockwise direction (see Figure 3-2). Here's what you can assume about points based on the quadrants they're in:

» All points in Quadrant I have a positive *x*-coordinate and a positive *y*-coordinate.

- >> All points in Quadrant II have a negative *x*-coordinate and a positive *y*-coordinate.

- >> All points in Quadrant III have a negative *x*-coordinate and a negative *y*-coordinate.

- >> All points in Quadrant IV have a positive *x*-coordinate and a negative *y*-coordinate.

- >> All points along the *x*-axis have a *y*-coordinate of 0.

- >> All points along the *y*-axis have an *x*-coordinate of 0.

Figure 3-2 also shows the location of points *A*, *B*, *C*, and *D*:

- >> Point *A* is in Quadrant I and has coordinates (2, 3).

- >> Point *B* is in Quadrant II and has coordinates (–1, 4).

- >> Point *C* is in Quadrant III and has coordinates (–5, –2).

- >> Point *D* is in Quadrant IV and has coordinates (7, –6).

The GMAT won't ask you to pick your favorite quadrant, but you may be asked to identify which quadrant a particular point belongs in.

Slip-sliding away: Slope and linear equations

The coordinate plane presents the exciting experience of visually representing linear equations in two variables, a topic you are already familiar with from the earlier section "Getting in sync: Simultaneous equations." You should know the formulas for finding the slope and the slope-intercept equation. Lucky for you, we discuss these formulas in the following sections.

Taking a "peak": The slope of a line

If a line isn't parallel to one of the coordinate axes, it either slants down or slants up from left to right. The measure of the steepness of the line's slant is its *slope*. In the following sections, we explain how to find the slope of a line and explore the different types of slope in a coordinate plane.

THE FORMULA FOR SLOPE

A simple way to remember the slope formula is to think, "rise over run." Here's the formula:

$$slope(m) = \frac{\text{Rise}}{\text{Run}} = \frac{\text{Change in Vertical Coordinates}}{\text{Change in Horizontal Coordinates}} = \frac{y_2 - y_1}{x_2 - x_1}$$

where (x_1, y_1) and (x_2, y_2) are two distinct points on the line and $x_1 \neq x_2$. The formula is just the ratio of the vertical change between two points and the horizontal change between those same two points. For example, the slope of the line through the points $(-1, -3)$ and $(1, 5)$ is

$$m = \frac{y_2 - y_1}{x_2 - x_1} = \frac{5 - (-3)}{1 - (-1)} = \frac{8}{2} = 4.$$

WARNING

When you subtract the values, remember to subtract the *x* and *y* values of the first point from the respective *x* and *y* values of the second point. Don't fall for the trap of subtracting $x_2 - x_1$ to get your change in the run but then subtracting $y_1 - y_2$ for your change in the rise. That kind of backward math will mess up your calculations, and you'll soon be sliding down a slippery slope.

TYPES OF SLOPE

>> A line with a negative slope slants down from left to right.

>> A line with a positive slope slants up left to right.

>> A horizontal line has a slope of 0 and coincides with or is parallel to the *x*-axis.

>> The slope of a vertical line is undefined.

REMEMBER

If you are given two distinct points (x_1, y_1) and (x_2, y_2) on a line, you can use the definition of slope to find the equation of the line. First, calculate the slope: $m = \frac{y_2 - y_1}{x_2 - x_1}$. When provided with the slope value *m* and the known point (x_1, y_1), any other point (x, y) on the line must satisfy the equation $m = \frac{y - y_1}{x - x_1}$, which you can transform into an equivalent linear equation of your desired form.

Using the slope-intercept form for linear equations

The equation $y = mx + b$ is the *slope-intercept form* of the equation of a line. In the slope-intercept form, the coefficient *m* is a constant that indicates the slope of the line, and the constant *b* is the *y*-intercept (that is, the point where the line crosses the *y*-axis). A line with the equation $y = 4x + 1$ has a slope of 4 and a *y*-intercept of 1. Its graph (shown in Figure 3-3) is a visual representation of all ordered pairs that are solutions to $y = 4x + 1$.

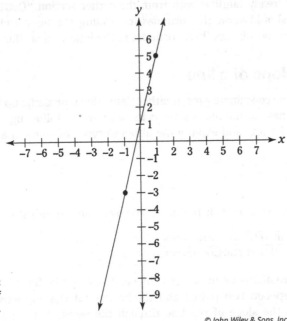

FIGURE 3-3:
The graph of
$y = 4x + 1$.

© John Wiley & Sons, Inc

The GMAT may give you an equation of a line and ask you to choose the graph that correctly shows it. You can figure out how the line should look when it's graphed by starting with the value of the *y*-intercept, marking points that fit the value of the slope, and then connecting these points with a line.

Whenever you get an equation for a line that doesn't neatly fit into the slope-intercept form, go ahead and play with the equation a little bit (sounds fun, doesn't it?) so it meets the $y = mx + b$ form that you know and love. For instance, to put the equation $\frac{1}{3}y - 3 = x$ in slope-intercept form, you simply manipulate both sides of the equation and solve for y, like this:

$$\frac{1}{3}y - 3 = x$$
$$\frac{1}{3}y = x + 3$$
$$y = 3(x + 3)$$
$$y = 3x + 9$$

The new equation gives you the slope of the line, 3, as well as the y-intercept, 9. Pretty handy! Here's a sample question to provide you with an idea of how the slope-intercept form may be tested on the GMAT.

What is the equation of a line with slope $-\frac{3}{4}$ and y-intercept 8?

(A) $4x + 3y = 32$

(B) $-3x + 4y = 16$

(C) $3x - 4y = 32$

(D) $3x + 4y = 16$

(E) $3x + 4y = 32$

In the slope-intercept form, $y = mx + b$, m is the slope, and b is the y-intercept. Plug the values the problem gives you into the equation: $y = -\frac{3}{4}x + 8$

This isn't an answer choice, but all options have the same form of $ax + by = c$. So, you need to convert your equation to that form. Move the terms around by multiplying all terms on both sides by 4 and adding $3x$ to both sides, like this:

$$y = -\frac{3}{4}x + 8$$
$$4y = -3x + 32$$
$$4y + 3x = 32$$

Choice (E) is the correct answer.

Manipulating Statistics and Sets

The GMAT tests what you know about groups (sets) of numbers. These question types are usually pretty easy, so you could probably work out the answers to most of the GMAT set questions given enough time. But, of course, you don't have all the time in the world on the GMAT, so in this section, we provide some shortcuts to help you answer set questions quickly.

You may find the statistics and probability questions on the GMAT a little more challenging. But don't worry: In this section, we go over the concepts you need to know, which include determining probability, statistical averages, and variations from the average. The statistics questions you'll encounter on the GMAT aren't particularly complex, but giving this subject your full attention will pay off.

Joining a clique: Groups

Group problems concern populations of individuals or objects and the ways they are grouped together into categories. The questions generally ask you to either find the total of a series of groups or determine how many individuals or objects make up one of the subgroups.

You can find the answer to most group problems by using your counting skills, but counting is time-consuming, and you want to work smarter, not harder, to solve these questions. If only two groups are involved, solving the problem comes down to applying simple arithmetic using a handy rule and nothing else.

TIP

Here's the rule for solving problems involving only two groups:

$$\text{Group 1} + \text{Group 2} - \text{Both Groups} + \text{Neither Group} = \text{Grand Total}$$

So, if you're told that out of 110 students, 47 are enrolled in a cooking class, 56 take a welding course, and 33 take both cooking and welding, you can use the rule to find out how many students take neither cooking nor welding. Let Group 1 be the number of cooks and Group 2 be the number of welders. Let x be Neither Group, the number that take neither cooking nor welding. Plug the known values into the rule and set up an equation to solve:

$$\text{Group 1} + \text{Group 2} - \text{Both Groups} + \text{Neither Group} = \text{Grand Total}$$
$$47 + 56 - 33 + x = 110$$
$$70 + x = 110$$
$$x = 40$$

Of the 110 students, 40 take neither cooking nor welding. Here's an example of how group problems may appear on the GMAT.

EXAMPLE

One-third of all U.S. taxpayers may deduct charitable contributions on their federal income tax returns. Forty percent of all taxpayers may deduct state income tax payments from their federal returns. If 55 percent of all taxpayers may not deduct either charitable contributions or state income tax, what portion of all taxpayers may claim both types of deductions?

(A) $\dfrac{3}{20}$

(B) $\dfrac{9}{50}$

(C) $\dfrac{1}{5}$

(D) $\dfrac{7}{25}$

(E) $\dfrac{17}{60}$

Use the rule to determine the correct portion of taxpayers who may claim both deductions. Group 1 can be the $\dfrac{1}{3}$ who claim charitable deductions, and Group 2 can be the percentage of those who deduct state income tax payments. The Grand Total is 100% of the U. S. taxpayers. Let x be Both Groups, the portion of all taxpayers who may claim both types of deductions.

TIP

Before you begin calculating, check the answer choices. Every answer appears as a fraction. Because your final answer will be in the form of a fraction, change references to percents into fractions. Converting percents to fractions is easy; put the value of the percent over a denominator of 100.

So, 40% is the same as $\frac{40}{100}$, which reduces to $\frac{2}{5}$; 55% is the same as $\frac{55}{100}$, which equals $\frac{11}{20}$; and 100% equals 1. Plug the values into the rule and solve:

$$\text{Group 1} + \text{Group 2} - \text{Both Groups} + \text{Neither Group} = \text{Grand Total}$$

$$\frac{1}{3} + \frac{2}{5} - x + \frac{11}{20} = 1$$

To add and subtract fractions, find a common denominator for all fractions and then convert the fractions, so all have the same denominator (see Block 4 for more about performing operations with fractions). The common denominator for this problem is 60.

$$\frac{20}{60} + \frac{24}{60} - x + \frac{33}{60} = \frac{60}{60}$$

$$\frac{77}{60} - x = \frac{60}{60}$$

$$x = \frac{17}{60}$$

The correct answer is Choice (E).

Setting up sets

A *set* is a collection of numbers, letters, objects, or other things. The things in a set are its *elements*, or *members*. An *empty set*, or *null set*, means that nothing is in that set. GMAT questions about sets are usually fairly simple to answer as long as you know a little terminology and how to read a Venn diagram. The following sections explore all you need to know about sets.

Set terminology

The terms *union*, *intersection*, *disjoint sets*, and *subset* describe how two or more sets relate to one another through the elements they contain.

>> The *union* of two sets contains the set of all elements of both sets. For example, the union of sets $A = \{0, 1, 2, 3, 4, 5, 6, 7, 8, 9\}$ and $B = \{2, 4, 6, 8, 10\}$ is $S = \{0, 1, 2, 3, 4, 5, 6, 7, 8, 9, 10\}$.

>> The *intersection* of two sets is the set of the elements that are common to both sets. For example, the intersection of sets $A = \{0, 1, 2, 3, 5, 6, 7, 8, 9\}$ and $B = \{2, 4, 6, 8, 10\}$ is $S = \{2, 6, 8\}$.

>> *Disjoint sets* are two or more sets with no elements in common. For example, set A and set B are disjoint sets if set $A = \{0, 2, 6, 8\}$ and set $B = \{1, 3, 5, 7\}$.

>> A *subset* is a set all of whose elements are also elements of another set. If all the elements of set $B = \{2, 3, 5, 7\}$ also appear in set $A = \{0, 1, 2, 3, 5, 6, 7, 8, 9\}$, then set B is a *subset* of set A. Note: Every set is a subset of itself.

>> A Venn diagram is a visual depiction showing how two or more sets are related.

Getting a visual: Venn diagrams

The GMAT often illustrates the concept of sets with Venn diagrams, such as those presented in Figure 3-4. Venn diagrams provide visual representations of union, intersection, disjoint sets, and subsets. You can draw Venn diagrams to help you answer GMAT questions about sets.

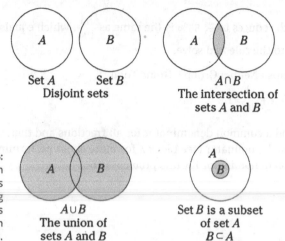

FIGURE 3-4:
Venn
diagrams
showing
relationships
between
two sets.

Set A   Set B
Disjoint sets

A∩B
The intersection of
sets A and B

A∪B
The union of
sets A and B

Set B is a subset
of set A
B⊂A

GMAT quantitative reasoning questions regarding sets are usually straightforward. Here's an example.

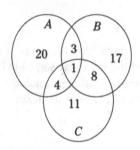

Given the Venn diagram, what are the number of elements in the intersection of sets A and B?

(A) 0

(B) 3

(C) 4

(D) 16

(E) 53

The number of elements in the intersection of sets A and B is the number of elements that are common to both sets. The portion of the diagram that represents the intersection is where the A circle and the B circle overlap. When you add the values in this intersection, you find that the number of elements that are common to both set A and set B is 4. The correct answer is Choice (C).

If you chose Choice (B), you ignored the one element that's common to all three sets. You must include that one element, however, because it's a common element of sets A and B. Choice (E) conveys the number of elements in the union of sets A and B rather than their intersection.

Dealing with permutations and combinations

The GMAT may test you on the number of ways a set's elements (or a group's members) can be arranged, so you're likely to see some permutation and combination problems. When you calculate *permutations*, you figure out the number of ways a set's elements can be arranged in a specific order. Determining *combinations* is similar to finding permutations, except that the order of the arrangements doesn't matter. In the following sections, we provide explanations and examples of each type of problem. But first, let's count.

Counting without listing

Suppose you're planning a fun outfit for the day. You can choose one of five different tops and one of four different pairs of pants; how do you figure out the total number of outfit combinations? Well, we have just what you need: The *multiplication principle*! Simply multiply the number of choices for each category: 5 (tops) multiplied by 4 (pants), which gives you a grand total of 20 possible outfit combinations.

Positioning with permutations

Permutations problems ask you to determine how many arrangements are possible given a specific set of distinct numbers and a particular order for the arrangements. For example, figuring out the number of possible seven-digit telephone numbers is a permutation problem. And the answer is huge (10^7) because you have 10 possible digits (0 to 9) to fill each of the seven places (although some possible numbers are useless, like 000-0000).

REMEMBER

Order matters when you set up permutations. Even though two different phone numbers in the same area code may have the same combination of numbers, such as 345-7872 and 543-7728, the numbers ring two different phones because you input them in a different order.

Consider the elements of $S = \{a, b, c\}$. You can arrange these three elements in six different ways: *abc, acb, bac, bca, cab,* and *cba.* Even though each group contains the same elements, these groupings are completely different permutations because they convey different orderings of the three elements. Writing out the number of possible orderings of a set of three letters isn't too difficult, but what if you had to figure out the number of orderings for a set of 11 numbers? That problem would take more time than anyone would care to spend and certainly more time than you have to finish the GMAT. Luckily, you can rely on factorials to figure out permutations.

TIP

For any integer $n > 1$, *n factorial* is written $n!$ and is the product of all positive integers from 1 through n. Also, by definition, $0! = 1! = 1$. For example, $5!$ is $5 \times 4 \times 3 \times 2 \times 1 = 120$.

Instead of listing the possible permutations for the set of three letters $\{a, b, c\}$, use a factorial. The number of ways three different elements (the letters in the set) can be arranged in as many different orders as possible is $3!$, which equals $3 \times 2 \times 1 = 6$. So, the number of possible permutations of the three letters is 6.

Suppose you have more than three elements. Maybe a photographer wants to know how many different ways to arrange five people in a single row for a wedding photo. The number of possible arrangements of the five-person wedding party is $5! = 5 \times 4 \times 3 \times 2 \times 1 = 120$. In general, for a set n of distinct elements, the number of different orderings of the elements of the set is $n!$ As you can see, more possible arrangements exist as the number of objects in the arrangement increases. Give it a shot!

EXAMPLE

Sophia is arranging four different dance trophies in a row on her bookshelf. How many different ways can she arrange the four trophies?

(A) 4

(B) 8

(C) 24

(D) 100

(E) 40,320

Because there are four trophies, the number of arrangements or permutations is $4! = 4 \times 3 \times 2 \times 1 = 24$. Thus, the correct answer is Choice (C).

WARNING

You can eliminate Choices (A) and (B) because they're too small. You know that more than four arrangements must exist, because there are four trophies. Choice (B) is 4×2, which isn't much better. In permutations, you know the number gets large in a hurry, but not as large as Choice (E), which is 8 factorial.

Permutations get a little more challenging when you have a fixed number of objects, n, to fill a limited number of places, r, and you care about the order the objects are arranged in. For example, consider the predicament of a big-league baseball coach of a 20-member baseball team who needs to know the number of different batting orders that these 20 ball players can fill in a 9-slot batting lineup. Luckily, there's a permutation formula that will save the coach's day!

The number of permutations of n distinct things taken r at a time is written $_nP_r$. (To help you remember the formula, think of a certain public radio station that has these call letters.) The formula looks like this:

$$_nP_r = \frac{n!}{(n-r)!}$$

Substitute $n = 20$ and $r = 9$ into the formula to figure out the possible number of batting orders:

$$_{20}P_9 = \frac{20!}{(20-9)!} = \frac{20!}{(11)!}$$

The GMAT won't expect you to calculate the permutation beyond this point. Here's an example of how complex permutations may appear on the GMAT.

EXAMPLE

A lawn care company has five employees that it schedules on a given day to work the lawns of any ten possible homes. How many different ways can the company assign the five employees to the ten homes if each employee provides lawn care service for just one home?

(A) 50

(B) $\dfrac{2!}{1!}$

(C) 120

(D) $\dfrac{10!}{5!}$

(E) 10!

This question may seem counterintuitive to the formula, which calculates n number of things taken r at a time to get the number of permutations. This problem appears to be taking a smaller number of things, r (the number of employees), and finding out how many times they can be spread around a greater number of places. That's what makes this question a little tricky.

TIP

This problem may look backward, but it really follows the same formula. Rather than thinking of how to spread five workers over ten houses, think of how many ways you can arrange the ten houses over the more limited number of workers and apply the formula:

$$_nP_r = \frac{10!}{(10-5)!} = \frac{10!}{(5)!}$$

The correct answer is Choice (D). With a calculator, you can figure out that 30,240 ways exist to assign employees. If you chose Choice (A), you simply multiplied the number of workers times the number of houses. But that's not the correct calculation. Choice (C) is what you get if you calculated 5!, which isn't the complete answer. Likewise, Choice (E) is incomplete.

WARNING

Don't let Choice (B) trip you up. You can't simplify factorials like you can common fractions:

$$\frac{10!}{5!} \neq \frac{2!}{1!}$$

If this problem was difficult for you, take heart: You won't see too many of these kinds of questions on the GMAT.

Coming together: Combinations

Combinations are a lot like permutations, only easier. You form a *combination* by extracting a certain number of persons or things from a larger total sample; for example, how many different three-member committees could you form from a pool of seven potential committee members? You can apply a formula to figure out the number of combinations. The formula is the number of ways to choose r objects from a group of n objects when the order of the objects doesn't matter, and it looks like this:

$$_nC_r = \frac{n!}{r!(n-r)!}$$

Suppose a pollster randomly approaches three different people from a group of five mall walkers. To figure out how many possible combinations of three different people the pollster can annoy, Substitute $n = 5$ and $r = 3$ into the combination formula:

$$_5C_3 = \frac{5!}{3!(5-3)!} = \frac{5!}{3!(2)!} = \frac{120}{6 \times 2} = \frac{120}{12} = 10$$

TIP

The factorial 5! is $5 \times 4 \times 3 \times 2 \times 1 = 120$, the factorial 3! is $3 \times 2 \times 1 = 6$, and the factorial 2! is $2 \times 1 = 2$. Therefore, from the five mall walkers, the pollster can create ten different combinations of three people to poll.

Because you can't use a calculator in the quantitative reasoning section, GMAT combination problem solving questions won't get too complex. The test-makers won't make you perform overly complex calculations on your low-tech note board.

Meeting in the middle: Mean, median, and mode

At least a few GMAT math problems will require you to evaluate data sets consisting of numbers. To evaluate data correctly, you need a measure of their *central tendency*. A *measurement of central tendency* is a single numerical value that describes a data set by attempting to provide a "central" or "typical" value of the numbers in the set. Common statistical measures for describing a central tendency include the *average* or (arithmetic) *mean*, the *median*, and the *mode*.

Summing it up mean-ingfully

The average is a common and useful statistical measure of central tendency. The *average* or *mean* of a set of n numbers is the sum of the n numbers divided *by n*:

$$\text{average or mean} = \frac{\text{Sum of the } n \text{ Numbers}}{n}$$

For example, the average of the five numbers 25, 43, 40, 60, and 12 is $\frac{12 + 25 + 40 + 43 + 60}{5} = \frac{180}{5} = 36$.

You can plug known values into this formula to solve for the other values. For example, if the GMAT tells you the average of five numbers is 40, you can use the formula to figure out their sum like this:

$$40 = \frac{\text{Sum}}{5}$$
$$\text{Sum} = 40 \times 5 = 200$$

Feeling median-ly split

The *median* is the middle value or the average of the middle pair of values in an *ordered* set of data. For a small data set, you can easily determine the median using a two-step process. First, put the numbers in order, from least to greatest (or greatest to least). Next, find the value that falls exactly in the middle of the other data values. If you have an odd number of values, just select the middle value. If you have an even number of values, find the two middle values and average them. The outcome is the median. Here are two examples.

To find the median of the five numbers 25, 43, 40, 60, and 12, order them from least to greatest: 12, 25, 40, 43, 60. The median is 40, the middle number in this list.

To find the median of the six numbers 3, 15, 8, 6, 8, and 5, order them from least to greatest: 3, 5, 6, 8, 8, 15. The median is $\frac{(6+8)}{2} = \frac{14}{2} = 7$, the average of 6 and 8, the two middle numbers.

Modeling the mode

The *mode* is the number (or numbers) that occurs with the highest frequency in a data set. A data set can have a single mode (just one number has the highest frequency), multiple modes (two or more numbers have the same highest frequency), or no mode (all numbers occur the same number of times). For example, the mode of the list of numbers 1, 1, 2, 4, 7, 7, 7, 9 is 7 because it occurs 3 times, the highest frequency of any number in the list. The list of numbers 51, 60, 60, 60, 72, 72, 75, 75, 75, 80 has two modes 60 and 75.

TIP

Questions about mode may contain words like *frequency* or ask you how often a value occurs. For example, you may be asked what income occurs most frequently at a certain company. If more people in the company have an income of $30,000 than any other income amount, the mode is $30,000.

Tuning into the frequencies

The number of times a value occurs in a data set is its frequency. A *frequency table* is a way to organize and present data in a tabular form. It shows the number of occurrences or frequency of each unique value in a data set. For example, look at this data set of 20 numbers:

40, 0, 0, 30, 20, 10, 10, 0, 10, 40, 10, 50, 0, 20, 0, 50, 20, 0, 0, 10

You can make a frequency table showing each unique value and its frequency:

Data Value	Frequency
0	7
10	5
20	3
30	1
40	2
50	2
Total	**20**

A frequency table simplifies the computation of statistical measures.

$$\text{Mean} = \frac{7 \times 0 + 5 \times 10 + 3 \times 20 + 1 \times 30 + 2 \times 40 + 2 \times 50}{20} = \frac{320}{20} = 16$$

$\text{Median} = \frac{10 + 10}{2} = 10$, the average of the 10th and 11th values

Mode = 0, the number with the highest frequency

You'll likely see a bunch of questions on the GMAT that ask you to figure out the central tendency of a set of values. Here's an example of one that asks about a mean.

EXAMPLE

George tried to compute the average (arithmetic mean) of his eight statistics test scores. He mistakenly divided the correct sum of all his test scores by seven and calculated his average to be 96. What was George's actual average test score?

(A) 80

(B) 84

(C) 96

(D) 100

(E) 108

The question asks you for George's average score on eight tests and gives the average of those eight scores when they're divided by seven. You know that his average must be less than 96 because you're dividing by a larger number, so you can automatically eliminate Choices (C), (D), and (E). Just use the formula for averages to determine George's average score for eight tests.

1. Figure out the sum of all George's test scores, using what you know from his incorrect calculation: $\frac{\text{Sum}}{7} = 96$

$\text{Sum} = 672$

2. Find George's actual average based on the sum of all his scores: $\text{Average} = \frac{\text{Sum}}{8} = \frac{672}{8} = 84$

The correct answer is Choice (B).

Solving range and standard deviation problems

Besides knowing the main concepts of central tendency, you also need to know about *variability* or *dispersion* of values in statistics. The two types of dispersion you'll deal with on the GMAT are *range* and *standard deviation*, which we explore in the following sections.

Scouting out the range

The easiest measure of dispersion to calculate is the *range*. The range is the difference between the greatest and least values in the data. For example, the range of the five numbers $12, 11, -5, 13, -2$ is $13 - (-5) = 13 + 5 = 18$. Simple as that!

Watching out for wanderers: Standard deviation

Another form of dispersion to know for the GMAT is *standard deviation*. The standard deviation is a measure of how dispersed the data set is in relation to the mean. Generally, the greater the spread of the numbers away from the mean, the greater the standard deviation. Although the range (see preceding section) can give you an idea of the total spread, standard deviation is a more reliable indicator of dispersion because it considers all the data, not just the two on each end. Standard deviation is a most widely used statistical measure for quantifying the dispersion of a data set.

To find the standard deviation of the five numbers 2, 4, 5, 6, and 8, do the following steps:

1. **Calculate the mean:** $\dfrac{2+4+5+6+8}{5} = \dfrac{25}{5} = 5$

   Find the differences between each of the *n* numbers and the mean:

   $(2-5) = -3; (4-5) = -1; (5-5) = 0; (6-5) = 1; (8-5) = 3$

2. **Square each difference:** $9, 1, 0, 1, 9$

3. **Find the average of the squared differences:** $\dfrac{9+1+0+1+9}{5} = \dfrac{20}{5} = 4$

4. **Determine the nonnegative square root of this average:** $\sqrt{4} = 2$

The standard deviation is 2.

TIP

Suppose you get a score of 76 on a test where the mean grade is 70 and the standard deviation of all the grades is 3. Your score is comparatively better in this situation than if you get a 76 on a different test, where the mean grade is still 70, but the standard deviation is 6. In the first situation, your score is 2 standard deviations above the mean (because $70 + 2 \times 3 = 70 + 6 = 76$), indicating you did very well relative to the others who took the test. But in the second situation, your score is only 1 standard deviation above the mean (because $70 + 1 \times 6 = 70 + 6 = 76$), indicating your score isn't as good relative to the others.

TIP

A small standard deviation means that the data values are more tightly clustered around the mean. A large standard deviation means that the data values are more scattered away from the mean.

EXAMPLE

Here's what a standard deviation question on the GMAT may look like.

I. {55, 56, 57, 58, 59}

II. {41, 57, 57, 57, 73}

III. {57, 57, 57, 57, 57}

Which of the following lists Sets I, II, and III in order from least standard deviation to greatest standard deviation?

(A) I, II, III

(B) I, III, II

(C) II, III, I

(D) III, I, II

(E) III, II, I

The set with the least standard deviation is the one that has the least total amount of deviation — in absolute terms! — from the mean, which in all three sets is 57. The values in Set III are all the same, so Set III has the least standard deviation and should be listed first. Eliminate Choices (A), (B), and (C) because they don't list Set III first. The standard deviation of the numbers in Set I is less than that of the numbers in Set II because clearly the combined absolute deviations from the mean of 55, 56, 57, 58, and 59 in Set I is less than the combined absolute deviations from the mean of 41, 57, 57, 57, and 73 in Set II. So, the set with the greatest standard deviation is Set II, which means it should be listed last. Choice (D) lists the sets in their proper order from least standard deviation to greatest standard deviation, so it's the correct answer.

Predicting the future: Probability

Probability is the measure of how likely a particular event will occur. You express probability as a percent, fraction, or decimal. You'd say that the probability of an event's occurrence falls between 0 percent and 100 percent or between 0 and 1, inclusive. If the probability of an event's occurrence is 0, or 0 percent, it's *impossible* for the event to occur. If the probability is 1, or 100 percent, the event is *certain* to occur. All other events are possible but uncertain and the probability of their occurrence falls somewhere between 0 and 1, or 0 and 100 percent.

Probability questions may ask you to determine the probability of the occurrence of one event or multiple events. We show you how to determine the probability for each type of question in the following sections.

Taking a chance

Probability deals with *random experiments, outcomes,* and *events.* A *random experiment* is a chance process that gives a single result that cannot be determined beforehand. Each individual possible result is an *outcome* of the experiment. You can assume that all the possible outcomes are known before the random experiment is performed, but which of the possibilities will in fact occur is uncertain. An *event* is a collection of outcomes from a random experiment. For situations where all possible outcomes are equally likely, the probability (P) that the event E occurs, represented by $P(E)$, is defined as

$$P(E) = \frac{\text{Number of Outcomes in } E}{\text{Total Number of Possible Outcomes}}$$

If you roll a six-sided die, what are your chances of rolling a four? The number of outcomes is 1 because four dots appear on only one side of the die. The total *possible* outcomes is 6 because the die has six sides. Your odds of rolling a four are $\frac{1}{6}$ or about 17%.

Fishing for a complement

The *complement* of an event E is the event that E does <u>not</u> occur. The probability that E does not occur is $P(\text{not } E) = 1 - P(E)$. For example, if the probability that E occurs is 0.6, then the probability that E does not occur is $1 - 0.6 = 0.4$.

Conditioning the probability

A *conditional probability* is one where partial information regarding the outcome of a random event is known. The *conditional probability* of an event B given that an event A has already occurred is denoted $P(B \mid A)$, which is read as "the probability of B given A." This probability is calculated like this:

$$P(B \mid A) = \frac{\text{Probability that both } B \text{ and } A \text{ occur together}}{\text{Probability that } A \text{ occurs}}$$

Look at this example.

A box contains 10 chips, identical in size and shape. Six of the chips are green and four are red. Of the green chips, four are marked X and two are marked Y. Of the red chips, three are marked X and one is marked Y. Given that a chip drawn from the box is green, what is the probability that the chip is marked X?

To solve problems like this one, make a 2×2 table to organize the information:

	Green	Red	Total
X	4	3	7
Y	2	1	3
Total	**6**	**4**	**10**

Now let A be the event the chip is green, and B be the event the chip is marked X. Using the table, do the following steps:

1. **Determine the probability that the chip is marked X and is green:** $\frac{4}{10}$.

2. **Determine the probability that the chip is green:** $\frac{6}{10}$

3. **Determine the probability that the chip is marked X given that it is green:**

$$P(\text{marked X} \mid \text{given it's green}) = \frac{\left(\frac{4}{10}\right)}{\left(\frac{6}{10}\right)} = \frac{4}{6} = \frac{2}{3}$$

Another way to find this probability is to observe that once you know the chip is green, you don't have to concern yourself with the red chips at all. In other words, the number of outcomes is "reduced" to 6, rather than 10. There are 6 green chips, 4 of which are marked X, so the probability that the chip is marked X given that it's green is $\frac{4}{6} = \frac{2}{3}$.

Recognizing mutually exclusive events

Two events are *mutually exclusive* if they cannot occur at the same time; that is, they have no outcomes in common. For example, if you draw one marble from a box containing 10 red marbles and 5 green marbles, the event of drawing a red marble and the event of drawing a green marble are mutually exclusive because you can only get one or the other, but not both in one draw.

Gaining insight into independent and dependent events

Two events are *independent* if the occurrence of one does not affect the probability of the occurrence of the other. Knowing that one of the events has occurred does not give you any information about whether the other event will occur. For example, flipping a fair coin and rolling a fair six-sided die are independent events; the result of flipping the coin has no bearing on the outcome of rolling the die, and vice versa. Similarly, the probability of getting heads on a fair coin flip is always $\frac{1}{2}$, regardless of the outcome of the previous flip. Each coin flip is an independent event; that is, the outcome of one flip does not affect the outcome of the subsequent flips.

Two events that are not independent are *dependent*: that is, the occurrence of one impacts the probability of the occurrence of the other. A dependent event relies on another event happening first. For example, if a coin is flipped twice, the probability that both flips result in heads depends on what happens on the first flip. If the first flip is heads, the probability that both flips result in heads is $\frac{1}{2}$. On the other hand, if the first flip is tails, the probability that both flips result in heads is 0. Clearly, there is no chance of getting two heads in a row if the first flip is tails.

Juggling multiple probabilities

You can find the probability of multiple events by following several rules. Table 3-5 lists and describes each rule, shows the corresponding formula, and provides an example of when you'd use it.

TABLE 3-5 Finding the Probability of the Occurrence of Multiple Events

Rule	Circumstance	Formula	Example
Special Rule of Addition	The probability of the occurrence of either of two possible events that are mutually exclusive	$P(A \text{ or } B) = P(A) + P(B)$	The probability of rolling a 5 or 6 on one roll of a fair die
General Rule of Addition	The probability of the occurrence of either of two possible events that can happen at the same time	$P(A \text{ or } B) = P(A) + P(B) - P(A \text{ and } B)$	The probability of drawing a club or a queen from a well-shuffled deck of 52 playing cards
Special Rule of Multiplication	The probability of the occurrence of two events when the two events are independent of each other	$P(A \text{ and } B) = P(A) \times P(B)$	The probability of rolling a 5 followed by a 6 on two rolls of a fair die
General Rule of Multiplication	The probability of the occurrence of two events when the occurrence of the first event affects the outcome of the second event	$P(A \text{ and } B) = P(A) \times P(B \mid A)$	The probability of first drawing the queen of clubs from a well-shuffled deck of 52 playing cards, not replacing it, and then drawing the jack of diamonds on the next try

APPLYING THE SPECIAL RULE OF ADDITION

You use the special rule of addition to figure out the probability of rolling a die and coming up with either a 1 or a 2. You can't get both on one roll, so the events are *mutually exclusive* (which means that the events cannot occur at the same time). Therefore, the probability of rolling a 1 or a 2 in one roll is $P(A) + P(B)$:

$$P(A \text{ or } B) = \frac{1}{6} + \frac{1}{6}$$

$$P(A \text{ or } B) = \frac{2}{6}$$

$$P(A \text{ or } B) = \frac{1}{3}$$

APPLYING THE GENERAL RULE OF ADDITION

You use the general rule of addition to figure probability in the case of choosing sodas from a cooler. Imagine that three types of sodas are in a cooler. Colas are numbered consecutively 1 through 5, orange sodas are numbered 1 through 7, and grape sodas are numbered 1 through 8. Let event A stand for when a cola is taken out of the cooler and event B represent when a can with a number 4 is taken out. You want to know the probability of picking out *either* a cola *or* a can with the number 4 on it but *not* specifically a cola with the number 4 on it. Five of the 20 cans are colas, three display the number 4, and only one can is a cola with the number 4. So $P(A)$ is $\frac{5}{20}$, $P(B)$ is $\frac{3}{20}$, and $P(A \text{ and } B)$ is $\frac{1}{20}$. Plug the values into the formula and solve:

$$P(A \text{ or } B) = P(A) + P(B) - P(A \text{ and } B)$$

$$P(A \text{ or } B) = \frac{5}{20} + \frac{3}{20} - \frac{1}{20}$$

$$P(A \text{ or } B) = \frac{7}{20}$$

You can also express this probability as 0.35 or as 35%.

APPLYING THE SPECIAL RULE OF MULTIPLICATION

The probability of multiple independent events occurring together is the product of the probabilities of the events occurring individually. For example, if you're rolling two dice at the same time, here's how you find the probability of rolling a 1 on one die and a 2 on the other:

$$P(A \text{ and } B) = \frac{1}{6} \times \frac{1}{6}$$

$$P(A \text{ and } B) = \frac{1}{36}$$

APPLYING THE GENERAL RULE OF MULTIPLICATION

Suppose the outcome of the second event depends on the outcome of the first event. You then invoke the general rule of multiplication. The term $P(B|A)$ is a conditional probability, where the likelihood of the second event B depends on the fact that event A has already occurred. For example, to find the probability of drawing the ace of spades from a well-shuffled deck of 52 playing cards on one try and then drawing the king of spades on the second try — with the ace out of the deck — apply the formula, like this: $P(A \text{ and } B) = P(A) \times P(B|A)$.

WARNING

The vertical line between the B and A stands for the word "given"; it doesn't mean divide! Thus, $P(B|A)$ is read "the probability of B given A."

$$P(A \text{ and } B) = P(A) \times P(B|A)$$

$$P(A \text{ and } B) = \frac{1}{52} \times \frac{1}{51}$$

$$P(A \text{ and } B) = \frac{1}{2,652}$$

We wouldn't bet against the house on that outcome! The probability of drawing the king of spades on the second draw is slightly better than the probability of drawing the ace on the first draw, because you've already removed one card from the deck on the first draw. Here's a sample of how the GMAT may test your knowledge of probability rules.

EXAMPLE

A candy machine contains gumballs: three blue, two red, seven yellow, and one purple. The machine randomly distributes one gumball for each dime. Dara has exactly two dimes with which to purchase two gumballs. What is the chance that Dara will get two red gumballs?

(A) $\frac{2}{169}$

(B) $\frac{1}{13}$

(C) $\frac{2}{13}$

(D) $\frac{1}{156}$

(E) $\frac{1}{78}$

You need to treat getting the two red gumballs as two events. The occurrence of the first event affects the probability of the second because after Dara extracts the first red gumball, the machine has one fewer gumball. So, you apply the general rule of multiplication.

The chance of getting a red gumball with the first dime is 2 (the number of red gumballs) divided by 13 (the total number of gumballs in the machine), or $\frac{2}{13}$. When Dara tries to get a second red gumball, the first red gumball is already gone, which leaves only 1 red gumball and 12 total gumballs in the machine, so the chance of getting a second red gumball is $\frac{1}{12}$. The probability of both events happening is the product of the probabilities of the occurrence of each event:

$$P(A \text{ and } B) = P(A) \times P(B \mid A)$$
$$P(A \text{ and } B) = \frac{2}{13} \times \frac{1}{12}$$
$$P(A \text{ and } B) = \frac{2}{156}$$
$$P(A \text{ and } B) = \frac{1}{78}$$

Choice (E) is the correct answer. Choice (A) is $\frac{2}{13} \times \frac{1}{13}$, which would look right if you didn't subtract the withdrawn red gumball from the total number on the second draw. Choice (B) is the chance of drawing one red gumball from a machine with 13 gumballs and only 1 red gumball. In this problem, $\frac{1}{13}$ is also the chance of drawing the purple gumball. If you picked Choice (C), you found the chance of drawing the first red gumball.

Tackling Problem-Solving Questions

The GMAT Quantitative questions challenge your ability to reason, to think on your feet, and to make the best use of the information you're given in a limited timeframe. Having problem-solving strategies in place enables you to solve problems faster and with greater accuracy. We strongly recommend that you learn all of the following techniques, so you're prepared for all types of problem-solving questions:

>> **Examine all the information the question provides to make sure you know exactly what you're asked to do.** Some problems present you with tables, graphs, and scenarios, and some with just an expression to evaluate or an equation to solve. Don't jump into the answer choices until you've given the question a little thought. Isolate exactly what the problem asks you to solve for and what information the problem provides you. Especially for more complex questions and word problems, use your note board to keep track of what you know and what you have to find out.

>> **Eliminate obviously incorrect answer choices if possible.** Before you begin solving a more complex math problem, look at the answer choices to root out any clearly illogical options. You can then focus your problem solving, and you won't pick these answers later through mistaken calculations. You can find more tips for eliminating answer choices in Block 6.

>> **Use the information in the problem.** You can expect that a GMAT problem solving question contains enough information for you to figure out the correct answer. But you need to use what you're given (including the answer choices!). Pull out the numbers and other terms in a problem and write them on your note board in a way that makes the numbers meaningful. Depending on the problem, you may show relationships between quantities, draw simple diagrams, or organize information in a quick table.

» **Find the equation.** Some GMAT problems provide an equation for you. Others, such as word problems, might require you to come up with an equation using the language in the problem. Whenever you need to turn what you know into an equation, formulate the equation to solve from the information provided in the problem and write it down on your note board.

» **Know when to move on.** Sometimes you may confront a question that you just can't solve. Relax for a moment and reread the question to make sure you haven't missed something. If you still don't know what to do or if you can't remember the tested concept, eliminate all the answers you can and record your best guess. You can find more suggestions for successful guessing in Block 6.

Block 4

Excelling on the Data Insights Section

The Data Insights section of the GMAT has five question types: table analysis, two-part analysis, graphics interpretation, multi-source reasoning, and data sufficiency. We refer to the first four question types collectively as *integrated reasoning* (IR) questions. Data sufficiency questions are in a class of their own.

In this block, we cover all five question types. We start by introducing you to four distinctive IR question types. Then we take a deeper dive into graphics interpretation. Finally, we wrap up this block with guidance on how to approach data sufficiency questions.

Knowing What to Expect: Four Key Integrated Reasoning Question Types

IR questions are completely different from the five-option multiple-choice questions you're probably accustomed to. IR questions require you to actively explore, manipulate, and extract meaningful information from multifaceted data landscapes to derive insights and make informed decisions. This section gives you the strategies you need to sort out and make sense of these multifaceted questions.

Understanding what the IR questions are all about

Answering IR questions requires you to effectively apply a blend of the critical reasoning skills assessed in the verbal reasoning section and the math skills essential for problem solving in the quantitative reasoning section to real-world scenarios. Therefore, if you have adequately prepared for the GMAT's Quantitative and Verbal sections, you're likely to perform well with the IR questions. We explain the details of the IR questions and the purpose behind them in the next two sections.

Skills tested

The most common math computations in the IR questions involve these areas:

>> Basic statistics, such as average, median, mode, range, and standard deviation

>> Sets and counting methods

>> Probability, sequences, and series

>> Rates, ratios, and percents

>> Algebraic expressions, equations, and functions

You'll need to apply the following essentials of critical reasoning:

>> Basic elements of logical arguments — premises, conclusions, and assumptions

>> Complex mental processes — evaluate, infer, synthesize, and strategize

>> Critical analysis including supporting or weakening claims

>> Argument types — cause and effect, analogy, and statistical

You can review the necessary math concepts in Block 3. Read more about evaluating logical arguments in Block 2.

About the question types

Each IR question type requires synthesizing information (usually more info than necessary) from multiple sources to solve complex problems. Almost every question has multiple parts. To get credit for answering a question correctly, you have to answer *all* its parts correctly. You don't receive partial credit for getting just one part of the question correct.

Even though you may have personal knowledge related to the topic presented, always answer IR questions based *only* on the information provided to you.

WARNING

On average, you can expect to encounter a couple of each IR question type on the GMAT. However, the specific number and order of these questions may vary. Therefore, make sure you're ready to tackle all four question types during your test:

>> **Table analysis:** This three-part question type offers you a spreadsheet-like table of data. You can sort the table by one or more of its columns by clicking a column's heading from a drop-down menu. You use the data to make judgments (for example, Yes/No; True/False) about three statements, phrases, words, numerical values, or formulas. Each of your judgments has to be correct to get credit for the question.

>> **Two-part analysis:** Based on a short written scenario of a phenomenon, situation, or mathematical problem, you make two choices that, together or separately, meet one or more conditions presented in the question. You make your two selections in the first two columns from a list of options in the third column of a three-column response table. The top row of the response table labels the columns. You must pick one correct answer in the first column and one correct answer in the second column to get credit for the question. You can pick the same answer in both columns.

>> **Graphics interpretation:** A graphic, image, or other visual representation provides all the data you need to complete the missing pieces of information in one or two statements. You must select the best choice from a drop-down menu of several answer options to record your

answer for each missing piece of information. If there are two or more drop-down menus, you must select the best choices in all of them to get credit for the question.

>> **Multi-source reasoning:** These aptly named questions present you with two or three sources of information, each labeled with a tab that allows you to switch from one source to another. One or more sources will be in the form of a written passage. Other possible source types include tables, graphics, images, letters, and business documents. You click on a tab to see the information it provides. You integrate information from the sources to reach logical conclusions that provide answers to questions in either of two formats: standard five-option multiple-choice questions and three-part questions that ask you to indicate whether a statement, phrase, numerical value, or formula meets a certain condition. For the multiple-choice questions, you must select the correct choice from the five given answer options to get credit for the question. For three-part questions, you must answer all three parts correctly to get credit for the question.

To assist you with the mathematical computations you may need to make for data insight questions, the GMAT software provides you with a simple on-screen calculator. Whenever you need it, you click the blue box labeled CALCULATOR and something that looks like Figure 4-1 appears. You can move it anywhere on the screen by dragging it with your mouse. It stays open until you close it by clicking the X in the upper-right corner of the tool.

FIGURE 4-1:
The GMAT
calculator.

© John Wiley & Sons, Inc.

You select its functions by using your mouse. The number and operation keys work just like a regular calculator. You can clear a single entry with the CE (clear entry) key or just the right digit with the ← key. Start over again from scratch by clicking the C (clear) key, which wipes out the entry and all its associated computations. The MS (memory store) key stores a value to the memory. You can add values to the memory with the M+ key and subtract them with the M− key. To access the value in the memory, click MR (memory recall). To clear it, click MC (memory clear). The ± key changes a positive value to negative and a negative value to positive. Press the + key to add, the − key to subtract, the ÷ key to divide, and the × key to multiply. Press the = key to complete a computation. The % key changes a percent to a decimal, and the √ finds the non-negative square root of a number.

WARNING

Don't get too attached to the calculator; it's available only for the Data Insights section, so you won't be able to use it in the Quantitative section. Because using an on-screen calculator can be awkward, you'll likely answer most IR questions more efficiently by using estimation or doing quick calculations by hand on your note board. Save the calculator for only the most complex or precise computations.

Approaching each question type

Each of the four IR question types tests your analytical ability in a slightly different way, so your approach depends on the question format. This section outlines the important considerations for handling each type.

Table analysis

Table analysis questions present you with a table that contains several columns of data, similar to the one in Figure 4-2. As you can see, a little bit of explanatory material precedes the table, but don't waste too much time reading those words. Usually, everything you need to answer the question appears in the data table.

During Lexington Restaurant Week, participating eateries design a three-course meal that they will offer throughout the week at a set price of either $20, $30, or $40 a person, excluding drinks (unless otherwise noted), tax, and tip, as reported on the following table.

Sort By:	Restaurant
	Cuisine Type
	Price Per Meal
	Neighborhood
	Wine Included? (Y/N)
	Average Daily Number of Meals Sold

Restaurant	Cuisine Type	Price Per Meal	Neighborhood	Wine Included? (Y/N)	Average Daily Number of Meals Sold
Bendimere's	Steakhouse	$40	Downtown	N	150
Big Ben's Bistro	American	$30	Central	Y	175
Chang's	Asian	$20	Chinatown	N	142
Frank's House	American	$20	Downtown	N	175
Hadley's on the Beach	Seafood	$40	Uptown	Y	160
Meritage	American	$40	Uptown	N	152
Ocean View	Seafood	$40	Uptown	N	151
Pesce Blue	Seafood	$40	Downtown	Y	164
The Purple Parrot	Latin	$30	Northwest	Y	134
Sorbello's	Italian	$40	Old Town	Y	175
Sushi Fusco	Asian	$30	Old Town	N	100
Thai Time	Asian	$20	Northwest	N	87
Valenzuela's	Mexican	$20	Downtown	N	113

FIGURE 4-2: Sample table analysis format.

© John Wiley & Sons, Inc.

The *Sort By* feature at the top of the table allows you to organize the information by column heading, a capability that comes in handy when you analyze the three statements that follow the table. When you click on *Sort By*, a drop-down menu of all column headings appears. Clicking on the column heading in the menu causes the table to rearrange its data by that category. So, if you were to click on *Cuisine Type* in the drop-down menu in Figure 4-2, the table would rearrange the order of the rows alphabetically so that all the American restaurants would be listed first, followed by the Asian, Italian, Latin, Mexican, Steakhouse, and Seafood restaurants, respectively.

Using the information in the table, you decide whether the proper response to each statement is *True* or *False*, *Inferable* or *Not Inferable*, *Yes* or *No*, or some other similar either/or answer choice dictated by the specifications of the question. Then you indicate your choice by clicking on the radio button next to the appropriate answer.

These questions require you to manipulate data and make observations and calculations. Some of the most common calculations are statistical ones, such as percentages, averages, medians, and ratios, so table analysis questions can be some of the easiest IR questions to answer. Here's how to make sure you get them right:

>> **Jump to the question immediately.** Most of the information you need appears in the table, so you rarely need to read the introductory paragraph that comes before the table. Glance at the column headings to get an idea of the type of information the table provides, and then move promptly to the question.

>> **Read the question carefully.** You're most likely to get tripped up on these questions simply because you haven't read them carefully enough to figure out exactly what data they ask you to evaluate.

>> **Identify the relevant column heading.** Often, the key to answering a table analysis question is ordering the data properly. Quickly figure out which column provides you with the best way to arrange the data and sort by that column. For example, if you were asked for the neighborhood on the list with the most participating restaurants, you'd sort by *Neighborhood*.

>> **Make accurate computations.** Determine exactly what calculations the question requires and perform them accurately, either in your head or on the calculator. Based on Figure 4-2, for example, you could easily figure the restaurant with the greatest average daily number of meals sold by sorting by that column and glancing at the highest number. However, calculating which participating restaurant in the Downtown neighborhood brought in the greatest average daily gross revenue may require the calculator to multiply each restaurant's price per meal by its average daily number of meals sold.

>> **Make use of your note board.** Keep track of more complex calculations on your note board. As you calculate each Downtown restaurant's average daily gross revenue, for example, record the results on your note board. Then you can easily compare the four values without having to memorize them.

Now apply these strategies to a sample question.

For each of the following statements, select *Yes* if the statement is true based on the information provided in Figure 4-2. Otherwise, choose *No*.

EXAMPLE

Yes	No	
○	○	A. The average price per meal for all participating restaurants in the Downtown neighborhood was approximately $30.
○	○	B. The average price per meal for participating restaurants in the Uptown neighborhood was less than the average price per meal in the Downtown neighborhood.
○	○	C. Participating restaurants that included wine with the meal in the Uptown neighborhood sold more meals on average per day than participating restaurants that did not include wine with the meal.

Statement (A) references two columns, *Price Per Meal* and *Neighborhood*. Sorting by *Neighborhood* makes more sense because it lists all Downtown restaurants together so that you may better view and compare each Downtown restaurant's price per meal. After you've sorted by *Neighborhood*, the table looks like this:

Restaurant	Cuisine Type	Price Per Meal	Neighborhood	Wine Included? (Y/N)	Average Daily Number of Meals Sold
Big Ben's Bistro	American	$30	Central	Y	175
Chang's	Asian	$20	Chinatown	N	142
Bendimere's	Steakhouse	$40	Downtown	N	150
Frank's House	American	$20	Downtown	N	175
Pesce Blue	Seafood	$40	Downtown	Y	164
Valenzuela's	Mexican	$20	Downtown	N	113
The Purple Parrot	Latin	$30	Northwest	Y	134
Thai Time	Asian	$20	Northwest	N	87
Sorbello's	Italian	$40	Old Town	Y	175
Sushi Fusco	Asian	$30	Old Town	N	100
Hadley's on the Beach	Seafood	$40	Uptown	Y	160
Meritage	American	$40	Uptown	N	152
Ocean View	Seafood	$40	Uptown	N	151

This arrangement allows you to see that two participating restaurants in the Downtown neighborhood charged $20 per meal and two charged $40 per meal. The number of $20 meals sold by both restaurants is 288, and the number of $40 meals sold at the two other restaurants is 314. To find the average A, multiply $20 by 288 and $40 by 314. Add the two products and divide by the total number of meals sold (602):

$$A = \frac{(20 \times 288) + (40 \times 314)}{602} = \frac{5,760 + 12,560}{602} = \frac{18,320}{602} \approx 30.43$$

Because $30.43 is approximately $30, you can say that the average price of a Downtown meal was approximately $30. The answer is *Yes*.

You've already figured out the second calculation for Statement (B). The average price per meal at a Downtown restaurant is about $30. You can write $D = 30$ on your note board to remind you. All the Uptown restaurants charged $40 per meal, so the average price per meal in Uptown is greater than the average price in Downtown. Select *No*.

Statement (C) again focuses on one neighborhood, so you don't have to resort to the table. The one restaurant that included wine in the meal price sold 160 meals on average per day, which is more than the 152 and 151 sold by the other two restaurants in the neighborhood. The answer is *Yes*.

Table analysis questions may not require that you use all the data provided. For example, you didn't need to evaluate *Cuisine Type* for any of the question parts in the example question. Don't worry if you don't use the data in some columns at all. Part of the task in answering table analysis questions is knowing what data is important and what's irrelevant.

Two-part analysis

When you see a paragraph or two of information that sets you up to choose two pieces of information from a table with three columns, you know you're dealing with a two-part analysis question. The third column provides a list of possible answer choices for each part. You select the answer for the first part of the question in the first column and the answer to the second part in the second column. On the actual test, you will not be able to select more than one answer in a column. Also, in some cases, both the first and second parts could have the same answer choice.

Here are some tips to help you confidently answer two-part analysis questions:

>> **Read the explanatory paragraph carefully.** Reading the explanatory paragraph for these questions is absolutely essential. It provides the conditions you need to consider and clarifies what each part of the question asks for.

>> **Read all the answer options.** Don't attempt to answer the question without looking over the answer options first. Thoroughly consider each possibility offered in the third column.

>> **Answer using only the information provided.** Base your answers only on the information given in the question rather than your own personal knowledge of the topic.

>> **Be sure to mark your choices in the proper column.** The possible answers are in the third column, on the far-right side of the table. For the first question, choose an answer from the list by making a selection in the first column; for the second question, choose an answer from the list by making a selection in the second column.

>> **Verify that your answer selections are logical and coherent.** Check your answers against the conditions stated in the explanatory paragraph. Make sure your selections are the best among all those offered.

The GMAT usually uses the two-part analysis question type to test mathematical skills (such as figuring functions) and verbal logical reasoning abilities (such as strengthening and weakening arguments). Often the best way to figure out the answer for the math variety is to try each of the possible values to see which ones fulfill the requirements. Usually, the best way to answer the verbal type is by process of elimination.

The following two sample questions give you an example of a math two-part analysis and a verbal two-part analysis question.

The GMAT won't label the answer options in the third column with letters as we have here to make our explanations easier to follow. To select an option on the computerized test, you'll simply click the radio button next to the option.

A set of four expressions consists of these three expressions $\{2n+8, n+4, 6n-2\}$ and one additional expression. From the following expressions, select the one that could be the fourth expression in the set and the one that could be the resulting average of the four expressions in the set. Make only one selection per column.

Fourth Expression of the Set	Arithmetic Mean of the Set	
○	○	A. 2n
○	○	B. 3n + 2
○	○	C. 3n – 2
○	○	D. 12n + 8
○	○	E. 48n + 32
○	○	F. 4n + 8

Approach this question by trying out the possible answer choices as potential fourth expressions to see which, when it's included with the given expressions, results in an average that's another of the possible answer choices.

First, evaluate the three provided expressions. All contain one-digit values that are multiplied by n with a one-digit value added or subtracted from that term. So, evaluate similar expressions, such as choices (B), (C), and (F) before you consider less similar expressions, such as choices (A), (D), and (E).

If Choice (B), $3n+2$, were the fourth expression, the average of the four expressions would be

$$\frac{(2n+8)+(n+4)+(6n-2)+(3n+2)}{4}=\frac{12n+12}{4}=3n+3$$

Because $3n+3$ isn't one of the answer choices, you know that $3n+2$ can't be the fourth expression.

Try Choice (C), $3n-2$. If you wrote your calculations for $3n+2$ on your note board, you know that the first term of the average is the same because the $3n$ doesn't change.

$$\frac{(2n+8)+(n+4)+(6n-2)+(3n-2)}{4}=\frac{12n+8}{4}=3n+2$$

This value is a possible option. When the fourth expression in the set is $3n-2$, the average of the four expressions is $3n+2$. Select Choice (C) for the first column and Choice (B) for the second. Only one possible set of answers exists, so if you're confident about your calculations, you don't have to consider the other options. Submit your answer and move on.

EXAMPLE

Joseph: Health insurance premiums are growing at an alarming rate. This is, in part, because many hospitals and clinics bill for unnecessary diagnostics and tests that inflate the subsequent amount that insurers pay out to them. These expenses are then passed on to consumers in the form of increased insurance premiums. Therefore, reducing the number of unnecessary tests performed by hospitals and clinics will effectively curb the rise in health insurance premiums.

Ronald: Often, the unnecessary diagnostics that you speak of are the result of decisions made by doctors on behalf of their patients. Doctors usually choose the diagnostics that allow them to bill insurers for more money but may not necessarily benefit the patient in a meaningful way or influence the course of treatment chosen. As a result, in order to succeed in reducing the number of unnecessary tests, patients should be allowed to decide which course of diagnostics they would like to undergo.

In the following table, identify the unique assumption upon which each argument depends. Make only one selection in each column: one in the first column for the best representation of Joseph's assumption in his argument and one in the second column for the best representation of Ronald's.

Joseph	Ronald	
○	○	A. Doctors are generally able to determine with great reliability which diagnostic procedures and tests will yield the most effective results.
○	○	B. Tests and diagnostic procedures make up a significant portion of the bills that are sent to insurers.
○	○	C. Insurance companies in other industries, such as auto and home, have been able to reduce costs by reducing the number of unnecessary repairs and replacements on claims for automobiles and homes.
○	○	D. Patients are not as likely as doctors to choose the most expensive diagnostics and tests.
○	○	E. Health insurance premiums have increased twice as fast in the past 5 years as they have over an average of the past 25 years.

Whereas the sample math two-part analysis question required you to figure out the answers to both parts at the same time, this verbal reasoning sample question is more easily handled one column at a time. First, consider the assumption that's most likely part of Joseph's argument. Then consider the one that pertains to Ronald's. (An *assumption* is usually a statement that links the premise of an argument to its conclusion. For details on evaluating arguments, see Block 2.)

Following are the premises of Joseph's argument:

>> Hospitals and clinics are billing health insurance companies for unnecessary and expensive tests.

>> This practice has caused health insurance companies to pay inflated rates to hospitals and clinics.

>> The result is that health insurance companies are compensating by raising consumers' health insurance premiums.

Based on these premises, Joseph concludes that reducing unnecessary tests will significantly control the rise in health insurance premiums.

To find the assumption that provides a link between the cessation of the unnecessary tests and a significant effect on increasing healthcare premiums, begin by narrowing your options. Joseph doesn't mention doctors in his argument, so you can eliminate choices (A) and (D). Choice (E) addresses healthcare premiums but not unnecessary tests, so it's out. Choice (C) concerns other insurance industries, so it has nothing to do with Joseph's argument about healthcare premiums. The best option for Joseph is the assumption that unnecessary tests make up a significant portion of insurance billing. If they make up just a small portion, eliminating tests wouldn't have a significant impact on the rising cost of healthcare premiums. Mark Choice (B) in the column for Joseph.

Now evaluate Ronald's argument. Here are his premises:

>> Doctors order unnecessary tests to increase their earnings.

>> Patients should be able to choose their tests.

>> Putting the decision regarding diagnostics and tests in the patients' control would reduce the number of unnecessary tests.

So you're looking for the assumption that links patients' decisions to fewer unnecessary tests.

Notice that Ronald doesn't address healthcare premiums at all, so you can confidently eliminate Choice (E). Choice (B) is out because it doesn't relate to patients' decisions. Choice (C) doesn't work for the same reason that it doesn't work for Joseph. Ronald's argument concerns only healthcare. Of the two remaining options (choices [A] and [D]), only Choice (D) relates to patients' decisions. Only if patients make decisions differently than doctors do would putting patients in control lessen the number of unnecessary tests. So you mark Choice (D) in the column for Ronald.

Graphics interpretation

Not surprisingly, graphics interpretation questions require that you interpret a graphic or other image. You may see line graphs, bar graphs, pie charts, scatter plots, Venn diagrams, and other data representation. Based on the information displayed in the graphic, you fill in two separate blanks by selecting the best option from a drop-down menu for each blank. (In the example question later in this section, we include the answer options in parentheses.) You have to complete both blanks correctly to get credit for one graphics interpretation question.

The information you need to fill in the blanks comes primarily from the graphic, so make sure you know how to read graphics. Later in this block, section "Extracting Insights from Graphic Data" provides a review of the most common GMAT graphics to refresh your memory.

TIP Here are some other tips to help you efficiently move through graphics interpretation questions:

>> **Read any text that accompanies the graphic.** Text around the graphic may clarify its purpose. It also might provide information that you need to select a correct answer.

>> **Analyze the graphic to determine exactly what information it provides and how.** Observe the labels and examine numerical increments carefully.

>> **Click on Select One to view all the answer options.** To see the possible answers in the drop-down menu for each blank, you have to click on the box that says Select One. Filling in the blank is much easier when you're limited to just the several available choices. Don't attempt to answer the question without seeing the answer choices first.

>> **Eliminate illogical answer choices.** Approach the two parts of a graphics interpretation question much like you would a standard multiple-choice question. Eliminate obviously incorrect options and use your reasoning skills to select the best answer from the remaining choices.

>> **Make estimations.** The data in graphics are rarely precise, so most of your calculations are estimates or approximations that you can work out on your note board or in your head rather than on the calculator.

Here's a sample graphics interpretation question to consider.

Scientists, health professionals, and life insurance agents are interested in examining the percentage of people in a population who will live to a certain age. One way to measure this information is to look at the percentage of the population who have died after a certain number of years. The following graph displays the results of such a study.

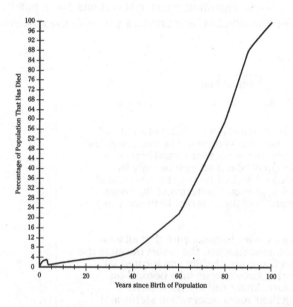

Approximately _____ (10, 40, 60, 80) percent of the population lives to at least 80 years of age. A person who was a member of the study population would still have an 80 percent chance of being alive at around a maximum age of _____ (15, 35, 55, 80) years.

Filling the first blank in the question tests your graph-reading skills. Find 80 years of age on the horizontal axis. Move your finger from the 80-year mark upward on the graph until you reach the plotted curve. Move your finger to the left to see that at 80 years, about 60 percent of people have died. Don't stop there and choose 60 percent, however. The question asks for how many are alive at the 80-year mark. Subtract 60 from 100 to get that approximately 40 percent of the population live to at least 80 years. The correct answer is 40 percent.

To complete the second blank, make sure you look at the answer choices first. Because the statement concerns the *maximum* value, consider higher ages first. The oldest option is 80, but it's very unlikely that 80 percent of people are alive at age 80, so try the next highest age, 55. Move along the graph until you reach 55 years. At 55 years of age, 20 percent have died, leaving a maximum of 80 percent alive. Ages above 55 can't be right, so 55 is the correct answer.

If you start with the first option of 15 years, you may be misled. Note that the graph shows you that at about 15 years of age, less than 5 percent of people have died, which means that more than 95 percent of the population are still alive. That's more than 80 percent, but the statement regards the *maximum* age where 80 percent of the population is still kicking, so 15 can't be correct.

Multi-source reasoning

Multi-source reasoning questions present two or three sources of information, labeled with tabs, each providing a distinct aspect of a given situation. The scenarios covered in these questions encompass a wide range of topics. You might encounter scientific phenomenon like black holes or plant photosynthesis, or you may be tasked with applying data to business-related situations, such as hiring decisions or event planning.

At least one of the tabs shows a written passage. Others may show additional written information or data presented in graphical form. You use the resources in the tabs to gather the necessary information to answer the questions posed. For example, Figure 4-3 shows the first tab for a sample multi-source reasoning scenario regarding guest reservations for a hotel's wedding block. The email in this tab sets up the situation and provides you with the guidelines for the reservation.

FIGURE 4-3: Sample multi-source reasoning format, Background Information tab.

The tabs shown: **Background Information** | **Contract Paragraph 3** | **Guest List**

The Pearson family is hosting the destination wedding of their daughter Emily and her fiancé, Matthew Voorhies. The event will take place on Saturday, September 8th, at the popular Grand Maryvale Resort, which is located on a tropical island accessible only by airplane. The resort has provided a block of rooms at a discounted rate to accommodate the wedding guests. The terms of the room discount are outlined in Paragraph 3 of the contract between the resort and Emily's father.

The Pearson and Voorhies families want to make sure that all who attend their wedding have accommodations at the resort because the island has few other hotels, and those are shabby and located far away from the resort. The resort is known to be fully booked on weekends in September. Therefore, Emily and Matthew have contacted each guest regarding their room reservation status and have recorded their statuses as of August 1st on a spreadsheet entitled Guest List.

© John Wiley & Sons, Inc.

Figure 4-4 shows what you find when you click on the second tab: language from the contract between the Pearson family and the resort.

Figure 4-5 shows what you find when you click on the third tab: a table showing the wedding guest list and their reservation status.

The multi-source reasoning questions appear in one of two formats: three-part table (similar to table analysis questions) or standard five-option multiple-choice. Keep in mind that you have to answer correctly all three parts of the first format to get credit for the one question. The multiple-choice format may be one of the easiest IR questions to answer. You can use the process of elimination to narrow the answers, and you have to choose only one correct answer to get full credit for the question.

The trickiest aspect of answering multi-source reasoning questions is sifting through the plethora of information to discover what's relevant. Depending on the scenario, you may have to juggle information in tables, diagrams, articles, and so on to come up with correct answers.

Background Information	Contract Paragraph 3	Guest List

III. For the Pearson/Voorhies Wedding, a hotel room block has been reserved at the Grand Maryvale Resort for the nights of September 7, 8, and 9. Instead of the regular room rate of $175 per night, guests who book as a part of the block for all three nights can pay a special rate of only $135 per night. Those who book for less than three nights will be charged $150 per night. Those who book rooms for the nights before or after the three nights specified by the hotel block must pay the regular nightly room rate for nights stayed beyond the three-night block discount. We can hold five rooms at a time for the attendees of the Pearson/Voorhies wedding — once the first five are filled, we will be able to release five more. We do not guarantee accommodations to wedding guests beyond these specifications.

FIGURE 4-4: Sample multi-source reasoning format, Contract tab.

© John Wiley & Sons, Inc.

Background Information	Contract Paragraph 3	Guest List

Name	Number Attending	Number of Rooms Needed	Nights Staying at Resort	Reservations Made?
The Rose Family	4	1	3	N
The Crawford Family	6	2	2	Y
The Fishers	2	1	1	Y
The Ball Family	5	2	3	Y
The Ranks Family	6	2	3	N
The Keppners	2	1	1	Y
The Albertsons	4	1	1	N
....	....	....	....	....

FIGURE 4-5: Sample multi-source reasoning format, Guest List tab.

© John Wiley & Sons, Inc.

TIP

Here are some pointers to help you with multi-source reasoning questions:

>> **Read the whole question carefully.** You're most likely to encounter difficulties with these questions simply due to not having carefully read them, thereby hindering your ability to figure out the specific task being asked of you.

>> **Summarize each tab.** As you read through the information in each tab for the first time, record pertinent points to help you remember which tab holds what type of data. That way you don't have to continually flip back and forth between screens as you answer questions. For example, summarize the contract details in Figure 4-4 on your note board with quick notations such as *9/7, 8, & 9 = $135/night; < 3 nights = $150/night; before/after 9/7 or 9/9 = $175/night.*

>> **Make connections.** After reviewing the information in each tab, synthesize facts and figures from one tab with related data from another. Make sure to record your observations on your note board. For example, as you examine the details in Figures 4-4 and 4-5, you can draw connections between the information in the table provided in the third tab and the room-charge specifications in the second tab. This strategy will help you figure out how much each guest will pay for resort rooms.

» **Rely on what the test gives you.** Some of the topics in multi-source reasoning scenarios may be familiar to you. Although familiarity may make the information more accessible to you, it may also influence you to answer questions based on what you know instead of what the exam tells you. For example, you shouldn't answer any questions about the Pearson wedding sample scenario based on what you know about hotel booking from your own experience as a front-desk manager.

Here's another sample multi-source scenario with a couple of questions to help you get more acquainted with the question type. This scenario has only two tabs, each conveying an opposing opinion from two scientists on a specific scientific phenomenon.

Scientist 1

Ancient ice cores from Antarctica indicate that the concentration of carbon dioxide in the atmosphere and global mean temperatures have followed the same pattern of fluctuations in levels over the past 160,000 years. Therefore, the increase in atmospheric carbon dioxide concentration from 280 parts per million to 360 parts per million that has occurred over the past 150 years points to significant and detrimental climatic changes in the near future. The climate has already changed: The average surface temperature of the earth has increased 0.6°C in the past hundred years, with the ten hottest years of that time period all occurring since 1980. Although 0.6°C may not seem large, changes in the mean surface temperature as low as 0.5°C have dramatically affected crop growth in years past. Moreover, computer models project that surface temperatures will increase about 2.0°C by the year 2100 and will continue to increase in the years after even if concentration of greenhouse gases is stabilized by that time. If the present trend in carbon dioxide increase continues, though, carbon dioxide concentration will exceed 1,100 parts per million soon after 2100 and will be associated with a temperature increase of approximately 10.0°C over the present mean annual global surface temperature.

Scientist 2

The observed increases in minor greenhouse gases such as carbon dioxide and methane will not lead to sizeable global warming. Water vapor and clouds are responsible for more than 98% of the earth's greenhouse effect. Current models that project large temperature increases with a doubling of the present carbon dioxide concentration incorporate changes in water vapor, clouds and other factors that would accompany a rise in carbon dioxide levels. The way these models handle such feedback factors is not supported by current scientific knowledge. In fact, there is convincing evidence that shows that increases in carbon dioxide concentration would lead to changes in feedback factors that would diminish any temperature increase associated with more carbon dioxide in the atmosphere. The climatic data for the last hundred years show an irregular pattern in which many of the greatest jumps in global mean temperature were too large to be associated with the observed increase in carbon dioxide. The overall increase of 0.45°C in the past century is well under what the models would have predicted given the changes in carbon dioxide concentration. As with the temperature models, recent increases in atmospheric carbon dioxide have not risen to the extent predicted by models dealing solely with carbon dioxide levels. The rate of carbon dioxide concentration increase has slowed since 1973. Improved energy technologies will further dampen the increase so that the carbon dioxide concentration will be under 700 parts per million in the year 2100.

Consider each of the following statements about atmospheric carbon-dioxide levels and determine whether Scientists 1 and 2 are both likely to agree by marking either *Yes* or *No*:

Yes	No	
○	○	A. Increasing carbon dioxide levels affect other factors.
○	○	B. Humans will never be able to stabilize atmospheric carbon dioxide levels.
○	○	C. The rate of increase in carbon dioxide levels will rise throughout the next 100 years.

Statement (A) is a nice, noncontroversial statement with which both scientists would agree. Scientist 1 stresses that rising carbon dioxide is linked to higher temperature (another factor), while Scientist 2 discusses *feedback factors,* which are factors that respond to carbon-dioxide changes and will, in turn, affect the carbon dioxide. Select *Yes* for Statement (A).

To answer Statement (B), notice that Scientist 2, who refers to improved energy technology, clearly disagrees with the statement, but so does Scientist 1, who mentions the possibility that carbon-dioxide levels will stabilize. Neither scientist would agree with Statement (B), so the answer is *No.*

Scientist 2 disagrees with Statement (C) and actually discusses a slowing down in the rate of carbon-dioxide-level increase. Because at least one of the scientists would disagree with the statement, the answer to Statement (C) is *No.*

The next question is in multiple-choice format.

Which of the following statements does only Scientist 1 support?

(A) A change in atmospheric water vapor could significantly affect global temperatures.

(B) The increase in atmospheric carbon-dioxide concentration from 280 parts per million to 360 parts per million that has occurred over the last 150 years is not expected to affect climactic change negatively in the future.

(C) Recent increases in atmospheric carbon dioxide have surpassed those predicted by temperature models dealing solely with carbon-dioxide models.

(D) Temperature fluctuations will match carbon-dioxide changes when carbon-dioxide changes are abrupt.

(E) Increases in carbon-dioxide concentration would lead to changes in feedback factors that would compound any temperature increase associated with more carbon dioxide in the atmosphere.

Focus on the information in the first tab. Scientist 1 mentions a match between carbon dioxide and temperature variations and then uses the recent large change in carbon-dioxide levels as evidence that significant changes in temperature will occur. Scientist 1 goes on to discuss how continued sharp increases in atmospheric carbon dioxide will lead to similar dramatic temperature increases. Scientist 1 implies that the recent carbon-dioxide changes have been unprecedented. The data during the past 160,000 years show a correspondence between temperature and carbon-dioxide fluctuations, but this correspondence has occurred in the absence of the dramatic changes the earth is now and soon will be experiencing. For Scientist 1 to use the fluctuation correspondence as evidence for what will soon happen, that scientist must assume that the correspondence will continue in light of current and near-future sharp changes. So Choice (D) is correct.

Choice (A) is supported by Scientist 2, and neither scientist would support choices (B), (C), or (E). In fact, Scientist 1 actually says that an increase in atmospheric carbon-dioxide concentration from 280 parts per million to 360 parts per million can cause "significant and detrimental climactic changes in the near future."

Extracting Insights from Graphic Data

A *graphic* is a visual representation or image that conveys information, data, or messages. Graphics can take various forms, including graphical displays like bar and line graphs, histograms, and pie charts. This section provides an overview of the different types of graphics commonly encountered in GMAT questions. Additionally, it offers guidance on effectively interpreting each type of graphic to maximize your efficiency in understanding the presented information. You read and interpret data provided in the graphic, and then you apply your analysis to draw conclusions about a bunch of scenarios.

Overall, graphics are an essential tool for visual representation of data, enabling you to impart tricky concepts in a way that's simple and easy to understand. So, buckle up and get ready to embark on an exciting journey of data visualization! Shall we begin?

Mastering graphics-focused questions with five simple steps

Regardless of the graphic you're working with in a Data Insights question, you'll follow a similar, five-step approach:

1. **Identify the type of graphic.**

Graphics display data in different ways, so start by recognizing which type you're dealing with. To make this step easy, we provide detailed information on each of the most common types of graphics on the GMAT within this section.

2. **Read the accompanying question and determine what it asks.**

Before you attempt to read the graphic, examine the question to figure out exactly what kind of information you need to answer it.

3. **Identify what you need to get out of the graphic to successfully answer the question.**

Refer to the graphic to discover where it conveys the specific data you need to answer the question.

4. **Read the graphic properly.**

Take a close look at the graphic and ensure that you comprehend its title. Examine the labels on the parts of the graphic and the legend to gain an understanding of what's being depicted.

For bar graphs, line graphs, histograms, and scatterplots note the labels on the horizontal and vertical axes, and their measurement scales. For line graphs, look for noticeable trends such as rising or falling values and periods of inactivity. Look for clusters, gaps, and outliers.

REMEMBER

5. **Answer the question.**

Use the data you've carefully extracted from the graphic to come up with the correct answer to the question. Where possible, use estimation to answer questions. However, be ready to do some simple arithmetic calculations (such as compute percentages, calculate an average, and more). Make sure the numbers add up correctly. Use the online calculator as needed.

Use only the information provided in the graphic and accompanying text. Do not answer based on your personal knowledge or opinion.

The remaining sections show you how to apply this approach to reading and interpreting a variety of graphics.

Translating information in tables

Tables show data organized into rows and columns, enabling you to conveniently observe and analyze accurate information. For example, a table can be an effective way of presenting average daily high and low temperatures in a given area, the number of male and female births that occur each year within a population, or the rankings of a band's top-ten hits.

The table displayed in Figure 4-6 presents the recorded scores of five gymnasts who took part in a local meet. It includes both the individual event scores and the all-around score of each gymnast. The data are precise rather than approximated, which allows you to come up with accurate analyses of the values. For example, you can see from the table that Kate just barely edged out Jess on the balance beam by a 0.005 difference in scores.

FIGURE 4-6:
Table similar to one you're likely to encounter in a Data Insights question.

Bayside Gymnastics Club Score Report					
Name	Vault Score	Uneven Bars Score	Balance Beam Score	Floor Exercise Score	All-Around Score
Kelsea Moore	16.250	15.500	15.100	14.985	61.835
Adrianne Rizzo	15.900	14.975	15.225	15.325	61.425
Kate McCaffery	16.000	14.600	15.000	13.995	58.595
Jess Hartley	15.875	13.966	14.995	15.000	59.836
Maggie Birney	16.100	13.920	15.100	13.870	58.990

© *John Wiley & Sons, Inc.*

When analyzing a table, pay particular attention to the column labels (called *headers*) as they name which variables are shown. Read carefully to differentiate values and determine, say, whether the numbers represent percentages or actual figures. For example, by taking a few moments to examine the values in the table depicted in Figure 4-6, you can ascertain that a gymnast's all-around score is the sum of that gymnast's other scores rather than their average. So, if a question asks you about a particular gymnast's average score for all events, you'd know to calculate this value instead of simply recording the given all-around score.

Not surprisingly, tables are the primary source of information in table analysis questions. These questions use tables to display data, usually a lot of it. You may also find tables in multi-source reasoning and two-part analysis questions. (For more details on answering Data Insights questions refer to the earlier section "Knowing What to Expect: Four Key Integrated Reasoning Question Types.")

Making comparisons with bar graphs

Bar graphs (also sometimes called *bar charts*) have a variety of uses. They're especially good for comparing data and approximating values. As the name suggests, they use rectangular bars, displayed either horizontally or vertically, to visually depict various data categories. The bars are labeled at the base, indicating the different categories they represent. The height or length of each bar indicates the corresponding quantity for that category of data.

You see bar graphs most frequently on the GMAT in graphics interpretation questions, but they may also appear in multi-source reasoning and two-part analysis questions. Simple bar graphs present the relationship between two variables. More complex bar graphs show additional data by displaying additional bars or by segmenting each individual bar. We show you how to read simple and complex bar graphs in the following sections.

Simple bar graphs

Bar graphs provide an excellent way to visualize the similarities and differences among several categories of data. Even a simple bar graph, such as the one in Figure 4-7, can convey a whole bunch of information.

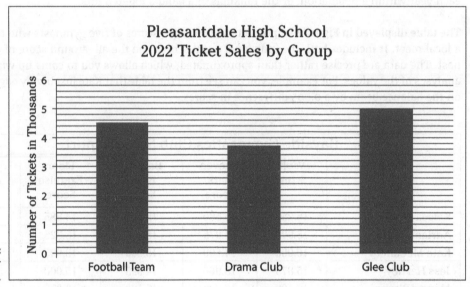

FIGURE 4-7:
Simple bar
graph.

The title of the bar graph in Figure 4-7 defines the overall category of information: 2022 ticket sales for Pleasantdale High School by group. You don't need a title for the horizontal axis. It's obvious from the graph's title that each bar provides the data for each school group. From the vertical axis label, you discover that the data represent number of tickets sold rather than the total revenue from those tickets. "In Thousands" means that each major horizontal gridline represents 1,000 tickets. Each of the four minor gridlines between each major gridline represents 200 tickets (the four lines divide the segments between the whole numbers into five parts, and $(1000 \div 5 = 200)$. So, the graph indicates that the number of drama club tickets sold was approximately 3,700 because the Drama Club bar ends between the third and fourth minor gridlines above the 3,000 mark. To find the total number of drama club tickets sold, add 200 for each of the three minor gridlines and half of that (100) as represented by the half space between the third and fourth minor gridlines: $3,000 + 3(200) + 100 = 3,700$.

Some GMAT bar graphs may display information for a range of values. An example appears in Figure 4-8. Based on this graph, you can figure that the minimum total number of tickets sold by all groups in 2022 was the sum of the lowest numbers for each group $(4,000 + 5,000 + 6,000)$, or 15,000 tickets. The maximum possible total of tickets sold by the three groups combined was the sum of the highest value for each category: $5,000 + 6,000 + 7,000$, or 18,000.

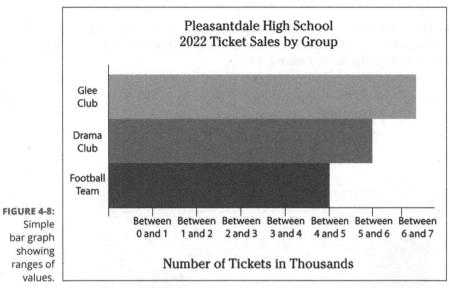

Pleasantdale High School
2022 Ticket Sales by Group

Glee Club

Drama Club

Football Team

Between 0 and 1 | Between 1 and 2 | Between 2 and 3 | Between 3 and 4 | Between 4 and 5 | Between 5 and 6 | Between 6 and 7

Number of Tickets in Thousands

FIGURE 4-8:
Simple bar graph showing ranges of values.

Graphs with many bars

Altering the design of a bar graph allows you to convey even more information. Graphs with multiple bars reveal data for additional categories. For example, Figure 4-9 compares the ticket sales totals for the three groups by year for three years.

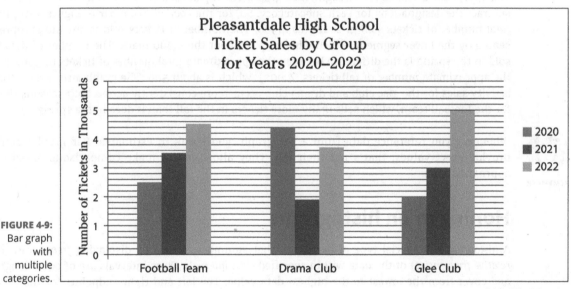

Pleasantdale High School
Ticket Sales by Group
for Years 2020–2022

Number of Tickets in Thousands

Football Team | Drama Club | Glee Club

2020
2021
2022

FIGURE 4-9:
Bar graph with multiple categories.

The legend designates which group the bars stand for. This graph allows you to easily make comparisons over the years and among the three groups. For example, it's easy to see that in 2020, glee club ticket sales were not only greater than they had been in previous years but also exceeded sales for either of the other two groups.

Segmented bar graphs

Graphs with segmented bars display the characteristics of subcategories. Each bar is divided into segments that represent different subgroups. The height of each segment within a bar represents the value associated with that particular subgroup. For example, Pleasantdale High can provide more specific comparisons of the ticket sales during different times of the year by using a segmented bar graph, such as the one in Figure 4-10.

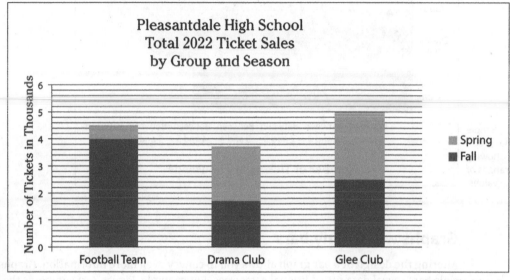

FIGURE 4-10:
Segmented bar graph with sub-categories.

You apply subtraction to read a segmented graph. The top of each bar is the total from which you subtract the designations for each subcategory. So, for the *Football Team* bar in Figure 4-10, the total number of tickets sold in 2022 was 4,500. The number of tickets sold in the fall is represented by the lower segment, which climbs up to about the 4,000 mark. The number of tickets sold in the spring is the difference between the approximate total number of tickets (4,500) and the approximate number of fall tickets (4,000), which is about 500. The graph also reveals that activity sales for the glee club and drama club occur more consistently across both seasons than for the football team, which sells many more tickets in the fall than it does in the spring.

REMEMBER

Whenever you reference data from a bar graph, you speak in estimates. Bar graphs don't provide exact values; that's not their job. They allow you to make comparisons based on approximations.

Honing in on histograms

A *histogram* is a special type of bar graph that summarizes data by displaying *frequencies* (or *relative frequencies*) of the data within specified *class intervals.* Class intervals are of equal length and cover from the lowest to the highest data value. The left and right endpoints for the class intervals are selected so that each data value clearly falls within one and only one class interval. The frequency of occurrence of the data values within a class interval is represented by a rectangular column. The height of the column is proportional to the frequency of data values within that interval. Unlike the bars in other bar graphs, the bars in a histogram are side-by-side (usually) with no space in between. In a *frequency histogram*, the scale for measuring the height of the bars is marked with actual frequencies (that is, raw counts). In a *relative frequency histogram*, the scale is marked with relative frequencies instead of actual frequencies. Looking at the histogram in Figure 4-11, can you determine how many students received 90 or above on the first test?

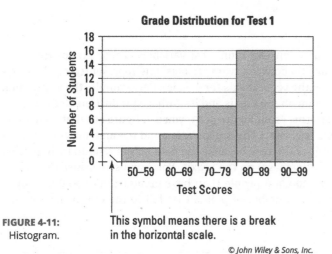

Grade Distribution for Test 1

This symbol means there is a break in the horizontal scale.

FIGURE 4-11:
Histogram.

The scale on the vertical axis shows the number of students who achieved the grade. The scale is marked in multiples of 2. The top of the bar for the interval 90–99 is halfway between 4 and 6, indicating that 5 students received 90 or above on Test 1.

Looking at line graphs

Another graph that crops up frequently in graphics interpretation questions is the *line graph*. Line graphs display information that occurs over time or across graduated measurements and are particularly effective in highlighting trends, peaks, or lows. Typically (but not always), the horizontal axis displays units of time or measurement (the independent variable), and the vertical axis presents the data that's being measured (the dependent variable).

Basic line graphs

The line graph in Figure 4-12 shows the garbage production for three cities for each of the four quarters of 2021. You can tell from the graph that Plainfield produced more garbage in every quarter than the other two cities did, and it's evident that all three cities produced less garbage in Quarter 3 than they did in the other quarters.

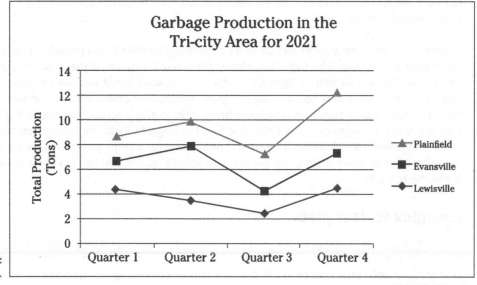

FIGURE 4-12:
Line graph.

Scatter plots

Scatter plots display the relationship between two numerical variables. These graphs display a bunch of points that show the relationship between two variables, one represented on the horizontal axis (or *x*-axis) and the other on the vertical axis (or *y*-axis). For example, the scatter plot in Figure 4-13 plots each city's population on the *x*-axis and its garbage production on the *y*-axis. Scatter plots show you trends and patterns. From Figure 4-13, you can figure out that, generally, a direct or positive relationship exists between a city's population and the amount of garbage it produces. The graph indicates that this is the case because the data points tend to be higher on the *y*-axis as they move to the right (or increase) on the *x*-axis. You can also surmise that of the 20 cities listed, more have fewer than 200,000 people than have greater than 200,000 people. That's because the graph shows a greater number of points that fall to the left of the 200,000 population line than to the right.

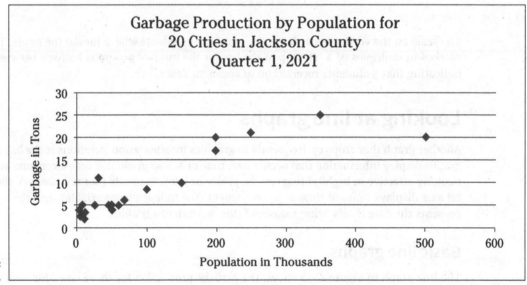

FIGURE 4-13: Scatter plot.

© John Wiley & Sons, Inc.

REMEMBER

When two quantitative variables are *positive correlated*, higher values of one are associated with higher values of the other, and lower values are associated with lower values as well. If they are *negatively correlated*, higher values of one are associated with lower values of the other, and vice versa.

Scatter plots also convey trend and pattern deviations. The GMAT may provide a scatter plot with or without a *trend line*. The trend line shows the overall pattern of the data plots and reveals deviations. The scatter plot in Figure 4-13 doesn't display a trend line, so you have to imagine one. You can lay your note board along the graph to help you envision the trend line if one isn't provided. Figure 4-14 shows you the trend line for the garbage production graph. With the trend line in place, you can more easily recognize that the largest city in the county deviates from the trend somewhat considerably. Its garbage production is less in proportion to its population than that of most other cities in the county. You know that because its data point is considerably below the trend line.

Complex scatter plots

Sometimes the GMAT crams even more information on a scatter plot by introducing another variable associated with the data. The values for this variable appear on a vertical axis on the right side of the graph. This type of graph is just a way of combining information in one graph that could appear on two separate graphs.

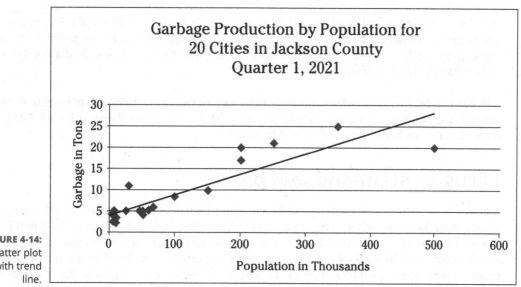

FIGURE 4-14:
Scatter plot
with trend
line.

© John Wiley & Sons, Inc.

Figure 4-15 shows you an example of a complex scatter plot. It adds another variable (average yearly income by population) to the mix. The average annual income for each city lies on the right vertical axis. The points for one set of data have different symbols than those for the other so that you can distinguish between the two sets. The legend at the right of the graph in Figure 4-15 tells you that garbage production is represented by diamonds, and the symbol for income is a square. The trend line for the relationship between city population and average yearly income has a negative slope, which shows you that the smaller the population, the greater the average yearly income. This trend indicates an inverse relationship between city population and average yearly income.

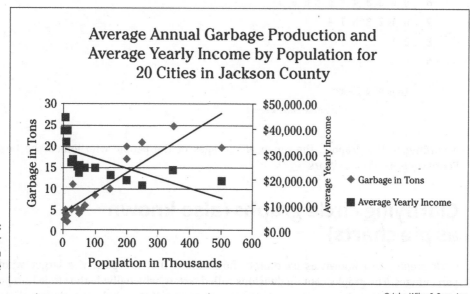

FIGURE 4-15:
Scatter
plot with
multiple
variables.

© John Wiley & Sons, Inc.

REMEMBER

The GMAT may ask you to identify the relationship between two variables as positive, negative, or neutral. If the trend line has a positive slope (that is, it slants upward from left to right), the relationship is positive; if it has a negative slope (that is, it slants downward from left to right), the relationship is negative. If the trend line is horizontal or the points are scattered without any recognizable pattern, the relationship is neutral, meaning that no linear correlation exists between the variables.

WARNING

When you encounter scatter plots and line graphs with more than two variables, make sure you keep your variables straight. So, if you're asked a question about garbage production, using Figure 4-15, you have to use the data represented by the left vertical axis and the diamond symbol rather than the right vertical axis and the squares.

Like bar graphs, line graphs display approximate values. Use the technique explained in the earlier section, "Simple bar graphs," to help you estimate the values associated with each data point from the axes labels and grid marks on these graphs.

Perusing stem-and-leaf plots

A *stem-and-leaf plot* is a visual display of data in which each data value is separated into two parts: a stem and a leaf. For a given data value, the leaf is the last digit and the stem is the remaining digits. For example, for the data value 49, 4 is the stem and 9 is the leaf. When you create a stem-and-leaf plot, include a *legend* that explains what is represented by the stem and leaf so that the reader can interpret the information in the plot; for example, 4|9 = 49. Note that a useful feature of a stem-and-leaf plot is that the original data is retained and displayed in the plot. Usually, the stems are listed vertically (from least to greatest), and the corresponding leaves for the data values are listed horizontally (from least to greatest) beside the appropriate stem. Figure 4-16 shows an example.

**Ages of 40 People Who Joined
the Fit-Past-Forty Club in February**

Stem	Leaf
4	1 2 6 8 9
5	1 1 2 3 3 6 7 7 7 7 7 8 9
6	0 0 3 3 4 4 5 6 8 8 9
7	0 1 2 3 5 7 8
8	0 1
9	0 3

Legend: 4|9 = 49

FIGURE 4-16: Stem-and-leaf plot.

According to the graphic, the range of the ages of the people who joined the health club in February is $93 - 41 = 52$ years.

Clarifying circle graphs (also known as pie charts)

Circle graphs, also known as *pie charts*, show values that are part of a larger whole, such as percentages. The graphs contain divisions called *sectors*, which divide the circle into portions that are proportional to the quantity each represents as part of the whole 360-degree circle. Each sector becomes a piece of the *pie*; you get information and compare values by examining the pieces in relation to each other and to the whole pie.

When a graphics interpretation question provides you with a circle graph and designates the percentage values of each of its sectors, you can use it to figure out actual quantities. The circle graph in Figure 4-17 tells you that Plainfield has more Republican affiliates than Democrat and that Democrats constitute just over twice as many Plainfield residents as Independents do.

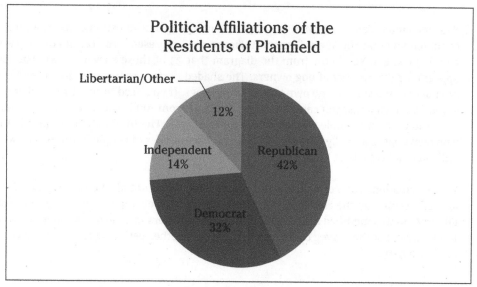

FIGURE 4-17:
Circle graph
or pie chart.

© John Wiley & Sons, Inc.

When you know one of the quantities in a circle graph, you can find the value of other quantities. For example, if a multi-source reasoning IR question provides you with both the scatter plot in Figure 4-13 and the circle graph in Figure 4-17 and tells you that the city of Plainfield is the city in Figure 4-13 with the highest population, you can use information from both graphs to discover the approximate number of Plainfield residents who are registered Democrats. The city with the largest population in Figure 4-13 has around 500,000 residents. Figure 4-17 tells you that 32 percent of Plainfield residents are Democrats. So just about 160,000 ($=500,000 \times 0.32$) Democrats reside in Plainfield.

Venturing into Venn diagrams

Venn diagrams, like the one depicted in Figure 4-18, consist of interconnected circles — typically, two or three in number — and are a great way to show relationships that exist among sets of data. Each circle represents a distinct data set while the overlap among the circles visually demonstrates the connections among the data.

Individuals Surveyed: 100

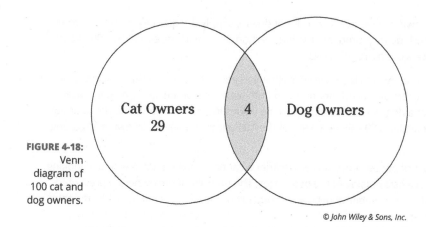

FIGURE 4-18:
Venn
diagram of
100 cat and
dog owners.

© John Wiley & Sons, Inc.

You encounter Venn diagrams in graphics-interpretation questions. For example, the GMAT could tell you that the Venn diagram in Figure 4-18 represents the results of a survey of 100 cat and dog owners. You know from the diagram that 33 of those surveyed own cats, but no value appears for the number of dog owners. The shaded portion represents the intersection: the four members of the survey who own both cats and dogs. If you need to find the number of those surveyed who own dogs, you can't simply subtract 33 from 100 because that doesn't take into consideration the four people who own both types of pets. The total number of people in the survey who own dogs is actually $(100 - 33) + 4$, or 71. The number of people in the survey who own dogs only, and not cats, is $71 - 4$, or 67.

Your calculations can get a little more complicated when not all the members of the general set are represented by the circles in the Venn diagram. For example, say the survey represented in Figure 4-18 was modified a bit to represent 100 pet owners instead of 100 cat and dog owners. The 100 members of the survey could own cats, dogs, or other pets. The results of this survey appear in Figure 4-19.

Individuals Surveyed: 100

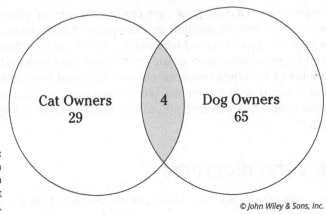

FIGURE 4-19:
Venn
diagram
of 100 pet
owners.

© John Wiley & Sons, Inc.

Based on this diagram, the GMAT could pose questions that ask for the number of people who own only cats but not dogs, the number of people who own at least one cat or one dog, or the number of those surveyed who own neither a cat nor a dog. Here's how you'd solve for these three cases:

>> The number of pet owners who own cats but not dogs is simply the quantity in the cat-owner circle that doesn't include the number in the intersection of the two circles. Of the 100 people surveyed, 29 own cats but don't own dogs.

>> The total number of cat owners is 33, which is what you get when you add the 4 cat and dog owners to the 29 owners of cats but not dogs. To find how many of the surveyed pet owners own at least a cat or a dog, you just need to add the values in each circle and add the quantity in the shaded intersection: $(29 + 65) + 4 = 98$. Of the 100 people surveyed, 98 own at least one cat or one dog.

>> Figuring the number of pet owners who own neither a cat nor a dog means that you're looking for the quantity that exists outside of the two circles. The number of pet owners represented inside the circles plus the number of pet owners outside of the circles is equal to 100, the total number of pet owners surveyed. You know the number of people represented by the space inside the circle; it's the same number as those who own at least a cat or a dog (98). The number of pet owners who don't have a cat or a dog is simply $100 - 98$ or 2.

So to evaluate Venn diagrams correctly, keep track of the total members in the set and what they represent. Information in the question will allow you to assess whether the circles represent the total number of members or whether a subset of members resides outside of the circle, so reading carefully will allow you to accurately interpret the Venn diagram. When you've successfully figured out the general set and the subsets, extracting information from Venn diagrams is easy.

Taking on Data Sufficiency Questions

As noted earlier, in the section "Knowing What to Expect: Four Key Integrated Reasoning Question Types," the Data Insights section of the GMAT consists of five types of questions: table analysis, two-part analysis, graphics interpretation, multi-source reasoning, and data sufficiency. The first four types were extensively discussed in that previous section. This section focuses specifically on data sufficiency questions, which have a format that's unique to the GMAT.

Data sufficiency questions can be manageable if you familiarize yourself with effective approaches before you encounter them on the GMAT. However, if you don't know much about these questions, getting confused and making careless mistakes is easy. Fortunately, you've decided to read this book to get a sneak peek. Thereafter, your knowledge should be more than sufficient for data sufficiency!

You don't need the solution to find the answer

Unlike the traditional math problems you've seen throughout your life, data sufficiency questions don't actually require you to solve the problem. Instead, you have to analyze the data in two statements and determine whether at some point there is *sufficient* information for you to answer the question.

For each data sufficiency problem, you have a question and two statements, labeled (1) and (2). Your job is to decide whether each of the statements gives you enough information to answer the question using general math skills and everyday facts (such as the number of days in a week and the meaning of *clockwise*). If you need a refresher in the math concepts tested on the GMAT, review Block 3. And if you need help analyzing tables, graphs, and similar data representations, check out the section earlier in this block called "Extracting Insights from Graphic Data."

WARNING

Don't make foolish assumptions when you answer data sufficiency questions. Keep in mind that your job is to determine whether the information given is sufficient, not to try to make up for the lack of data! You're used to having to come up with an answer to every math problem, so if the statements lack just a little information, you may be tempted to stretch the data to reach a solution. Don't give in to temptation. Deal only with the information expressly as it's stated, without making unwarranted assumptions.

The five answer choices for data sufficiency questions are the same for each question:

(A) Statement (1) *alone* is sufficient, but Statement (2) *alone* is *not* sufficient.

(B) Statement (2) *alone* is sufficient, but Statement (1) *alone* is *not* sufficient.

(C) *Both* statements *together* are sufficient, but *neither* statement *alone* is sufficient.

(D) *Each* statement *alone* is sufficient.

(E) Statements (1) and (2) *together* are *not* sufficient.

The computer doesn't actually designate the answer choices with the letters A through E, but the choices appear in this order (you choose the correct one with your mouse or keyboard), and we refer to them as A, B, C, D, and E to make the discussion simpler.

It's possible that just one of the statements gives enough data to answer the question, that the two statements taken together solve the problem, that both statements alone provide sufficient data, or that neither statement solves the problem, even with the information provided by the other one. That's a lot of information to examine and apply in two minutes and fifteen seconds—the average time per question for the Data Insights questions! Don't worry. You can overcome brain block by following a step-by-step approach to these questions.

Steps to approaching data sufficiency questions

Take a methodical approach to answering data sufficiency questions, and follow this series of steps:

1. **Evaluate the question to make sure you know exactly what you're supposed to solve.**

Read the initial information and the question carefully. If you can, decide what kind of information you need to solve the problem.

2. **Examine one of the statements and determine whether the data in that one statement is enough to answer the question.**

Start with the first statement or whichever one seems easier to evaluate. Record your conclusion on the note board.

3. **Examine the other statement and determine whether it has enough information to answer the question.**

While performing this step, ignore information given in the statement you started with. Record your conclusion on the note board.

4. **Evaluate what you've written on your note board.**

- If you recorded *yes* for both statements, pick the fourth answer, which we designate as Choice (D).

- If you recorded *yes* for (1) and *no* for (2), select the first answer, Choice (A) in this book.

- If you recorded *no* for (1) and *yes* for (2), choose the second answer, Choice (B) for our purposes.

- If you've written *no* for both statements, go on to the next step.

5. **Consider the statements together to determine whether the data given in both is enough information to answer the question.**

- If the answer is *yes,* select the third answer, Choice (C).

- If the answer is *no,* choose the last answer, Choice (E).

You can boil this method down to a nice, neat chart, like the one shown in Figure 4-20.

Don't think *too* hard about whether an answer provides sufficient information to solve a problem. Data sufficiency questions aren't necessarily designed to trick you. For example, you deal only with real numbers in these questions, and if a line graph looks slanted, it is.

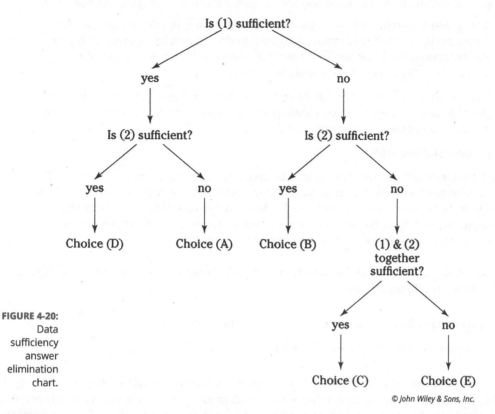

FIGURE 4-20:
Data
sufficiency
answer
elimination
chart.

© *John Wiley & Sons, Inc.*

TIP

A statement is sufficient to answer the question if it provides only one possible answer for the question. If the information in a statement allows for two or more answers, the statement isn't sufficient.

EXAMPLE

David and Karena were among a group of runners who were raising money for a local charity. If David and Karena together raised $900 in the charity race, how much of the money did Karena raise?

1. David raised $\frac{4}{5}$ as much money as Karena did.

2. David raised 5 percent of the total money raised at the event.

Use the steps and/or the chart in Figure 4-20 to solve the problem:

1. Know what you have to solve for.

The question asks you to figure out how much money Karena raised for charity. The question gives you the total money raised by David and Karena together ($D + K = \$900$) but doesn't specify how much David raised. Check out the statements to see whether either or both of them let you know how much David came up with. If you have David's amount, you only need to subtract it from $900 to get Karena's amount.

2. Examine Statement (1) to determine whether it lets you solve for Karena's total.

You determined that you needed data that would allow you to separate the money raised by Karena from that raised by David. Knowing that David raised $\frac{4}{5}$ as much money as Karena allows you to set up a formula to solve for Karena's portion. Let K stand for Karena's contribution and substitute $\frac{4}{5}K$ for D in the equation $D + K = \$900$. Your new equation is

$\frac{4}{5}K + K = \$900$. This equation has only one variable, and that variable stands for how much Karena raised. Therefore, you know you can solve the problem by using just the data from Statement (1). You don't need to actually figure out what K stands for. Just write (1) is *yes* on your note board. You know that the correct answer is either Choice (A) or Choice (D), but you have to look at Statement (2) to know which.

TIP If a question like this one appears at the end of the section and you're pressed for time, you can guess between choices (A) and (D), knowing that you have a 50 percent chance of answering correctly without even reading Statement (2).

3. **Examine Statement (2).**

Statement (2) tells you that David raised 5 percent of the total money raised at the event. The question doesn't tell you how much total money was raised at the event, so you can't use this information to figure out how much David raised. And if you don't know how much David raised, you can't figure out how much Karena raised. Jot down (2) is *no* on the note board. Because (1) is *yes* and (2) is *no*, the answer has to be Choice (A).

TIP If you've read both statements and determined that either Statement (1) or Statement (2) is sufficient alone, two things are true:

>> You're done with the question and can move on to the next one.

>> The answer can't be Choice (C) or Choice (E).

Both Choices (C) and (E) apply to the statements when they're considered together. You don't need to consider the statements together if either statement is sufficient alone. Your only possible choices if *either* statement is sufficient are Choice (A) if only Statement (1) is sufficient, Choice (B) if only Statement (2) is sufficient, and Choice (D) if each statement alone is sufficient.

WARNING Don't evaluate whether both statements together answer the problem unless you've determined that neither is sufficient alone. The only time you consider together is when you've answered *no* to both individual statements. For instance, say the example question replaced Statement (1) with this information: "The event raised a total of $8,000." Statement (1) wouldn't be enough to answer the question. But because Statement (2) tells you that David raised 5 percent of the total event money, you can answer the question using the data from both statements. Statement (1) provides the total amount, and Statement (2) allows you to figure out how much David raised based on that amount. If you subtract that amount from $900, you'll have Karena's total.

Choice (E) would be correct if Statement (1) said, "The event raised more money this year than last year." In this case, neither statement, nor the two together, could answer the question.

Don't waste time trying to come up with the actual numeric answer if you don't have to. When you look at a question like the example, you may be tempted to solve the equation and figure out how much Karena raised. Don't give in! Finding the number just wastes precious time, and no one gives you extra credit for solving the problem! Instead, use your valuable time to solve other questions in the Data Insights section.

EXAMPLE Office Solutions employs both male and female workers who work either full time or part time. What percentage of its employees work part time?

1. Twenty percent of the female employees at Office Solutions work part time.

2. Thirty percent of the workforce at Office Solutions is male.

Decide whether the statements are sufficient for answering the question, and then select one of the answer choices that follow.

(A) Statement (1) *alone* is sufficient, but Statement (2) *alone* is *not* sufficient.

(B) Statement (2) *alone* is sufficient, but Statement (1) *alone* is *not* sufficient.

(C) *Both* Statements *together* are sufficient, but *neither* statement *alone* is sufficient.

(D) *Each* statement *alone* is sufficient.

(E) Statements (1) and (2) *together* are *not* sufficient.

Here's an example of how word problems may appear as data sufficiency questions. Apply the steps in the same way you do for solving linear equations:

1. Find out what to solve for.

The question asks you to find the percentage of part-time employees at Office Solutions. You know two facts at this point: (1) Office Solutions employs a certain number of males (m) and a certain number of females (f), and (2) a certain number of employees work either full time (F) or part time (P). That undertaking creates four unknown variables. The question doesn't tell you anything about how many total people (T) Office Solutions employs, so you have another unknown. Here's what you know in mathematical terms: $F + P = T$ and $f + m = T$.

2. Examine Statement (1).

The first statement gives you the percentage of female part-time employees but tells you nothing about the percentage of male part-time employees. It takes care of only two of the unknown variables; you're missing half of what you need to solve the problem. Statement (1) isn't sufficient. Write (1) is *no* on the note board, and eliminate choices (A) and (D).

3. Examine Statement (2).

This statement concerns male employees at Office Solutions, but not females, so it's insufficient by itself. Record your finding as (2) is *no*. The answer can't be Choice (B).

4. Evaluate what you've written on your note board.

You have double *no*s, so consider Statement (2)'s sufficiency when paired with Statement (1).

5. Consider the two statements together.

One statement provides a percentage for females and the other offers a percentage for males. You may be on your way to finding the percentage for both.

WARNING

Read the statements carefully. You may be tempted to think that Statement (2) offers the other half of the solution, but this statement tells you the percentage of *all* males who work at the company, not just the ones who work part time.

You can't determine the total percentage of part-time workers if you don't know the ratio of male full-time to male part-time workers. Neither statement is sufficient and the two together don't cut it. *Correct answer:* Choice (E).

BLOCK 5
Taking a (Shortened) Practice Test

Practice is crucial for performing well on the GMAT. This short practice test consists of three sections: Data Insights, Quantitative, and Verbal. Each section has a time limit of 20 minutes, and you're free to complete them in any order that you choose. However, keep in mind that after you start a section, you cannot move on to the next one until time for that section expires. In total, you're required to answer eight Data Insights questions, nine Quantitative questions, and ten Verbal questions within the allotted time for each.

After you complete the test, check your answers with the answer key and read the answer explanations in the "Answers and Explanations" section at the end of this block.

Section 1: Data Insights

TIME: 20 minutes for 8 questions

DIRECTIONS: Choose the best answer from the five choices provided.

Climate Description: Jorworth is a city in the foothills of a large mountain range. It has a semi-arid climate and receives significantly more rainfall during the summer months than the winter. Brief afternoon thunderstorms are common in July and August when the city receives its heaviest rainfall. The city experiences drastic day-to-day variability of weather conditions due to its location next to a mountain range. During the winter, Jorworth receives an annual average of 42 inches of snow.

Within the mountain range that surrounds Jorworth, is a nearby city called Vocton. Vocton has a humid climate and receives more evenly distributed rainfall throughout the year than Jorworth. Vocton also receives significantly more snowfall than Jorworth, with an annual average of 176 inches.

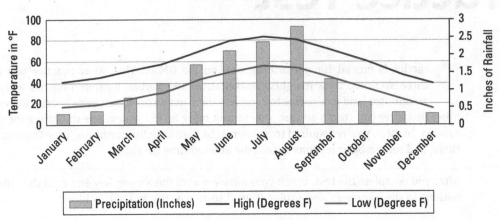

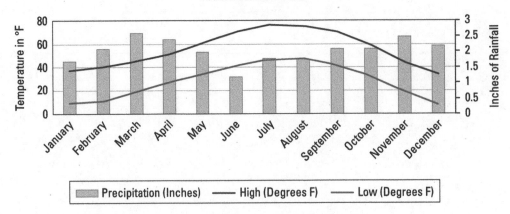

1. For each of the following statements, select whether the validity of the statement can or cannot be determined based on the information given in the sources.

Can Be Determined	Cannot Be Determined	
○	○	Jorworth receives more average annual rainfall than Vocton.
○	○	The average low temperature in July is lower in Vocton than in Jorworth.
○	○	Thunderstorms are common in Vocton during its rainiest months.

2. The following table shows the number of items sold at a store throughout a given week:

	Books	Games	Computers	Movies	Appliances	Furniture
Sunday	34	13	1	51	0	20
Monday	46	31	0	42	1	7
Tuesday	81	18	3	62	0	5
Wednesday	72	27	6	37	2	13
Thursday	78	16	3	48	1	6
Friday	63	14	4	36	0	19
Saturday	79	17	12	60	3	24

For each of the following statements, select whether the statement is consistent or inconsistent with the information given in the table.

Consistent	Inconsistent	
○	○	Average furniture sales were lower on weekend days than on weekdays.
○	○	The day with the highest number of books sold also had the highest number of movies sold.
○	○	The total number of appliances sold throughout the week was less than the total number of games sold throughout the week.

GO ON TO NEXT PAGE

3. The following graph shows the distribution of blood types among a population. There are four blood groups: A, B, AB, and O. Each blood group is further divided into positive and negative to differentiate the eight different blood types.

BLOOD TYPE

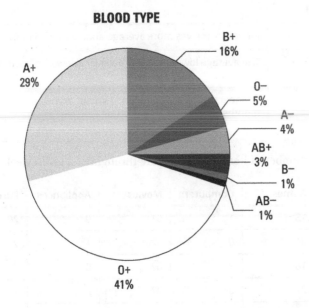

Refer to the pie chart to complete BOTH of the following statements.

If a member of the population is chosen at random, the chance that they will have neither type A nor a negative type of blood is:

(A) 21%

(B) 57%

(C) 60%

(D) 71%

There are more members of the population with type _____ blood than type O blood.

(A) A

(B) A or AB

(C) A or B

(D) B or AB

4. Richard mixes 4 ounces of each of three beverages to create a 12-ounce drink. Any flavor that is present in one of the beverages he mixes will also be present in his final drink. He is developing two new mixtures: a daytime and a nighttime drink. For his daytime drink, Richard wants something sweet with a caffeine content of at least 80 milligrams (mg). For his nighttime drink, Richard wants something herbal with a caffeine content of less than 60 mg. Richard only mixes a maximum of two beverages that have a common flavor.

Following are the beverages that Richard uses to create his drinks, each listing the flavors they will add to his mixture and the caffeine content in 8 fluid ounces.

- **Mack's Cola (Sweet & Spicy, 20 mg caffeine)**
- **Fizzer Soda (Citrus & Sweet, 60 mg caffeine)**
- **Lemonade (Citrus & Sour, 0 mg caffeine)**
- **Orange Juice (Citrus & Sweet, 0 mg caffeine)**
- **Green Tea (Earthy & Herbal, 50 mg caffeine)**
- **Oolong Tea (Herbal & Sweet, 70 mg caffeine)**
- **Coffee (Bitter & Earthy, 100 mg caffeine)**

Select the mix of ingredients Richard used in his daytime drink and the mix of ingredients he used in his nighttime drink.

Daytime Drink	Nighttime Drink	
○	○	Mack's Cola, Fizzer Soda, and Green Tea
○	○	Mack's Cola, Oolong Tea, and Coffee
○	○	Mack's Cola, Lemonade, and Orange Juice
○	○	Fizzer Soda, Lemonade, and Green Tea
○	○	Fizzer Soda, Orange Juice, and Oolong Tea
○	○	Lemonade, Green Tea, and Coffee

Elephant Lifespan Study: Over the last 50 years, a study was conducted on elephant lifespans in the wild and in captivity. The goal of the study was to document the quantitative effects of captivity on elephant lifespans, as well as to understand some of the reasons that lifespans were affected.

The elephants in the wild were found to face greater threats from poachers, lack of food, and natural disasters. While these threats were not present for the elephants in captivity, they faced issues of their own. Some of the elephants were kept in small, confined spaces without enough space to maintain the full range of activity that they would enjoy in the wild. When the elephants were born in captivity, they weren't always left with their mother as long as they would have been in the wild. Oftentimes, elephants were transported to a new zoo or habitat in less than ideal conditions. All of these factors had contributing effects on the lifespans of the animals studied.

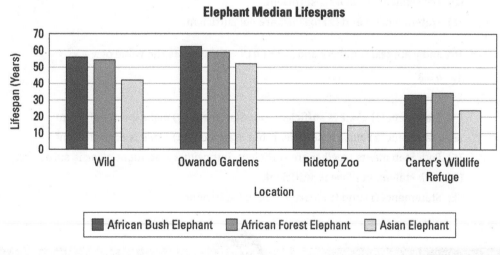

5. For each of the following statements, if the statement is supported by the sources, select *Supported*. Otherwise, select *Not Supported*.

Supported	Not Supported	
○	○	Half of the elephants studied at Owando Gardens had a lifespan of at least 50 years.
○	○	The elephants' lifespans were reduced in captivity due to natural disasters.
○	○	None of the elephants studied at Ridgetop Zoo lived longer than 20 years.

6. Suppose a jar contains 24 tokens, each of which is blue, green, orange, or red, all identical except for color. If a token is randomly drawn from the jar, what is the probability that the token drawn is blue or orange?

   1. The probability is $\frac{1}{2}$ that the token drawn is green or red.

   2. The probability is $\frac{1}{3}$ that the token drawn is orange.

   (A) Statement (1) *alone* is sufficient, but Statement (2) *alone* is *not* sufficient.

   (B) Statement (2) *alone* is sufficient, but Statement (1) *alone* is *not* sufficient.

   (C) *Both* Statements *together* are sufficient, but *neither* statement *alone* is sufficient.

   (D) *Each* statement *alone* is sufficient.

   (E) Statements (1) and (2) *together* are *not* sufficient.

7. Joe uses three different modes of transportation to travel a total of 225 kilometers to visit his aunt. How many kilometers does Joe travel by bus?

   1. Joe rides his bike 5 kilometers to the bus station where he boards the bus to take him to the train station. He then takes the train 10 times the distance he has traveled by bus.

   2. The distance Joe travels by bike is $\frac{1}{4}$ the distance he travels by bus, and his train ride is 40 times longer than his bike ride.

   (A) Statement (1) *alone* is sufficient, but Statement (2) *alone* is *not* sufficient.

   (B) Statement (2) *alone* is sufficient, but Statement (1) *alone* is *not* sufficient.

   (C) *Both* Statements *together* are sufficient, but *neither* statement *alone* is sufficient.

   (D) *Each* statement *alone* is sufficient.

   (E) Statements (1) and (2) *together* are *not* sufficient.

8. If x and y are real numbers and $(a)^{2x}(a)^{2y} = 81$, what is the value of $x + y$?

   1. $a = 3$
   2. $x = y$

   (A) Statement (1) *alone* is sufficient, but Statement (2) *alone* is *not* sufficient.

   (B) Statement (2) *alone* is sufficient, but Statement (1) *alone* is *not* sufficient.

   (C) *Both* Statements *together* are sufficient, but *neither* statement *alone* is sufficient.

   (D) *Each* statement *alone* is sufficient.

   (E) Statements (1) and (2) *together* are *not* sufficient.

DO NOT TURN THE PAGE UNTIL TOLD TO DO SO **STOP** **DO NOT RETURN TO A PREVIOUS TEST**

Section 2: Quantitative

TIME: 20 minutes for 9 questions

DIRECTIONS: Choose the best answer from the five choices provided.

$$\frac{10xy + 15x}{2y + 3} + 3y = 1$$

1. If $x = 4$ and $y \neq -1.5$, what is the value of y?

   (A) $-\frac{19}{3}$

   (B) $-\frac{3}{19}$

   (C) $\frac{3}{19}$

   (D) $\frac{1}{3}$

   (E) $\frac{19}{3}$

2. A stand at a farmer's market is selling peaches individually and in cartons. An individual peach costs $1. When bought in a carton of 30, the price of each peach is discounted by 10 percent. Since it is the end of the growing season, there is a sale going on where the price is further discounted by 60 percent. What is the price of two cartons of peaches?

   (A) $9.00

   (B) $10.80

   (C) $18.00

   (D) $21.60

   (E) $32.40

3. The table shows the peak price each year for stocks from five different companies. Which stock had the greatest increase in peak price from Year 1 to Year 3?

	Year 1	Year 2	Year 3	Year 4	Year 5
OMK	$5.12	$6.86	$9.12	$6.20	$7.31
RRW	$30.51	$32.84	$45.18	$40.08	$47.12
LKP	$15.12	$25.32	$32.10	$31.12	$34.19
AWL	$130.54	$162.18	$154.96	$151.83	$183.39
TCK	$62.48	$71.31	$73.99	$79.42	$83.14

   (A) OMK

   (B) RRW

   (C) LKP

   (D) AWL

   (E) TCK

GO ON TO NEXT PAGE

4. If $y = 1$, what is the value of the following expression: $(4^{y+z})(16)(4^{-z})$?

(A) 4

(B) 16

(C) 64

(D) 128

(E) 256

5. When $x \neq 0$, $\left(\dfrac{2}{x} + \dfrac{1}{3}\right)\left(\dfrac{x}{2}\right)$ can be simplified to which one of the following?

(A) $1 + \dfrac{x}{6}$

(B) $\dfrac{3x - 2}{3}$

(C) $\dfrac{1}{6} + x$

(D) $\dfrac{1}{3}$

(E) $\dfrac{3x}{2x + 6}$

6. If $x - y = 8$ and $5x + y = -8$, then $x + y =$

(A) -2

(B) -8

(C) 2

(D) 3

(E) 8

7. If $y = \dfrac{x}{2}$ and $x \neq 0$, which one of the following is equal to $\dfrac{y}{2x} + \dfrac{x}{4}$?

(A) $\dfrac{4x^2 + x}{4}$

(B) $\dfrac{x + 1}{4}$

(C) $\dfrac{x + 4}{2x}$

(D) $x^2 + 1$

(E) $\dfrac{1}{4}$

8. Anthony runs a business manufacturing machine parts. If Anthony's business manufactured 80,000 machine parts last year and 88,000 machine parts this year, how many parts must the business produce next year to maintain the same percent growth from year to year?

(A) 88,000

(B) 88,800

(C) 96,000

(D) 96,800

(E) 100,000

9. Patrick and Mel are each selling shirts at a rock concert to promote their favorite bands. It costs each of them the same amount to produce each shirt. Mel is selling her shirts for $60. If Patrick is making 20 percent more profit than Mel, and his profit is $24 per shirt, how much is Patrick charging for his shirts?

(A) $48.00

(B) $62.00

(C) $64.00

(D) $68.80

(E) $72.00

Section 3: Verbal

TIME: 20 minutes for 10 questions

DIRECTIONS: Follow these directions for each of the two question types:

- **Reading comprehension questions:** Choose the best answer to every question based on what the passage states directly or indirectly.

- **Critical reasoning questions:** Pick the answer choice that best answers the question about the argument provided.

Questions 1–6 refer to the following passage, which is excerpted from *Playing against Nature: Integrating Science and Economics to Mitigate Natural Hazards in an Uncertain World,* by Seth Stein and Jerome Stein (John Wiley & Sons, Inc. 2014).

Natural hazards are the price we pay for living on an active planet. The tectonic plate subduction producing Japan's rugged Tohoku coast gives rise to earthquakes and tsunamis. Florida's warm sunny weather results from the processes in the ocean and atmosphere that cause hurricanes. The volcanoes that produced Hawaii's spectacular islands sometimes threaten people. Rivers that provide the water for the farms that feed us sometimes flood.

Humans have to live with natural hazards. We describe this challenge in terms of hazards, the natural occurrence of earthquakes or other phenomena, and the risks, or dangers they pose to lives and property. In this formulation, the risk is the product of hazard and vulnerability. We want to assess the hazards — estimate how significant they are — and develop methods to mitigate or reduce the resulting losses.

Hazards are geological facts that are not under human control. All we can do is try to assess them as best we can. In contrast, risks are affected by human actions that increase or decrease vulnerability, such as where people live and how they build. We increase vulnerability by building in hazardous areas, and decrease it by making buildings more hazard resistant. Areas with high hazard can have low risk because few people live there. Areas of modest hazard can have high risk due to large population and poor construction. A disaster occurs when — owing to high vulnerability — a natural event has major consequences for society.

The harm from natural disasters is enormous. On average, about 100,000 people per year are killed by natural disasters, with some disasters — such as the 2004 Indian Ocean tsunami — causing many more deaths. Although the actual numbers of deaths in many events, such as the 2010 Haiti earthquake, are poorly known, they are very large.

Economic impacts are even harder to quantify, and various measures are used to try to do so. Disasters cause losses, which are the total negative economic impact. These include direct losses due to destruction of physical assets such as buildings, farmland, forests, etc., and indirect losses that result from the direct losses. Because losses are hard to determine, what is reported is often the cost, which refers to payouts by insurers (called insured losses) or governments to reimburse some of the losses. Thus, the reported cost does not reflect the losses to people who do not receive such payments.

1. The main idea of the first paragraph is best expressed as

   (A) the factors that make an area desirable are also those that can pose the most risk.
   (B) the Hawaiian Islands would not exist if not for powerful and explosive volcanoes.
   (C) floods, volcanoes, and earthquakes pose threats to the natural environment.
   (D) humans must learn to live with natural hazards such as volcanoes and tsunamis.
   (E) natural hazards are most prevalent in areas that are sunny and warm.

2. Which one of the following might the author of the passage consider an "indirect loss" associated with a disaster?

   (A) Desecration of a library due to vandalism
   (B) Damage to a school building in a fire
   (C) Loss of retail clothing sales due to a mall flood
   (D) Death of a ranch's livestock due to a volcanic eruption
   (E) Destruction of a pavilion due to a hurricane

3. According to the passage, an important distinction between hazards and risks is

   (A) risks occur naturally, while hazards arise because of human actions.
   (B) hazards result from risks, and risks result from vulnerability.
   (C) hazards can lead to disasters, while risks cannot.
   (D) hazards are not under human control, while risks usually are.
   (E) risks are harder to quantify than hazards.

4. The passage is primarily concerned with

   (A) describing the causes and impacts of natural disasters.
   (B) assessing the impact that disasters render on the global economy.
   (C) depicting the various ways human beings may endanger themselves.
   (D) raising awareness of the loss of human lives due to the severity and unpredictability of natural disasters.
   (E) explaining that natural disasters are not under human control.

5. Which one of the following best describes the purpose of the fourth paragraph in relation to the passage as a whole?

   (A) It uses numerical data and metrics to describe the economic impacts of natural disasters.
   (B) It emphasizes how little is known about how many lives are lost in natural disasters.
   (C) It outlines the differences between hazards and risks to set up information detailed in the remainder of the passage.
   (D) It provides sensory details about specific recent natural disasters that may be familiar to readers to evoke an emotional response.
   (E) It applies statistical data to emphasize the magnitude of damage created by natural disasters.

GO ON TO NEXT PAGE

6. Which one of the following logically follows the information given in the passage?

  (A) The number of unreported deaths in the 2010 Haitian earthquake exceeded the number of unreported deaths in the 2004 Indian Ocean tsunami.

  (B) In the years 2010 and 2004, there were more deaths than average due to natural disasters.

  (C) The number of deaths due to natural disasters along Japan's tectonic plate is greater on average than those experienced on islands such as Hawaii or Haiti.

  (D) Economic costs are more frequently unreported than numbers of deaths in any given natural disaster.

  (E) Areas of high hazard, such as Japan's Tohoku coast, may have a lower risk of natural disaster costs than areas where hazard incidents are lower.

7. The size of oceanic waves is a function of the velocity of the wind and of *fetch*, the length of the surface of the water subject to those winds. The impact of waves against a coastline is a function of the size of the waves and the shape of the sea bottom. The degree of erosion to which a coastline is subject is a function of the average impact of waves and the geologic composition of the coastline.

If these statements are true, which one of the following must also be true?

  (A) The degree of erosion to which a coastline is subject is related to the shape of the sea bottom.

  (B) The size of oceanic waves will not fluctuate far from an average for any given stretch of ocean.

  (C) The fetch of winds is related to the shape of the sea bottom.

  (D) The size of oceanic waves is related to the shape of the sea bottom.

  (E) The average velocity of the wind in an area plays no role in the degree of erosion to which a coastline is subject.

8. Health insurers are largely immune to the factors that are limiting profit in many sectors of the healthcare economy. Consumers have shown a willingness to pay almost any price for health insurance premiums. Capital demands, which are the responsibility of doctors and hospitals, are increasing dramatically, even as cost-containment measures, largely encouraged by the insurers and their friends in government, have forced new levels of fiscal discipline upon hospitals and doctors. Patients still need MRI scans and buildings to conduct them in, but hospitals are limited in how much they can charge patients for the use of these facilities.

Which one of the following most accurately describes the role that the statement "patients still need MRI scans and buildings to conduct them in" plays in the argument?

  (A) It is a specific example of a general condition described during the argument.

  (B) It is used to counter a consideration that may be taken to undermine the argument.

  (C) It is used to indirectly support the claim made by the argument.

  (D) It describes a social side effect of the benefit with which the argument is concerned.

  (E) It introduces the conclusion that the argument intends to support.

9. Forcing businesses to furnish employees with paid leave for family concerns, such as family leave or leave to care for a sick child, is a terrible idea. If a business allows employees to take this time off, the workers will take advantage of the privilege and come to work as little as possible. This will destroy productivity and workplace morale.

Which one of the following, if true, most seriously weakens the argument?

(A) European countries guarantee employees generous family leave and paid vacation time, but the European standard of living is slightly below that of the United States.

(B) Most male workers refuse to take family leave even though it is allowed under federal law and their employers encourage it; they fear they may anger co-workers and harm their chances for promotion if they take time off for what is still seen as a frivolous reason.

(C) The Family and Medical Leave Act requires employers to grant employees 12 weeks a year of unpaid leave for family purposes; although employers save money because the leave is unpaid, they often must spend money to find a replacement for the employee who takes time off.

(D) In some workplaces, the loss of a single employee at a busy time of year can be devastating, even if that employee plans to return after a few weeks; allowing family leave can overwhelm the employees who stay on the job.

(E) Allowing employees to take leave for family matters reduces absenteeism, improves morale, and surprisingly increases productivity because the employees who are granted leave tend to work much harder and more efficiently when they come back to work.

10. Software engineers know that a poorly written application can consume more memory than it should and that running out of memory can cause an application to crash. However, if a crashing application causes the whole operating system to crash, the fault lies with the operating system.

Which one of the following, if true, is least helpful in establishing that this conclusion is properly drawn?

(A) Operating systems with generous amounts of memory are less susceptible to crashing, even when applications are poorly written.

(B) Operating systems can isolate the memory used by individual applications, even when an application uses a large amount of memory.

(C) An operating system can monitor an application's consumption of memory and act when that consumption gets too high.

(D) Techniques for programming operating systems to catch and manage memory errors are well defined and well known among programmers.

(E) Because many applications can run simultaneously under a single operating system, the operating system should have a well-defined method of managing memory consumption.

Answer and Explanations

Examine the information for the questions you missed as well as those you answered correctly. You may find tips and techniques you haven't thought of before in one of the answer explanations. If you're short on time or just want to quickly check your answers, head to the end of this block for an abbreviated answer key.

Section 1: Data Insights

1. *Statement 1: Jorworth receives more average annual rainfall than Vocton.* **Can be Determined.** Look at the climate data for the two cities to estimate each city's total annual rainfall.

   Jorworth receives about 0.5 inches of rainfall in January, February, March, October, November, and December. This is a total of 3 inches so far. Add 1 inch of rainfall for April, 1.5 inches for May and September, 2 inches in June, and 2.5 inches in July and August for a total of 14 inches. Divide by 12 to get an average of 1.17 inches per month.

   Vocton receives less than 1.5 inches of rainfall in June; most of the other months' rainfall is significantly greater. Therefore, Vocton's monthly average must be higher than 1.17 inches per month, and therefore its annual average rainfall is also higher than Jorworth's. The statement is contradictory to the data, which can be determined from the given sources.

   Statement 2: The average low temperature in July is lower in Vocton than in Jorworth. **Can Be Determined.** Jorworth's average low temperature in July is about 55 degrees. Vocton's average low temperature in July is about 45 degrees — 10 degrees lower than Vocton's.

   Statement 3: Thunderstorms are common in Vocton during its rainiest months. **Cannot Be Determined.** Thunderstorms are mentioned only in the context of Jorworth. Nothing is ever said about thunderstorms in Vocton.

2. *Statement 1: Average furniture sales were lower on weekend days than on weekdays.* **Inconsistent.** The two days with the highest number of furniture sales were Sunday and Saturday, with 20 and 24 sold respectively, so furniture sales were, on average, higher on the weekend than on weekdays.

   Statement 2: The day with the highest number of books sold also had the highest number of movies sold. **Consistent.** The highest number of books was sold on Tuesday, with a total number sold of 81. On Tuesday, 62 movies were sold, which is the highest number of movies sold on any of the days. The data in the table agrees with the statement.

   Statement 3: The total number of appliances sold throughout the week was less than the total number of games sold throughout the week. **Consistent.** Only seven appliances were sold during the week. Many more than seven games were sold, with the lowest number in a day being 13. The data in the table supports the statement.

3. *First Blank: If a member of the population is chosen at random, the chance that they will not have type A or a negative type of blood is* <u>*60 percent*</u>. The types of blood that are not A and are not negative are: O+, 41 percent; B+, 16 percent; AB+, 3 percent. Totaling these three types, you get 60 percent. So, 60 percent of the population has neither an A blood type nor a negative blood type.

   Second Blank: There are more members of the population with type <u>*A or B*</u> *blood than type O blood.* 46 percent of the population has type O blood (41 percent with O+ and 5 percent with O−). The first choice is wrong because only 33 percent of the population has type A blood (29 percent with A+ and 4 percent with A−). The second choice is incorrect because only

37 percent of the population has type A or type AB blood (33 percent with type A, 3 percent with AB+, and 1 percent with AB−). The third choice is correct because 50 percent of the population have type A or B blood (33 percent with type A plus 16 percent with type B+ plus 1 percent with type B−). The fourth choice is incorrect because only 21 percent of the population has type B or AB blood (17 percent with type B and 4 percent with type AB).

4. The daytime drink needs more than 80 mg of caffeine. The only mixture in the list that meets that criterion is Mack's Cola, Oolong Tea, and Coffee with a total caffeine content of $\frac{20mg}{2} + \frac{70mg}{2} + \frac{100mg}{2} = 95mg$ and, thanks to Mack's Cola, it's sweet. The nighttime drink needs to have an herbal flavor, so it must contain either Green Tea or Oolong Tea; that eliminates the third item in the list (Mack's Cola, Lemonade, and Orange Juice). It must have a caffeine content of less than 60mg; the only other mixture on the list that meets that criteria is the fourth selection down — Fizzer Soda, Lemonade, and Green Tea with a caffeine content of $\frac{60mg}{2} + \frac{0mg}{2} + \frac{50mg}{2} = 55mg$.

5. *Statement 1: Half of the elephants studied at Owando Gardens had a lifespan of at least 50 years.* **Supported.** The bar graph for Owando Gardens shows that all elephant species had a lifespan over 50 years. Since half of the elephants studied in each group had a lifespan of greater than 50 years, half of the elephants studied overall at Owando Gardens also did.

Statement 2: The elephants' lifespans were reduced in captivity due to natural disasters. **Not Supported.** The study text states that in the wild elephants faced threats from poachers, lack of food, and natural disasters. It goes on to say that these were not present for animals in captivity. The contributing factors given for animals in captivity do not include natural disasters.

Statement 3: None of the elephants studied at Ridgetop Zoo lived longer than 20 years. **Not Supported.** Although the bar graph for Ridgetop Zoo shows median lifespans for all three elephant species lower than 20 years, they don't indicate the maximum life span of any elephants in those groups. Individuals in each group may have lived longer than 20 years. The data does not tell you enough about the lifespans of the animals studied to prove this statement.

6. **A.** For this problem, you work with probabilities:

   1. **Find out what to solve for.**

      You're asked to find the probability that the token drawn is blue or orange.

   2. **Examine Statement (1).**

      Statement (1) gives you that the probability is $\frac{1}{2}$ that the token drawn is green or red. From this information, you know that $\frac{1}{2}$ of the tokens are green or red. Thus, $\frac{1}{2}$ of the tokens are blue or orange. So, the probability is $\frac{1}{2}$ that the token drawn is blue or orange. Problem solved! Statement (1) is sufficient. Write (1) is *yes* on your note board and eliminate choices (B), (C), and (E). You know that the correct answer is either choice (A) or (D), but you have to assess Statement (2) to know which.

   3. **Examine Statement (2).**

      Statement (2) gives you that the probability is $\frac{1}{3}$ that the token is orange, which tells you that $\frac{1}{3} \times 24 = 8$ of the tokens are orange. However, there is no information about how many of the remaining 16 tokens are blue, green, or red. Without additional information, you cannot obtain an exact value of the probability that the token drawn is blue or orange. Statement (2) is not sufficient. Write (2) is *no* on your note board. Because (1) is *yes* and (2) is *no,* the answer has to be Choice (A).

7. D. This data sufficiency question is essentially a simple addition problem.

1. Find out what to solve for.

You know the total distance Joe travels to his aunt's is 225 kilometers and that he takes different types of transportation, one of which is a bus. Lucky guy! The question asks for the length of Joe's bus ride. That's your unknown, so designate the number of kilometers by bus as x.

2. Examine Statement (1).

From Statement (1), you learn that the other modes of transportation are bike (b) and train (t). Great news! It also tells you the exact length of Joe's bike ride (5 kilometers) and that his train ride is 10 times his bus ride. So $t = 10x$. You can set up an equation with this information: $5 + x + 10x = 225$. The equation has only one variable, the unknown length of the bus ride. You know you can solve a linear equation with only one variable, so Statement (1) is sufficient. Write (1) is *yes* on your note board, and eliminate choices (B), (C), and (E).

3. Examine Statement (2).

Create an equation from the information in the second statement. If Joe's bike ride (b) is $\frac{1}{4}$ as long as his bus ride (x), then $b = \frac{1}{4}x$. If the train trip (t) is 40 times the length of the bike ride (b), then $t = 40b$. This gives simultaneous equations. Substitute $\frac{1}{4}x$ for t in the train ride equation: $t = 40\left(\frac{1}{4}x\right)$. So the equation for the bike ride plus the bus ride plus the train trip is this: $\frac{1}{4}x + x + 40\left(\frac{1}{4}x\right) = 225$

This equation has only one variable, so you know you can solve for x. You don't have to actually solve for x; you just need to know that you can solve for x, to know that Statement (2) is also sufficient. Write (2) is *yes*. So, each statement alone is sufficient. *Correct answer:* Choice (D).

8. A. This question contains a bunch of unknown variables, so you may think you can't solve for much. You may be surprised!

1. Find out what to solve for.

Take a few seconds to evaluate the equation. You're given two factors with exponents, and their product is equal to a perfect square. Both factors have the same base (a), and both contain an exponent with a factor of 2. The problem asks you to find the sum of the other two factors in the exponents of the terms.

2. Examine Statement (1).

From the information in the first statement, you can substitute 3 for a in the equation:

$$(3)^{2x}(3)^{2y} = 81$$

The terms have the same base, so you add the exponents when you multiply the terms:

$$3^{2x+2y} = 81$$

Now extract the common factor in the exponent:

$$3^{2(x+y)} = 81$$

Square 3 to get 9:

$$9^{(x+y)} = 81$$

Because $9^2 = 81$, you know that the exponent $(x + y)$ must equal 2.

You could also find the value of $x + y$ by rewriting 81 as a base and exponent:

$$3^{2x+2y} = 3^4$$

When the bases are equal, the exponents are equal:

$$2x + 2y = 4$$
$$x + y = 2$$

Either way, the information in Statement (1) is sufficient to tell you the value of $x + y$. Write (1) is *yes* on your note board, and eliminate Choices (B), (C), and (E).

3. Examine Statement (2).

This statement tells you that x and y are equal, so you may be tempted to draw from the information in the last statement and assume that x and y each equal 1. Well, that could be true if $a = 3$. But you no longer know that $a = 3$.

WARNING

You can't carry over the information from one statement to evaluate the sufficiency of the other. It's true that x and y could each equal 1, but they could also each equal 0.5. Start fresh with each statement.

If x and y are equal, then you can substitute x for y in the equation, simplify, and solve for a:

$$(a)^{2x}(a)^{2x} = 81$$
$$a^{4x} = 81$$
$$a^{4x} = 3^4$$
$$a^x = 3$$
$$a = \sqrt[x]{3}$$

Since a is equal to the xth root of 3, the possible values of x, y, a, and, of course, $x + y$, are infinite. For example, if $x = 2$, then so does y, and $a = \sqrt{3}$. If x and y each equal 3, then $a = \sqrt[3]{3}$, and so on. Because Statement (2) results in more than one value for $x + y$, it can't be sufficient to answer the question. Write (2) is *no* on your note board. So, Statement (1) alone is sufficient, but Statement (2) alone is not sufficient. *Correct answer:* Choice (A).

Section 2: Quantitative

1. A. $-\dfrac{19}{3}$

This question gives you an equation with variables x and y, and asks you to solve for the value of y. It gives you a value of x and says that $y \neq -1.5$. Looking at the first part of the expression, you may notice that you are able to factor the numerator. Factor out the common factor of $5x$:

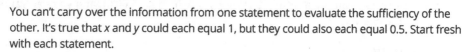

$$\frac{10xy + 15x}{2y + 3} + 3y = 1$$
$$\frac{5x(2y + 3)}{2y + 3} + 3y = 1$$

Because you know that $y \neq -1.5$, you know that the denominator is not equal to 0, so you are able to cancel out the common factor of $(2y + 3)$. Now you have $5x + 3y = 1$.

Rearrange the equation to solve for y:

$$y = \frac{1-5x}{3}$$

When you insert 4 for x, you arrive at the conclusion that $y = -\frac{19}{3}$, Choice (A).

2. D. $21.60

In this price discount problem, you will need to apply multiple price discounts to the original price of the peaches to calculate the final price. The problem tells you that each peach costs $1, so a carton of 30 peaches would therefore cost $30. But the problem says that the price is discounted by 10% when the peaches are bought in a carton of 30. If the discount is 10%, then multiply the cost of the peaches by $1-10\%$, which is 90%. So, two cartons of peaches would be 60 peaches, and the price would be $\$60 \times 90\% = \$54$.

The problem tells you that there is an additional discount of 60%. To apply the additional discount, simply multiply $54 by 40% (which is $1-60\%$), and you get $21.60. Choice (D) is the answer.

3. D. AWL

This data-interpretation question presents you with a table showing peak prices of various stocks over the course of five years. The question is asking you to find which stock had the greatest increase in peak price from Year 1 to Year 3. Looking at the peak prices for OMK, you can see that they were $5.12 in Year 1 and $9.12 in Year 3. This is an increase of $4. Use estimation to evaluate the rest of the table.

Continuing down the table, you can see that the peak price of RRW increased by about $\$45.00 - \$30.00 = \$15.00$, and the peak price of LKP increased by about $\$30.00 - \$15.00 = \$15.00$.

If you don't find an answer with a greater increase, you'll have to evaluate these two options more carefully later. But there are still two more stocks to evaluate. Looking at AWL, its peak price increased by about $\$155.00 - \$130.00 = \$25.00$. AWL is now the highest increase in peak price you've seen and is higher than TCK, which increased from around $62.00 to $74.00, an increase of only about $12.00.

Of all the stocks, the peak price of AWL, Choice (D), increased the most from Year 1 to Year 3.

4. C. 64

This question concerns exponents. You are given an expression and asked for the value of the expression if $y = 1$. Look for a way to make the bases of the terms the same. Because $16 = 4^2$, you can rewrite the expression as

$$4^{y+z} \times 4^2 \times 4^{-z}$$

Since exponents with the same base can be added together, you can simplify the expression to

$$4^{y+z+2-z}$$

The z terms cancel out and you are left with 4^{y+2}. You know that $y = 1$, so the expression becomes 4^3, or 64. The answer is Choice (C).

5. A. $1+\dfrac{x}{6}$

The first fraction involves addition, so you'll need to find a common denominator. The simplest common denominator for 3 and x is $3x$. So, multiply the first fraction by $\dfrac{3}{3}$ and the second fraction by $\dfrac{x}{x}$ to create equivalent fractions that have the common denominator. Then add:

$$\frac{2}{x}+\frac{1}{3}=\frac{6}{3x}+\frac{x}{3x}=\frac{6+x}{3x}$$

Multiply this new fraction by $\dfrac{x}{2}$:

$$\left(\frac{6+x}{3x}\right)\left(\frac{x}{2}\right)=\frac{6x+x^2}{6x}$$

Simplify:

$$\frac{6x+x^2}{6x}=\frac{6x}{6x}+\frac{x^2}{6x}=1+\frac{x}{6}$$

And you're done! The answer is Choice (A).

6. B. -8 To find the value of $x+y$, first, find the value of x by adding the two equations to eliminate y. The equation for the first line is $x-y=8$, and the equation for the second line is $5x+y=-8$:

$$\begin{aligned} x-y &= 8 \\ 5x+y &= -8 \\ \hline 6x &= 0 \\ x &= 0 \end{aligned}$$

When you know that $x=0$, solve for y by substituting x into either equation:

$$\begin{aligned} 5x+y &= -8 \\ 0+y &= -8 \\ y &= -8 \end{aligned}$$

Therefore, $x+y=0+-8=-8$, Choice (B).

7. B. $\dfrac{x+1}{4}$

You are given $y=\dfrac{x}{2}$, so you can insert $\dfrac{x}{2}$ for y in $\dfrac{y}{2x}+\dfrac{x}{4}$ to get the expression solely in terms of x: $\dfrac{y}{2x}+\dfrac{x}{4}=\dfrac{\left(\dfrac{x}{2}\right)}{2x}+\dfrac{x}{4}$. Simplify by performing division in the first fraction: $\dfrac{x}{2}\times\dfrac{1}{2x}=\dfrac{x}{4x}$, which simplifies to $\dfrac{1}{4}$ when you cancel x from the numerator and denominator.

Then add to find the correct answer:

$\dfrac{1}{4}+\dfrac{x}{4}=\dfrac{1+x}{4}=\dfrac{x+1}{4}$, Choice (B).

8. D. 96,800

This is a percent change problem dealing with the number of parts produced in different years. Knowing that Anthony's business made 80,000 parts last year and 88,000 parts this year, you can calculate the percent growth using the percent change formula, which is the difference between the two values divided by the original value, expressed as a percent:

$$\frac{\text{parts produced this year} - \text{parts produced last year}}{\text{parts produced last year}} = \frac{88,000 - 80,000}{80,000} = \frac{8,000}{80,000} = \frac{1}{10} = 10\%$$

To maintain 10% growth next year, the business will need to produce the same number of parts as last year + 10% more, which you can express as 110% or 1.1 of 88,000: $88,000 \times 1.1 = 96,800$, which is Choice (D).

TIP

Make sure you use the new year's value when calculating the percentage increase for the upcoming year. Choice (C) reflects an increase of 8,000 parts, but that amount is 10% of the parts made last year and only about 9.1% of the parts made this year. To maintain 10% growth, the number of additional parts made next year must be greater than this year's.

9. C. $64.00

This is a profit question dealing with two different merchants each selling the same product.

You can eliminate Choice (A) right away. If Patrick makes more profit than Mel, he must be charging more than $60, the price Mel charges for her shirts.

A general equation for the profit of each merchant is that profit (p) is equal to selling price (s) minus cost (c). So, $p = s - c$. You can write a profit equation for each merchant to make solving the question easier. For Mel (M), $p_M = s_M - c_M$. Because Mel is selling her shirts for $60, $s_M = 60$ and $p_M = 60 - c_M$.

For Patrick (P), $p_P = s_P - c_P$. You know that Patrick's profit is $24, so $24 = s_P - c_P$.

If Patrick makes 20% more profit than Mel, then $p_P = 120\%(p_M) = 1.2(p_M)$. Find Mel's profit by substituting $24 for p_P in the equation:

$$24 = (1.2)p_M$$
$$\frac{24}{1.2} = p_M$$
$$20 = p_M$$

After you know Mel's profit is $20 per shirt, you can find the cost of her shirt:

$$p_M = 60 - c_m$$
$$20 = 60 - c_m$$
$$-40 = -c_m$$
$$40 = c_m$$

Because you know Patrick and Mel have the same shirt cost, you can now find out how much Patrick sells his shirt for:

$$p_P = s_P - c_P$$
$$24 = s_P - 40$$
$$64 = s_P$$

Patrick sells his shirt for $64.00, Choice (C).

Section 3: Verbal

1. **A. The factors that make an area desirable are also those that can pose the most risk.**

   The substantiating details in the paragraph describe situations where those factors that create desirable areas such as the Toboku coast, Florida, Hawaii, and productive farmlands are the same factors that create great destruction, so Choice (A) is the best answer.

   Choice (B) is too specific. Choice (C) mentions the destructive forces in the paragraph but not the concomitant desirability of the environments they also cause. Choice (D) requires too much speculation. The paragraph states that humans pay a price for living on Earth, but it doesn't state the requirement that they learn to live with the risks. The paragraph is less about humans and more about the kinds of natural risks on Earth. Choice (E) doesn't address all of the risks provided in the paragraph and is therefore too specific to be its main idea.

2. **C. Loss of retail clothing sales due to a mall flood**

   In the final paragraph of the passage, the authors discuss what they call direct and indirect losses. Direct losses, they note, are those that involve the destruction of physical assets; indirect losses are those that arise because of the direct ones. Choices (A), (B), (D), and (E) all involve the actual destruction of physical assets: a library, school building, livestock, and a pavilion, respectively.

   Choice (C), on the other hand, reports the loss of income due to a direct loss — a mall flood. Thus, only Choice (C) denotes an indirect loss because loss in sales isn't tangible and therefore isn't a physical asset.

3. **D. hazards are not under human control, while risks usually are**

   Skim the answer choices to determine whether any of them can be easily eliminated. Choice (B) isn't a true statement according to the information contained in the passage. The passage notes that ". . . risk is the product of hazard," which is the opposite of stating that hazards result from risks. You can also eliminate Choice (A) because it claims that risks occur naturally while hazards result from human interaction; the passage states that the opposite is true. So, you've narrowed options down to Choices (C), (D), or (E). Choice (C) makes another false statement — nowhere in the passage do the authors report that hazards, and not risks, can lead to disasters. Rather, they imply that the two together increase the risk of a disaster.

   Choice (D) sounds like a serious contender, and the first two lines of the third paragraph back it up. Just to be sure, however, take a look at Choice (E). The words "harder to quantify" may jump out at you because you find them in the final paragraph, but upon more scrutiny, you can determine that the author claims that "economic impacts," not risks, are hard to quantify. Choice (D) is the best answer.

4. **A. describing the causes and impacts of natural disasters**

   Eliminate answers that contain information that appears in just a part of the passage rather than the whole. The authors don't discuss economic impacts until the final paragraph, so Choice (B) isn't a strong contender for the passage's primary concern. The role of human beings in risk is covered early in the passage, but the passage also discusses that some hazards are simply beyond human control, so Choice (C) isn't the best expression of the primary purpose. Choice (D), too, only tells part of the story; in addition to loss of human life, the passage discusses financial costs. Choice (E) is also inaccurate; the authors note that hazards aren't under human control, but risks, at least to some degree, are.

   By process of elimination, Choice (A) is the best answer. This general summary statement incorporates information discussed in the entire passage.

5. **E. It applies statistical data to emphasize the magnitude of damage created by natural disasters.**

Choice (A) is incorrect because the numerical information in the fourth paragraph relates to human lives lost rather than economic impacts. Choice (B) mentions a specific detail in the fourth paragraph, but the detail provides supporting evidence rather than the primary purpose of the paragraph. Choice (C) provides a better description of the function of the third paragraph than the fourth. And you can eliminate Choice (D) because its statement isn't true; the paragraph gives numerical data about one event rather than sensory detail about several.

Only Choice (E) offers a plausible explanation for the function of the fourth paragraph in relation to the rest of the passage. The paragraph provides statistics regarding a specific event that provides an example of the colossal destruction a natural disaster can cause.

6. **E. Areas of high hazard, such as Japan's Tohoku coast, may have a lower risk of natural disaster costs than areas where hazard incidents are lower.**

The third paragraph clarifies that the highest cost risk isn't always associated with the greatest hazard. Places with less hazard risk may experience greater costs because the hazard affects more people, or the area is less prepared to withstand damage. Therefore, Choice (E) is correct.

The passage doesn't provide clear data regarding the number of reported and unreported deaths in the tsunami and earthquake disaster, so you can't definitively compare number of deaths in Choice (A). The passage says that the tsunami in 2004 caused many more deaths than average, but it doesn't say the same for the 2010 Haiti disaster, so Choice (B) is wrong. Because you don't have actual data for deaths due to natural disaster in Japan, Hawaii, and Haiti, you also can't pick Choice (C). The passage suggests that both economic costs and death totals are unreported for natural disasters, but it doesn't compare the two, so you can't justify Choice (D).

7. **A. The degree of erosion to which a coastline is subject is related to the shape of the sea bottom.**

Choice (A) makes sense because the impact of waves is related to the shape of the sea bottom, and the coast's erosion is related to the impact of waves. Choice (B) is wrong because the statements only state the factors (wind velocity and fetch) that influence wave size; there's nothing to suggest that wave size stays close to an average. Choice (C) doesn't work; if fetch is the length of the surface of the water, it shouldn't be related to the shape of the sea bottom. Choice (D) is wrong because the size of waves comes from wind and fetch, not the shape of the bottom. Choice (E) looks wrong, too. Wind velocity creates size of waves, size of waves affects impact, and impact affects erosion, so average velocity of wind playing no role in erosion doesn't make sense. Choice (A) is the best answer.

8. **A. It is a specific example of a general condition described during the argument.**

The argument is that because patients need medical care and hospitals, regardless of what those services cost, hospitals and doctors rather than insurers bear the brunt of cost-containment measures; the MRI statement provides an example. Choice (A) is a good answer; the statement is a specific example of capital demands (MRIs and buildings) of the general condition of fiscal discipline described in the argument.

Choice (B) doesn't work because the MRI statement doesn't counter an attack. Choice (C) isn't as good an answer as Choice (A). The author's claim or conclusion is that health insurers are still profiting from healthcare while doctors, hospitals, and patients are being increasingly squeezed, but the MRI statement doesn't indirectly support that claim. Choice (D) doesn't work. Patients' needing treatment isn't a social side effect but a normal event that remains consistent, regardless of changing circumstances. Choice (E) is wrong; the MRI statement doesn't introduce the conclusion about the immunity of health insurers. Choice (A) is correct.

9. **E. Allowing employees to take leave for family matters reduces absenteeism, improves morale, and surprisingly increases productivity because the employees who are granted leave tend to work much harder and more efficiently when they come back to work.**

To weaken the argument, look for an answer showing that allowing family leave doesn't hurt productivity or perhaps even helps it. Choice (A) doesn't affect the argument because standard of living isn't an issue, and it doesn't mention workplace productivity. Choice (B) could arguably weaken the argument because it provides evidence that workers may not abuse the privilege of leave — fathers aren't taking family leave at all, which weakens the conclusion that workers would work less if they had leave. On the other hand, if taking paternity leave angers co-workers, that strengthens the conclusion that family leave hurts workplace morale, so this isn't the best answer. Choice (C) strengthens the argument by showing that FMLA leave costs the employer money. Choice (D) also strengthens the argument by illustrating the destruction caused by one employee leaving for a while.

Choice (E) weakens the argument. If employers are worried about productivity and morale, this choice says that allowing leave increases productivity and morale. Choice (E) is the right answer.

10. **A. Operating systems with generous amounts of memory are less susceptible to crashing, even when applications are poorly written.**

Okay, you want to find the four answers indicating that operating systems are responsible for the smooth functioning of applications and can somehow manage their memory problems. The best way to do this is by process of elimination. If you can find four answers that show the operating system handling applications' memory issues, then the answer that's left over should be correct. Choice (B) helps the conclusion because it shows that operating systems are responsible for handling the memory used by individual applications. Choice (C) helps because it shows that operating systems can spot overuse of memory and stop it. Choice (D) helps because it tells you that programmers should know how to program an operating system that can prevent memory errors, which means all operating systems should be able to do this. Choice (E) helps the conclusion because it describes what an efficient operating system should be able to do.

Choice (A) is the only answer that doesn't put responsibility for memory management on the operating system; adding memory to the computer evidently can let the operating system off the hook. Choice (A) is the right answer.

Answer Key

Section 1: Data Insights

1. Statement 1: **Can Be Determined**

   Statement 2: **Can Be Determined**

   Statement 3: **Cannot Be Determined**

2. Statement 1: **Inconsistent**

   Statement 2: **Consistent**

   Statement 3: **Consistent**

3. First blank: **60 percent**

   Second blank: **A or B**

4. Daytime drink: **Mack's Cola, Oolong Tea, and Coffee**

   Nighttime drink: **Fizzer Soda, Lemonade, and Green Tea**

5. Statement 1: **Supported**

   Statement 2: **Not Supported**

   Statement 3: **Not Supported**

6. **A**

7. **D**

8. **A**

Section 2: Quantitative

1.	A	4.	C	7.	B
2.	D	5.	A	8.	D
3.	D	6.	B	9.	C

Section 3: Verbal

1.	A	4.	A	7.	A	10.	A
2.	C	5.	E	8.	A		
3.	D	6.	E	9.	E		

Block **6**

Ten Tips for Scoring Higher on the GMAT

By the time you take the GMAT, you'll have already given up hours of your free time study-ing for the test, researching business schools, and planning for the future. Add to that the 2 hours and 15 minutes you'll spend alone with the GMAT striving to prove yourself worthy of admission to an MBA program. Because you've invested so much of yourself, you may as well get the highest score you're capable of achieving, so invest just a tad bit more time developing the ten proven test-taking techniques we cover in this block.

Pace Yourself

If you time yourself during practice tests, you'll probably begin to know intuitively whether you're falling behind, so you may not need to rely on the GMAT's clock to set your pace. In fact, you may want to conceal the clock to prevent it from becoming a distraction or an obsession. You can then check the clock more strategically to make sure you have enough time to answer all the questions. We recommend checking the clock as follows:

>> Periodically — for example, after every five questions, which means revealing the clock four times during each section.

>> When you suspect that you're spending too much time on a question. If you're spending more than a couple minutes on a question, you may want to guess and come back to it later if you have some time left after answering all the other questions.

Guess and Move On

Remember that standardized tests aren't like tests in your undergraduate college courses. If you studied hard in college, you may not have had to do much guessing on your midterms and finals. On the GMAT, however, the software won't allow you to skip questions. So, if you stumble upon some really difficult questions that you're not sure how to answer, your best option may be to guess and move on.

TIP

If a question is taking too much time, you can use the bookmark feature to flag the question for review and edit after you complete the section (provided you have time remaining).

You don't need to know the correct answer for each question to do well on the GMAT. Almost everyone answers a few questions in each section incorrectly, and almost everyone has to guess on those really difficult questions. Don't worry if you have to guess; just be sure to make an educated guess — to improve your odds, eliminate as many wrong answers as possible before choosing from the remaining answers.

Take Advantage of the Review and Edit Option

The GMAT allows you to review and edit answers for up to three questions in each section before time runs out for that section. Also, while you're working through a section, you can use the bookmark feature to flag as many questions as you like, giving you the freedom to move on to other questions and return to flagged ones to review — provided you've submitted an answer for every question in the section (including those you've flagged) and have time remaining.

After you confirm your answer for the final question in a section, a "Question Review & Edit" screen will pop up (this screen will not appear if your time has run out). This screen displays a numbered list of the questions in the section, and a bookmark icon next to any questions you flagged. Click a question number to return to it. Knowing that you can change answers to three questions max, you must be strategic in deciding which questions are the most promising candidates to consider.

WARNING

Don't change an answer unless you have a good reason to do so! You should change an answer only if you're confident that your initial answer was incorrect and you have a good reason to believe that your new answer is correct. Generally, it is better to trust your instincts and stick with your initial choice unless, for example, you made a wild guess on a question or you realize that you misread the question or made a careless mistake.

Finish It! Completing Each Section

Your GMAT score is based on the number of questions you answer correctly, so if time expires before you've answered all the questions in a section, you miss out on potential points. Be sure to answer all questions in each section, even if you have to guess.

REMEMBER

Answer every question in each section! If you have only three or four minutes remaining in a section and more than five questions left, spend the remaining minutes marking an answer for every question, even if you don't have time to read them. You have a 20 percent chance of randomly guessing the correct answer to a five-option multiple choice question, which is better than not answering the question at all. If you have to guess randomly at the end of the section, mark the same bubble for each answer.

Give Each Question Equal Treatment

You may have heard that you should spend a lot of time on the first ten questions because your performance on them determines your ultimate score. Although your performance on the first ten questions *does* give the computer an initial estimate of your ability, in the end, these first questions aren't scored higher than any other questions. You'll still encounter all the questions in the section eventually, so you really have no reason to spend an unreasonable length of time on the first ten.

WARNING

If you spend too much time on the first ten questions and answer them all correctly, you'll have less time to answer the remaining questions in the section. You may even run the risk of running out of time before answering all the questions in the section, in which case you'd lose points for unanswered questions.

Make Time for the Last Ten Questions

One strategy is to spend less time on the first questions, leaving you more time to answer the final ten questions in each section correctly. (Ten questions remain when you hit question 11 of the Quantitative section, question 13 of the Verbal section, or question 10 of the Data Insights section.)

Here are the steps to follow for this approach:

1. **Work through the first 22 minutes and 30 seconds of each section at a good pace.**

   Allocate a little over two minutes per Quantitative question, slightly under two minutes per Verbal question, and precisely two minutes and 15 seconds per Data Insights question.

2. **Don't spend more than three minutes on any question during the first 25 minutes of a section.**

3. **When you have ten questions remaining in the section, check the time remaining and adjust your pace accordingly.**

TIP

   For instance, suppose you managed to answer the first 11 Quantitative questions in just 20 minutes. With 25 minutes remaining, you can allocate more time to each of the remaining ten questions. By doing so, you can avoid resorting to random guessing for the unanswered questions towards the end of the section. These additional seconds per question could be crucial in improving your accuracy when addressing the final ten questions. Moreover, you might even have surplus time to review and edit your answers for up to three questions.

WARNING

We're not suggesting that you rush through the first 20 minutes or so of each section so you can spend lots of time on the last ten questions. Instead, you should stick to a pace that gives you ample time to respond to each question. You can't afford to spend five or six minutes on a single question without sacrificing your performance on the rest of the test, so pace yourself in a way that enables you to answer all the questions as accurately as you can.

If you happen to have additional time when you get to the last ten questions, by all means, use it. You miss points for not finishing a section, but you don't get a prize for finishing early.

Use the Process of Elimination to Improve Your Odds

We've stressed that the key to success is to move through the test steadily so you can answer every question and maximize your score. Keeping this steady pace will probably require you to make some intelligent guesses, and intelligent guesses hang on your ability to eliminate incorrect answers.

Eliminating answer choices is crucial on the Verbal and Quantitative sections of the GMAT. These questions come with five answer choices, and usually one or two of the options are obviously wrong (especially in the Verbal section). As soon as you know that an answer choice is wrong, eliminate it. After you've eliminated that answer, don't waste time reading it again. By quickly getting rid of choices that you know are *wrong*, you'll be well on your way to finding the *right* answer!

Maintain Your Focus

Don't be surprised if 135 minutes of answering questions gets a little boring. We know the prospect is shocking! But don't let your mind wander. Keep your brain on a tight leash. This test is too important. Just remind yourself how important these two hours and fifteen minutes are to your future. Teach yourself to concentrate, and use your relaxation technique of choice to recenter yourself if you start to lose focus. You'll need those powers of concentration in that MBA program you'll soon be starting!

Take Time to Read the Questions

We hate to break it to you, but you probably aren't a superhero named "Speedy Reader." You'll be anxious when the test begins, and you may want to blow through the questions at record speed. Big mistake! You don't get bonus points for finishing early, and you have plenty of time to answer every question if you read at a reasonable pace. You may take pride in your ability to speed-read novels, and that skill may help you with the reading comprehension passages, but don't use it to read the questions. You need to read questions carefully to capture the subtle nuances baked into GMAT questions and understand exactly what you're being asked.

Many people who get bogged down on a few questions and fail to complete a section do so because of poor test-taking techniques, not because of slow reading. Do yourself a favor: Relax, read at a reasonable pace, and maximize your score!

Don't Sink All Your Time into the Hard Questions

Although you shouldn't try to work at lightning speed, remember not to get held back by a few hard questions, either. The difficulty of a question depends on the person taking the test. For everyone, even the high scorers, a few questions on a test are more challenging than others. When you confront a difficult question on the GMAT, do your best, eliminate as many wrong answers as you can, and then make an intelligent guess. Even if you had all day, you might not be able to answer that particular question. (However, if you believe you may have a shot at it, take your best guess and bookmark it in case you have time to return to it later.) If you allow yourself to guess and move on, you can work on plenty of other questions that you'll answer correctly.

Index

A

absolute value, 50–51, 76–77, 81–82
addition
  in algebra, 65–67
  basics of, 48–49, 50, 52
  decimals, 56
  with exponents, 52
  fractions, 58
algebra
  factoring polynomials, 70–71
  functions, 71–75
  operations, 65–69
  overview, 63
  solving problems
    absolute value equations, 76–77
    break-even problems, 87
    coordinate plane, 87–91
    distance problems, 85–86
    inequalities, 79–82
    linear equations with one unknown, 75–76
    mixture problems, 86
    overview, 75
    quadratic equations, 82–83
    simultaneous equations, 77–79
    word problems, 83–85
    work problems, 85
  terminology, 63–65
Aristotle, 27
assumptions, questions seeking, 29, 35–36
author tone, 12, 14, 17
average, 97

B

bar graphs, 123–126
bases, 52–54
break-even problems, 87

C

calculator, on-screen, 109–110
central tendency, 97–99
circle graphs (pie charts), 130–131
combinations, 94, 97
common factors, 70
complements, 101
conclusions
  drawing, 29, 33–35
  in logical arguments, 26–27
constants, 63
coordinate plane, 87–91

coordinates, finding, 88
critical reasoning questions
  essentials of informal logic, 26–29
  overview, 6, 25
  practice questions and answer explanations, 41–45
  question types, 29–40
  structure of, 25–26
  techniques for answering, 26

D

data insights section of GMAT. *See also* integrated reasoning questions
  data sufficiency questions, 5, 133–137
  graphics, 122–133
  overview, 5, 107
  practice test answers, 152–155, 162
  practice test questions, 140–144
data sufficiency questions, 5, 133–137
decimals, 56
deductive reasoning, 27–28, 33, 39
dependent events, 102
difference of two squares, 82–83
distance problems, 85–86
division
  in algebra, 67–69
  decimals, 56
  with exponents, 53
  fractions, 58–59
  overview, 49, 50, 51
domain, function, 72–74
drawing-conclusions questions, 29, 33–35

E

events
  defined, 101
  independent and dependent, 102
  multiple probabilities, 103–105
  mutually exclusive, 102, 103
exception questions, 18–20
exponents, 52–54
expressions, 63–64

F

factoring
  polynomials, 70–71
  to solve quadratic equations, 82
FOIL method, 68–69, 70
fractional exponents, 53
fractions, 56–59

frequency table, 98–99
functions, in algebra, 71–75

G

general rule of addition, 103–104
general rule of multiplication, 103, 104–105
Graduate Management Admission Test (GMAT)
  content of, 4–6
  deciding where to take, 3–4
  enhancing score on, 163–167
  navigating computerized test, 6
  overview, 1–2, 3
  preparing for, 7–8
  registering for, 4
  retaking, 9
  scoring, 8–9
graphics
  bar graphs, 123–126
  circle graphs, 130–131
  histograms, 126–127
  line graphs, 127–130
  mastering questions focused on, 122–123
  overview, 122
  stem-and-leaf plots, 130
  Venn diagrams, 131–133
graphics interpretation questions, 108–109, 116–117

H

histograms, 126–127

I

icons, explained, 2
inconsistencies, resolving, 38–39
independent and dependent events, 102
inductive reasoning, 28–29, 37–38, 39
inequalities, 79–82
inference and application questions, 14, 16
informal logic, essentials of, 26–29
integrated reasoning (IR) questions
  graphics interpretation questions, 108–109, 116–117
  multi-source reasoning questions, 109, 118–122
  overview, 5, 107
  question types overview, 108–110
  skills tested, 108
  table analysis questions, 108, 110–113
  two-part analysis questions, 108, 113–116
intervals of numbers, 80–81

About the Authors

Lisa Zimmer Hatch, M.A., and **Scott A. Hatch, J.D.,** have prepared teens and adults since 1987 to excel on standardized tests, gain admission to colleges of their choice, and secure challenging and lucrative professional careers. For more than 35 years, they have created and administered award-winning standardized test preparation and professional career courses worldwide for live lecture, online, and other formats through more than 500 universities worldwide.

Scott and Lisa have written the curriculum for all formats, and their books have been translated for international markets. Additionally, they wrote, produced, and appeared in the landmark weekly PBS *Law for Life* series. They continue to develop new courses for a variety of careers and extend their college admissions expertise to assist those seeking advanced degrees in law, business, and other professions. Together they have authored numerous law and standardized test prep texts, including *ACT For Dummies, 1,001 ACT Practice Problems For Dummies, LSAT For Dummies,* and *Paralegal Career For Dummies* (John Wiley & Sons, Inc.).

Lisa is currently an independent educational consultant and the president of College Primers, where she applies her expertise to guiding high school and college students through the undergraduate and graduate admissions and financial aid processes and prepares students for entrance exams through individualized coaching and small group courses. She prides herself in maximizing her students' financial aid packages and dedicates herself to helping them gain admission to the universities or programs that best fit their goals, personalities, and financial resources. She graduated with honors in English from the University of Puget Sound and received a master's degree in humanities with a literature emphasis from California State University. She holds a certificate in college counseling from UCLA and is a member of and the webinar manager for the Higher Education Consultants Association (HECA) and a member of the Rocky Mountain Association of College Admissions Counselors (RMACAC).

Scott received his undergraduate degree from the University of Colorado and his Juris Doctorate from Southwestern University School of Law. He's listed in *Who's Who in California and Who's Who Among Students in American Colleges and Universities* and is one of the Outstanding Young Men of America as determined by the United States Jaycees. He was also a contributing editor to McGraw-Hill's *Judicial Profiler* series and *The Colorado Law Annotated* series published by Lawyers Cooperative Publishing. He also served as editor of the Freedom of Information Committee Newsletter and functioned as editor of several national award-winning periodicals. His current law books include *A Legal Guide to Probate and Estate Planning* and *A Legal Guide to Family Law* in B & B Legal Publication's *Learn the Law* series.

In addition to writing law books, periodical articles, television scripts, and college curricula, Scott was editor of his law school's nationally award-winning legal periodical, winner of two first-place awards from the Columbia University School of Journalism, and another first-place award from the American Bar Association. He also contributed to Los Angeles's daily newspaper, *The Metropolitan News,* was an editorial assistant during the formation of the Los Angeles Press Club's Education Foundation, and served on the Faculty of Law at the City University of Los Angeles.

Sandra Luna McCune, PhD, is professor emeritus and a former Regents professor at Stephen F. Austin State University. She's currently a full-time author and math/statistics consultant.

Publisher's Acknowledgments

Executive Editor: Lindsay Lefevere
Compiling Editor: Joe Kraynak
Editor: Elizabeth Kuball

Production Editor: Tamilmani Varadharaj
Cover Design: Wiley
Cover Image: © bortonia/Getty Images